CONTINUING

REVELATION

CONTINUING

REVELATION

ESSAYS ON DOCTRINE

EDITED BY
Bryan Buchanan

SIGNATURE BOOKS | 2021 | SALT LAKE CITY

The opinions expressed in this book are not necessarily
those of the publisher.

Design by Jason Francis.

FIRST EDITION | 2021

LIBRARY OF CONGRESS CATALOGING-IN-PUBLICATION DATA

Names: Buchanan, Bryan (Bookseller), editor.

Title: Continuing revelation : essays on doctrine / edited by Bryan Buchanan.

Description: First edition. | Salt Lake City : Signature Books, 2021. | Summary:
                "Determining what is and what is not Mormon doctrine is a difficult
                endeavor. The Church of Jesus Christ of Latter-day Saints embraces
                four books of scripture as its canon, but also believes the church is led
                by a living prophet. Additions to the canon have been rare since the
                death of church founder Joseph Smith. Joseph Fielding Smith, tenth
                church president, said that if the prophet ever contradicts cannon,
                cannon prevails. On the other hand, Ezra Taft Benson, the church's
                thirteenth president, said that the living prophet's words are more
                important than cannon. Such messages create no shortage of confusion
                among church members. The question "What is doctrine?" opens the
                door for theologians and historians to wrestle over the answer, and to
                do so thoughtfully and insightfully. In Continuing Revelation, editor
                Bryan Buchanan has compiled essays that seek greater understanding
                about what doctrine is and why it matters"—Provided by publisher.

Identifiers: LCCN 2021014058 (print) | LCCN 2021014059 (ebook) | ISBN
                9781560852933 (paperback) | ISBN 9781560853992 (ebook)

Subjects: LCSH: Church of Jesus Christ of Latter-day Saints—Doctrines. |
                Revelation—Church of Jesus Christ of Latter-day Saints. |
                Revelation—Mormon Church. | Mormon Church—Doctrines.

Classification: LCC BX8643.R4 C66 2021 (print) | LCC BX8643.R4 (ebook) |
                DDC 230/.9332—dc23

                LC record available at https://lccn.loc.gov/2021014058
                LC ebook record available at https://lccn.loc.gov/2021014059

CONTENTS

EDITOR'S INTRODUCTION

A wise observer of Mormon Studies, Bridget Jack Jeffries, once noted: "An old adage among outsiders who study Mormonism states that determining what is and is not Mormon doctrine is a lot like trying to nail Jell-O to a wall—except that the latter feat is entirely possible while the former remains a struggle to this day."[1] To bolster her argument, she linked to instructions on how to go about nailing said Jell-O to a wall. Leaving this assessment aside, the fact is that serious study of Mormon ideas has flourished in the last two decades. Since the predecessor to this volume—*Line Upon Line: Essays on Mormon Doctrine*—was published more than thirty years ago, in 1989 (when I was nine years old), Mormonism is increasingly seen as a legitimate topic of scholarly analysis. University-level courses on Mormonism have proliferated and several Mormon Studies programs are now in place. As part of this burgeoning, methods and topics of interest have also matured. Cross-disciplinary approaches have led to a more robust field.

However, Jeffries is not wrong. The question at heart—what *is* Mormon doctrine[2]—remains a difficult one. Understanding why requires a few related side journeys:

1. Relatively speaking, Mormonism is a fresh-faced youth among world religions, not having the benefit of centuries (or even millennia) to wrestle with its complexities.

---

1. "Why We're Confused," *Times and Seasons*, www.timesandseasons.org, June 27, 2009. Jack, a non-Mormon observer of the field of Mormon theology, graduated from Brigham Young University and wrote a master's thesis on women and the Mormon idea of exaltation.

2. One point of clarification: this volume focuses on LDS thought, leaving other fruitful fields of exploration (Community of Christ, fundamentalist, other groups under the Mormon umbrella) for another day. For the purposes of this compilation, "Mormon" refers generally to all religious expressions linking to Joseph Smith, while "LDS" refers specifically to the Church of Jesus Christ of Latter-day Saints, headquartered in Salt Lake City, Utah.

2. Mormonism has generally eschewed, occasionally in borderline explicit fashion, systematic treatments of doctrine and theology. Only in recent decades has that changed somewhat.

3. With its identity so tenaciously constructed around the concept of continuing revelation, Mormonism has deliberately situated itself away from the closed-canon world of mainstream Christianity.

4. Continuing revelation, by definition, creates a fluid landscape that makes categorical assessment much more complex.

Working in a Mormon-focused bookstore, I am always amused to hear comments like, "FOUR commentaries on the Doctrine & Covenants—why so many?!" At their ripe old ages, religions such as Christianity and Islam—with their thousands of theologians and writers—have produced entire libraries of commentaries, systematic theologies, and doctrinal expositions. Mormonism has yet to complete its second century. While those years have been fairly robust in terms of per capita books published, particularly in recent decades, the process of historical maturity still needs time to unfold.

Mormonism has always had a complicated relationship with theologians. When future LDS Church apostle Orson F. Whitney prophesied of his people, "We will yet have Miltons and Shakespeares of our own,"[3] he most certainly did not add "and Thomas Aquinases and al-Ghazalis." True, Parley P. Pratt's *Key to the Science of Theology* (first published in 1855) has been a staple of Mormon bookshelves since it came off the press, but Pratt's book should be seen as more of an outlier than the norm. Gerald Bradford, who later directed the Neal A. Maxwell Institute at Brigham Young University, highlights some of the tensions, particularly as experienced by believers, thus:

> For the Church, there is only one man who holds the "keys." The "prophet, seer, and revelator" alone may come to know the things of God for the whole Church. Thus it is difficult to see how any Mormon theologian could mistake his role for that of the prophet. And it is doubly unfortunate if what a theologian says falls outside of what could count as meaningful discourse because not only does this render understanding difficult, if not impossible, but it also suggests that one may assume the ways of God are not reasonable. And revelation from God has always been viewed as reasonable.

---

3. "Home Literature," *Contributor* 9, 8 (June 1888): 300.

Secondly, consider an even more important reason. Mormonism, despite the well-meaning intentions of a few "rationalistic" theologians in the Church, is first and foremost a revealed religion. The message and influence of the gospel must ultimately be accepted on the basis of individual initiative under the influence of the Holy Spirit. I contend there is simply no place for the alternative view that as a result of systematic or creative theology the gospel can be said to be made "rational" in such a way that it would be accurate to speak of a person genuinely embracing it solely upon the dictates of reason alone.[4]

James Faulconer, a philosopher at BYU and seasoned observer of the state of Mormon theology, identified "the absence of official rational explanations or descriptions of beliefs and practices, and the presence of differing and inconsistent explanations for and descriptions of belief within the membership of the church." The result, he argues, is that "we are 'a-theological'—which means that we are without a church-sanctioned, church-approved, or even church-encouraged systematic theology." Reflecting a perspective that is certainly not unique among Mormons, he judged "that is as it should be because systematic theology is dangerous."[5]

Despite this history, the last quarter century is marked by renewed effort to engage Mormon doctrine. Authors like Terryl Givens, Adam Miller, and Joseph Spencer have moved extended, nuanced conversations on theology and doctrine squarely into "safe"—or "safer"—territory.[6]

*

The Greek word for "doctrine" used in the New Testament, *didache,* comes from a causative verb, *didasko*—in essence causing someone to learn. In that spirit, the contributors to this volume marshaled their talents to cause you, as reader, to engage Mormon doctrine anew.

---

4. M. Gerald Bradford, "On Theology," *BYU Studies* 14, 3 (Spring 1974): 8–9.

5. "Rethinking Theology: The Shadow of the Apocalypse," *FARMS Review* 19, 1 (2007): 179.

6. See, for example, Givens's *Wrestling the Angel: The Foundations of Mormon Thought: Cosmos, God, Humanity* (New York: Oxford University Press, 2015) which Catholic observer Stephen Webb characterized as "an exceptional representation of a Mormon systematic theology," one that he felt "will go a long way toward calming Mormon theological worries that system building can assume creedal dimensions." "Toward a Mormon Systematic Theology Essay on *Wrestling the Angel* by Terryl L. Givens," *BYU Studies Quarterly* 54, 1 (2015): 143–44.

"Well, what *is* our doctrine?" So begins Loyd Isao Ericson's lead essay on "The Challenges of Defining LDS Doctrine." David H. Bailey focuses on the key Christian concepts of omnipotence, omniscience, omnipresence, and omnibenevolence and their roles in LDS thought in "LDS Theology and the Omnis: The Dangers of Theological Speculation." In a similar vein, Steven L. Peck looks at a longstanding discussion throughout Christianity in "Crawling Out of the Primordial Soup: A Step toward the Emergence of an LDS Theology Compatible with Organic Evolution."

In addition to situating Christian ideas and discussions within LDS thought, essays in this volume treat uniquely Mormon concepts. Boyd Petersen addresses the Mormon perspective on the pre-mortal conflict with the "great dragon ... and his angels" in "'To Destroy the Agency of Man': The War in Heaven in LDS Thought." One potential complication in a religion that relies on continual updates from its leaders is that some concepts are seen as settled by some but remain in flux for others. Shannon Flynn suggests that a central idea in Mormon doctrine may not be as concrete as previously thought in "Three Sub-degrees in the Celestial Kingdom?"

Part of the recent flourishing of scholarship relating to LDS theology is the welcome exploration of the role and perspectives of women and the LGBTQ community. Blaire Ostler examines a particularly underdeveloped topic in "Heavenly Mother: The Mother of All Women." A notable element of Mormonism in the last quarter century is the increasing place of dissent as a topic of discussion, which is investigated by Kelli D. Potter in "Mormonism and the Problem of Heterodoxy."

Bridging the topics of gender and ritual studies is an important emphasis in contemporary scholarship. Susanna Morrill does just that in "Women at the Gates of Mortality: Relief Society Birth and Death Rituals." One observer of contemporary Mormon culture has commented on the interplay of ritual and theology, noting that "Mormons have apparently come to maintain such unity as prevails on the basis of conformity to and acceptance of the crucial rites, more than through linguistic discourse about doctrine."[7] Two essays in this collection explore that dynamic: Samuel R. Weber in "'Shake Off the Dust of Thy Feet': The Rise

---

7. John L. Sorenson, "Ritual as Theology and as Communication," *Dialogue: A Journal of Mormon Thought* 33, 2 (Summer 2000): 127.

and Fall of Mormon Ritual Cursing" and "'Satan Mourns Naked Upon the Earth': Locating Mormon Possession and Exorcism Rituals in the American Religious Landscape, 1830–1977," by Stephen C. Taysom.

I am proud of the lineup in *Continuing Revelation*—some of these authors I have known and respected for years while, in other cases, this marks my introduction to them. My thanks to the crew at Signature Books, all of whom I count as friends. Signature is to be commended for reanimating this essay series—the original run has a place of honor on my bookshelves. Signature's work in commissioning an entire generation's worth of compilations and documentary histories has made Mormon Studies all the more rich. I greatly appreciate the invitation to join the fold.

… I hold that it is entirely compatible with the genius of the church to change its procedure, forms, and interpretations as changes in thought, education, and environment of people from time to time seem to warrant, provided, of course, that no violence is done to the elemental concepts of truth which lie at the basis of our work. I would not discard a practice merely because it is old. Indeed, I believe that one of the tests of worth is the test of time. But, on the other hand, I would not hang on to a practice or conception after it has outlived its usefulness in a new and ever-changing and better-informed world. …

Dogmatism and bigotry have been the deadliest enemies of true religion in the long past. They have made it forbidding, shut it up in cold grey walls … out of the sunlight and fragrance of the growing world. They have garbed it in black and then in white, when in truth it is neither black nor white any more than life is black or white, for religion is life abundant, glowing life, with all its shades, colors, and hues, as the children of men reflect in the patterns of their lives the radiance of the Holy Spirit in varying degrees.

—Elder Stephen L Richards, "Continuing Revelation and Mormon Doctrine," in *Line Upon Line: Essays on Mormon Doctrine,* ed. Gary James Bergera (Salt Lake City: Signature Books, 1989), 184, 185.

ONE

THE CHALLENGE OF DEFINING LDS DOCTRINE

LOYD ISAO ERICSON

The dramatic growth of the Church of Jesus Christ of Latter-day Saints in recent decades has prompted unprecedented inquiry into the beliefs and practices of the nearly 200-year-old church. Scrutiny has risen sharply from critics and the news media in the twenty-first century as the church has been highlighted in the national media by events such as the 2002 Salt Lake City Winter Olympics, the FLDS polygamy cases, Mitt Romney's campaign for the United States presidency, the Ordain Women movement, and its involvement with LGBTQ legislation. A review of the data predictably shows a range of views from gross misrepresentation to sincere inquiry regarding the official teachings of the church—an understandable response given the sharp divergence between many Latter-day Saint teachings and those of traditional Christians. Furthermore, as the church has grown in population so have the number of members within the church who actively study, theorize, and speculate about their beliefs. The availability of information and communication over the internet has greatly accelerated these inquiries. As a result, a frequent question from outside the LDS faith is "What do Mormons really believe?"[1] and the reply from within may be equally asked, "Well, what *is* our doctrine?"

This essay analyzes recent attempts to grapple with the questions of LDS doctrine in the effort to show the challenges involved in establishing precise criteria to distinguish doctrine from beliefs, teachings, policies, etc. Furthermore, these models point to deeper theological issues that emerge in the attempt to reconcile infallible doctrinal truths

---

1. For example, see John Ankerberg and John Weldon, *What Do Mormons Really Believe? What the Ads Don't Tell You* (Eugene, Oregon: Harvest House Publishers, 2002).

with the growth of understanding implied in Mormonism's concept of modern revelation. This essay does not seek to resolve these issues, but to help clarify the questions for future work and discussion.

THE AUTHORITATIVE MODEL

The most common approach to providing criteria for determining LDS doctrine is what I call the *authoritative model,* which attempts to define doctrine by appeal to what is commonly assumed to be authoritative sources and leaders. This model has been expressed by Robert L. Millet, a professor of religion at Brigham Young University, in his essay, "What Do We Really Believe? Identifying Doctrinal Parameters within Mormonism,"[2] and is promoted in an official LDS Newsroom commentary on the church's website.[3] Departing from this authoritative model, Nathan B. Oman, a professor law at the College of William and Mary, has proposed a hermeneutic approach modeled after judicial practices of interpreting law. In this approach, particular doctrines are appealed to in an attempt to provide boundaries or parameters of doctrinal possibility.[4] However, I argue that both models face problems in their attempts to (1) live up to their own criteriological goals, (2) accommodate adequately the breadth of LDS theology, and (3) avoid question-begging arguments.

2. Robert L. Millet, "What Do We Really Believe? Identifying Doctrinal Parameters within Mormonism," in *Discourses in Mormon Theology: Philosophical and Theological Possibilities,* ed. James M. McLachlan and Loyd Ericson (Salt Lake City: Greg Kofford Books, 2007), 265–81. A previous version of this essay was also published in "What Is Our Doctrine?" *The Religious Educator: Perspectives on the Restored Gospel* (Provo, Utah: BYU Religious Studies Center), 4, 3 (2003): 15–33. Also selections from this essay, including his authoritative model, are included in his books *Getting at the Truth: Responding to Difficult Questions about LDS Beliefs* (Salt Lake City: Deseret Book, 2004), 43–63, and *What Happened to the Cross? Distinctive LDS Teachings* (Salt Lake City: Deseret Book, 2007), 52–65.

3. See LDS Newsroom, "Approaching Mormon Doctrine" (May 4, 2007), in *Newsroom,* retrieved Mar. 6, 2008, at newsroom.churchofjesuschrist.org/ldsnewsroom/eng/commentary/approaching-mormon-doctrine. For a similar, but slightly more restricted, authoritative model, see Stephen E. Robinson, *Are Mormons Christians?* (Salt Lake City: Bookcraft, 1991), 13–18.

4. Nathan B. Oman, "Jurisprudence and the Problem of Church Doctrine," *Element* 2, 1 (Fall 2006): 1–19. See also Nathan B. Oman, "A Defense of the Authority of Church Doctrine," *Dialogue: A Journal of Mormon Thought* 40, 4 (Winter 2007): 1–28. In the latter essay, Oman examines the authoritative role that church doctrine plays in the lives of members. While I agree that doctrine can and does play an authoritative role among believers, the role that it plays depends on how each member personally interprets church doctrine. This latter essay still begs the question of whether or not doctrine may be established for the whole church and whether it does so as a matter of policy, current teaching, or absolute truth.

The authoritative model appeals to the commonly held belief that there are authoritative sources to which someone may turn as a definitive source of doctrine. According to Millet, a doctrine is something that is (1) "found within the four standard works and/or within official declarations or proclamations"; (2) "taught or discussed in general conference or other official gatherings by general Church leaders"; (3) "found in the general handbooks or approved curriculum of the Church"; or (4) in "the content of the temple endowment." Furthermore, some overriding criteria are that church doctrines are found in (5) "the teachings of the Church *today*"; are (6) "central and saving doctrine[s] ... , not tangential and peripheral concepts"; and have (7) "what might be called 'sticking power,' i.e., [they are] taught and discussed and perpetuated over time." Finally, Millet places a heavy emphasis on contemporary sources, repeatedly pointing out that statements of the past should not necessarily be considered doctrine as (8) "not everything that was ever spoken or written by a Church leader in the *past* is part of what we teach *today*."[5] Thus if a belief or teaching is confirmed by these criteria then it could be confidently claimed to be doctrine.[6]

However, the appeal to a criterion of authoritative sources faces challenges. First, no justification is provided as to why that particular set of criteria should be used over any other. If there are, in fact, saving doctrines or saving practices tied to certain doctrines, then the method by which one determines this (as opposed to one that is merely tangential or non-doctrinal) would seem to be of equal importance. For example, Millet briefly mentions the old teaching that plural marriage is essential for salvation.[7] On the authoritative model, such a teaching

---

5. Millet, "What Do We Really Believe?" 266–67, 273, emphasis added. Millet uses the word "today" at least eighteen times throughout his essay to emphasize that statements of current leaders should be given doctrinal authority over those of past leaders.

6. Compare to *Newsroom*, "Approaching Mormon Doctrine," where it states that (1) "doctrine resides in the four 'standard works' of scripture"; (2) "is established by the First Presidency ... and the Quorum of the Twelve Apostles"; (3) "in official Church publications"; (5) "relevant to the circumstances of [the] day"; (6) "might be considered core doctrines"; (7) "is consistently proclaimed"; and (8) a "single statement by a single leader on a single occasion ... is not meant to be officially binding for the whole church." The omission of temple rituals as a source of doctrine may be to avoid providing justification for the media to cite the sacred rites.

7. Millet, "What Do We Really Believe?" 267.

would not be considered doctrine as it is no longer taught by the LDS Church today; whereas, the present teaching that monogamous marriage is essential for salvation (and polygamous marriage is grounds for excommunication) would qualify as a true doctrine. As adherence to the former teaching could prove damning while adherence to the latter could prove saving, the method by which someone could distinguish between the two would be equally as important for salvation. Yet Millet does not offer scriptural, official, or authoritative justification to support such criteria.

Even if such criteria are justifiable through scriptural and other authoritative sources, they face the problem of overcoming the fact that the relevance of those sources as justification for the criteria would be based on the criteria they are attempting to justify. This circularity is a challenge because similar reasoning could be used to establish a variety of methodologies for determining what qualifies as authentic LDS doctrine. For example, I could claim that doctrine is that which is contained in the scriptures or taught in a sermon by Brigham Young. I could then appeal to Young's sermon where he states that he has "never yet preached a sermon and sent it out to the children of men, that they may not call scripture,"[8] and then use that to justify my criteria. Just as with the authoritative model, the validity of my *Young model* would depend on the criteria of this model to grant doctrinal authority to the sources I use to justify my criteria.

Another example is found in the widespread belief that contemporary LDS Church leaders are correct in pronouncing doctrine because God would not allow a modern-day prophet to lead the Saints astray. Wilford Woodruff's well-known quote is often invoked in support of this claim: "[T]he Lord will never permit me or any other man who stands as president of this Church to lead you astray."[9] This assurance, like the others, faces the bootstrapping question as to whether it is an infallible criterion for knowing what to accept as authentic doctrinal teaching.

The authoritative model also suffers from the problem of interpretation. As Oman points out, scripture is not an unproblematic source for

8. Brigham Young, Jan. 2, 1870, *Journal of Discourses*, 26 vols. (London/Liverpool: LDS Booksellers Depot, 1854–86), 13:95.
9. Wilford Woodruff, in Sixty-first Semiannual General Conference of the Church, Monday, Oct. 6, 1890, Salt Lake City, reported in *Deseret Evening News*, Oct. 11, 1890, 2.

determining doctrine because multiple interpretations may come from a single verse.[10] For example, Latter-day Saints and traditional Christians both appeal to the Bible as a source of their beliefs, yet as any LDS-Christian dialogue shows, what they believe the Bible to actually mean varies tremendously. This is the same frustration Joseph Smith felt when he observed that "the teachers of religion of the different sects understood the same passages of scripture so differently as to destroy all confidence in settling the question by an appeal to the Bible" (JS-H 1:12). The presence of modern, living prophets in the LDS Church addresses this problem, but as the history of the Church of Jesus Christ of Latter-day Saints shows, their words, like the scriptures, are themselves subject to varying interpretations.[11]

Finally, the appeal to "sticking power" as a measure of doctrine is also problematic because it places a time limit on doctrine and requires a democratic process that could oppose new doctrines that may arise through modern revelation. The scriptural record gives numerous accounts of prophets and leaders speaking against the iniquities of the people and the church, as well as promulgating new doctrines. The requirement of consistency or "sticking power" negates many of these as they were rejected by the people and church. If not outright rejected, with this criterion it would take some amount of time and general acceptance before a particular belief could be considered doctrine. For example, after the June 1978 revelation was announced that gave the priesthood to all men and access to the temple to all men and women regardless of skin color, at what point would the change have garnered enough "sticking power" to be considered doctrine? One hour? One day? One year? Furthermore, how much acceptance must the change gain before it is doctrine? Must it have unanimous approval, or need it only have minimal acceptance? Such a requirement would seem to vitiate the view that church leaders are able to reveal new doctrine.

---

10. Oman, "Jurisprudence and the Problem of Church Doctrine," 6.

11. For a recent example, see then-Elder Russell M. Nelson's February 2003 *Ensign* article, "Divine Love," where he writes, "While divine love can be called perfect, infinite, enduring, and universal, it cannot correctly be characterized as unconditional" (20). What Nelson meant by this was largely discussed and debated by LDS thinkers. For an example of a discussion of this article, see the June 29, 2007, blog entry, "Your Friday Firestorm #3," on the Mormon blog *By Common Consent*, www.bycommonconsent.com/2007/06/29/your-friday-firestorm-3, accessed May 11, 2009.

THE INTERPRETIVE MODEL

Oman does not make explicit appeals to authoritative sources. Instead he employs a model analogous to the judicial practice of appealing to previously decided legal cases to provide an interpretive basis for judging a new case. Oman points out that judges are often presented with difficult legal cases where the obvious ruling is unclear and no precedent had been established for determining the proper and best ruling for the new case. In this situation the judge must "look at the previously decided cases and construct the best possible argument that he can to justify them."[12] On this approach, a new case must be decided by reference to its consistency with previous cases, but there is some hermeneutic flexibility in deciding *how* this consistency is understood.

Centuries ago, when a judge was unable to make a clear ruling he "could rule *dubitante*, simply declaring that the law was unclear and leave the case undecided."[13] Similarly, Oman proposes that when a question arises as to whether or not a certain teaching or belief is LDS doctrine, we would need to appeal first to "some easily identifiable core cases of Church Doctrine from which we can reason."[14] By appealing to these "brute facts" of doctrine, we "can simply reason on the basis of clear cases, fitting the new question into a story that will place things in their best possible light."[15] If a clear answer is still not available, like the ruling of *dubitante*, we ascertain that while the answer may not be clear, possible answers would fall within certain boundaries or limits of doctrine.

To illustrate, Oman examines one of the most debated questions within the LDS Church—are caffeinated beverages doctrinally prohibited by the Word of Wisdom? Acknowledging no clear answer, Oman goes back to "the brute fact that we all agree that the Word of Wisdom is Church Doctrine and that it forbids drinking coffee, tea, and alcohol."[16] Just as a judge looks into the reasons behind rulings for previous cases, we would attempt to look at the reasons behind the prohibition of coffee and other foods or substances in the Word of Wisdom. From

---

12. Oman, "Jurisprudence and the Problem of Church Doctrine," 9.
13. "Jurisprudence," 10, emphasis in original.
14. "Jurisprudence."
15. "Jurisprudence."
16. "Jurisprudence," 11.

this we might conjecture that the Word of Wisdom is not merely a prohibition of certain chemical substances because chocolate (which contains caffeine) and cold medicines (which may contain some alcohol) do not appear to be proscribed. Neither does the canonized Word of Wisdom bar narcotics and other drugs that were prevalent at the time it was revealed. Instead we might decide that "a better account is that the prohibition is meant as a reminder or symbol of the covenant that [we] make with God and an open-ended admonition to be healthy."[17] On this approach, the specific prohibitions of the Word of Wisdom are akin to the Jewish practices of circumcision and Sabbath adherence as signs of a covenant with God. We also might interpret that the broader teachings of the Word of Wisdom should be applied to our entire lifestyle by eating healthy and avoiding over-consumption. Thus caffeinated beverages are not specifically prohibited but, like all foods and substances, should be consumed, limited, or proscribed based on what would be a healthy diet and lifestyle.

While Oman's interpretive model largely avoids the criteriological problems of the authoritative model, it suffers from the assumption that there are "clear instances" of LDS doctrine that are easily identifiable. In the legal basis for Oman's analogy, the judge assessing a new case appeals to "previously decided cases" of law. In such instances, there are clear, public, and officially documented rulings that were formally made within an established and accepted framework of law. However, analogous instances of "previously decided cases" of LDS doctrine are more difficult to identify. This is because a formalized framework of understanding and ruling upon church doctrine has never been established. While there exists a codified framework of policy and procedures under church government, a framework for defining "easily identifiable core cases" of church doctrine does not exist—especially one that is universally accepted and understood by members of the church.[18] According to Oman, such a framework is akin to the *Catechism of the Catholic Church*, to which a Catholic easily turns as a reference point to

---

17. "Jurisprudence."
18. While the *Church Handbook of Instructions* lays out the ecclesiastical policies of the church, to which a leader could (and is instructed to) turn to clarify matters of policy, it is not designed to clarify points of doctrine.

mitigate a dispute between points of doctrine. However, Oman readily admits that the LDS Church "has no analogous volume."[19]

One could argue that while the LDS Church does not presently possess a framework, it *could* create one to provide this analogous source.[20] However, this is problematic for at least two reasons. First, like Millet's authoritative model, the creation of a committee to establish church doctrine authoritatively would not have the doctrinal basis to justify itself. And second, as Oman points out, such a committee would still need an authoritative criterion to determine doctrine. It would still require that "Church Doctrine exists as some body of identifiable, authoritative teachings *independent of correlation or whoever else is expounding it.*"[21]

Oman provides two examples of what he considers to be easily identifiable cases of LDS doctrine: "Jesus is the savior of mankind"[22] and the Word of Wisdom prohibits the consumption of coffee, tea, and alcohol.[23] In the former, what it means for Jesus to be the savior of humankind is widely disputed. Both BYU professor Stephen Robinson and I may affirm that "Jesus is the savior of mankind"; however, it also may be that we believe the phrase to mean two very different things— even to the extent that Robinson might not consider my understanding and affirmation of that phrase to be sufficient for my salvation. If we take into account the many different beliefs of Jesus, salvation, and the Atonement, there are scores of different understandings of what it means for Jesus to be the savior of humankind, even though the same scriptures and sources are appealed to. This is often the assertion of critics of the LDS Church—that Latter-day Saints use the same language of traditional Christianity but do not mean the same thing, and that these mistaken beliefs are detrimental to salvation.

Similarly, the assumption that the prohibition of coffee, tea, and alcohol is an easily understood doctrine does not take into account the varying interpretations of what that actually means. Does the prohibition include de-caffeinated coffee, frozen lattes, coffee ice cream, chocolate-covered

---

19. Oman, "Jurisprudence and the Problem of Church Doctrine," 2.

20. This might be something like the Correlation Committee, which effectively serves this purpose by virtue of what it determines is to be included and excluded from teaching churchwide curricula.

21. Oman, "Jurisprudence and the Problem of Church Doctrine," 3, emphasis added.

22. "Jurisprudence," 9.

23. "Jurisprudence," 11.

espresso beans, green tea, chai teas, herbal teas, iced teas, and kava?[24] What about the prohibition of alcohol? The revealed text of the Word of Wisdom distinguishes between "strong drinks," which "are not for the belly," and "mild drinks" of barley and other grains, which are promoted (D&C 89:7, 17). Yet, there is no easily identifiable interpretation of this to which one can point.[25] Also, the alcohol prohibition does not forbid cough syrups and other medicines that contain alcohol.

Oman's interpretive model depends on the *assumed* ability to appeal to easily identifiable brute facts of church doctrine; however, upon examination, these supposed clear cases of doctrine are not so clear. This is because no accessible and widely accepted framework for determining doctrine has been established. Instead of clear cases of doctrine, we have vague and abstract terms with no definitive understandings of what they actually mean. While Oman shies away from authoritative models, his proposal of an interpretive model *presupposes* authoritative criteria to establish a framework from which to interpret.[26]

PROBLEMS OF DEFINING DOCTRINE

The authoritative and interpretive models both suffer from a definitional problem for determining doctrine in that each fails to define

---

24. In August 2019, the church's *Newsroom* released a statement that "Church leaders have clarified that several substances are prohibited by the Word of Wisdom, including vaping or e-cigarettes, green tea, and coffee-based products." See "Statement on the Word of Wisdom," Newsroom, Aug. 15, 2019, www.newsroom.churchofjesuschrist.org/article/statement-word-of-wisdom-august-2019. The statement references a nameless article in the church's magazine for teens published that same month. See "Vaping, Coffee, Tea, and Marijuana," *New Era*, Aug. 2019, www.churchofjesuschrist.org/study/new-era/2019/08/vaping-coffee-tea-and-marijuana.

25. A historical reading of the text would probably make the same distinction regarding the drinks that exists today—that strong drinks are drinks with a high alcohol-content such as whiskey, rums, spirits, etc., while mild drinks are drinks with low alcohol-content such as malted beers and stouts. For example, in an 1875 sermon, Brigham Young equated "mild drinks" with beer as he urged the Saints to avoid purchasing beer for primarily economical reasons: "The same may be said of money spent in the purchase of beer. *It is a mild drink*, and is very pleasant and agreeable to a great many; but when a man pays his fifty cents, his dollar or his ten dollars for beer it goes into the hands of the grocery keepers and they send it off, and it does no good to the community. The beer itself does no good, it injures the system of those who habitually indulge in the use of it, and, whether they think of and realize it, or not, they will be brought to account for the means they have thus wasted." Brigham Young, Aug. 31, 1875, *Journal of Discourses*, 18:72; emphasis added. See also Oman, "Authority of Church Doctrine," 11.

26. See especially Oman, "Jurisprudence and the Problem of Church Doctrine," 2–7.

what it is determining. In asking the question, "Is 'x' a doctrine?," whatever "x" may be is carefully examined and defined, but the term *doctrine* is left unexplored or deficiently defined. This lack of a definition is problematic as it often leads to a confusing conflation of *beliefs, teachings, policies, doctrine,* etc. This is especially true when the ordinary usage of these terms in LDS discourse is not considered, or when these terms are applied both descriptively and prescriptively without acknowledging a difference in usage.[27]

In his "What Do We Really Believe?" Millet recounts an experience of an LDS woman who approached him and claimed that Latter-day Saints do not technically believe in the virgin birth of Jesus, but that it is an LDS belief that Jesus was conceived through sexual relations between God and Mary.[28] Appealing to his authoritative criteria, Millet convinced her that the church does not believe the very thing that she, a Latter-day Saint, claimed to be church doctrine. This may be familiar to the experiences and frustrations of many Latter-day Saints who have to defend their personal beliefs from critics who claim to better understand what they *actually* believe.[29]

Thus when Millet asks what Latter-day Saints really believe, he is not asking a descriptive question of what the Saints believe. Rather, he is posing a prescriptive question of what the Saints *ought* to believe. In other words, he equates beliefs with doctrine or teaching. However, this prescriptive use may cause confusion because for most Saints the question, "What do you believe?" asks them to describe their beliefs, not to theorize about what they should believe. In fact, it is common for Saints in Sunday school or other such forums to begin a statement with, "Well, this may not be doctrine, but I believe that …"[30] From this, it

27. While I acknowledge that there is a wide variation of how these terms are used within the LDS Church, by "ordinary usage" I refer especially to the usage employed by LDS general authorities when speaking to members. This, I believe, best represents how terms are applied for the majority of Latter-day Saints. Oman similarly appeals to "ordinary usage" when trying to pinpoint doctrine. See Oman, "Jurisprudence and the Problem of Church Doctrine," 5.

28. Millet, "What Do We Really Believe?" 270.

29. For example, see the introduction in Ankerberg and Weldon, *What Do Mormons Really Believe*, 7: "We have written this book to help clarify what Mormons *actually* believe, not what they give us the impression of believing" (emphasis added). See also Robinson, *Are Mormons Christian?*, 9–10.

30. For an example, see Elder Jeffrey R. Holland's April 2009 general conference talk where he makes it clear that he is referring to his own thoughts and feelings, and not

seems that a belief is not necessarily an official teaching or doctrine, but is rather something that is believed even though it may not be taught by the church. For example, many Saints hold various beliefs that they would not claim to be doctrine or officially taught by the church—such as the belief that Jesus was married, that we should not drink caffeinated sodas,[31] that the Earth is no older than 13,000 years, that God has multiple wives, or that the three Nephites possess the cure to cancer.

Now, it could be the case that Millet is trying to be descriptive with his question and that his use of the plural subject ("What do *we* really believe?") is meant to ask what it is that *all* Latter-day Saints believe. However, such a question seems to go against his need for an authoritative model—as establishing what all Saints believe is more easily learned through a questionnaire than through his criteria. Furthermore, if all Saints did believe in the actual virgin birth of Jesus, then Millet has had no need to correct this Latter-day Saint woman of her incorrect belief. As with Oman's appeal to easily identifiable cases of doctrine, we are hard-pressed to find a single particular doctrine on which all Saints agree.

Furthermore, just as a Latter-day Saint may hold a belief that is not doctrine or taught by the church, for most Saints, there is not a necessary relationship between their beliefs and truth. A statement of belief by a Latter-day Saint does not require that it be believed to be true. It would not be uncommon to hear a Saint say, "I believe 'x', though it may not be true," just as it would not have been uncommon to hear someone say prior the 2016 election, "I believe that Hillary Clinton will win the US presidency, though she could lose to Donald Trump."

Similarly, what is officially taught in the LDS Church does not seem to be considered co-extensive with doctrine either. Oman points out that while the scriptures are taught in church, there are many things in them that are not considered doctrine. For example, the scriptural and revealed form of the Word of Wisdom is given as guidance and not

speaking for the church: "Indeed, *it is my personal belief* that in all of Christ's mortal ministry the Father may never have been closer to His Son than in these agonizing final moments of suffering." Holland, "None Were with Him," *Ensign,* May 2009, 86.

31. For a discussion on the consumption of caffeine for Latter-day Saints, see Thomas J. Boud, "The Energy Drink Epidemic," *Ensign,* Dec. 2008, 48–52; also Russell Wilcox, "Energy Drinks: The Lift That Lets You Down," *New Era,* Dec. 2008, 3–33; "Vaping, Coffee, Tea, and Marijuana."

as commandment (D&C 89:2), prohibits the consumption of meat except in times of winter and famine (vv. 12–13), and seems to support the consumption of mild alcoholic beverages (v. 17). Yet most Saints do not consider these to be doctrine. Likewise, what has been taught in the past by LDS leaders is not necessarily doctrine either (as Millet emphasizes). But what about that which is taught in general conference or is "found in the general handbooks or approved curriculum of the Church today," as Millet argues?[32] It seems that, similar to beliefs, official teachings are not necessarily co-extensive with truth or doctrine. Latter-day Saints sometimes comment (though perhaps not publicly) that they do not agree with something said in general conference, published in the *Ensign,* or taught as part of a gospel doctrine course—claiming that an interpretation of scripture is incorrect, that a particular statement does not ring true, or that something is just their opinion and not doctrine. Even general authorities have been known to disagree with things taught by colleagues in general conferences and other official gatherings.[33]

This is an important distinction that Millet's and the *LDS Newsroom* commentary's authoritative model seems to lack—for many faithful, believing Saints, that which is officially taught in the church's curriculum and spoken of by church leaders is not *necessarily* true doctrine. In fact, Millet explicitly equates teachings with doctrine when he says that "doctrine means teaching. If the general authorities do not teach something today, it is not part of our doctrine today. This does not, however, mean that a particular teaching is untrue."[34] While this may be a technical definition, it does not fit the ordinary usage of "doctrine" in LDS discourse. As mentioned, a particular teaching may be such that any given faithful member might say, "Yes, that is taught, but I believe it is a poor interpretation or just his opinion. I don't believe it to be true doctrine."

---

32. Millet, "What Do We Really Believe?" 267.

33. See, for example, Gary James Bergera, *Conflict in the Quorum: Orson Pratt, Brigham Young, Joseph Smith* (Salt Lake City: Signature Books, 2002), esp. 169–87; D. Michael Quinn, *The Mormon Hierarchy: Extensions of Power* (Salt Lake City: Signature Books/Smith Research Associates, 1997), 66–115; and Richard Sherlock and Jeffrey E. Keller, "The B. H. Roberts/Joseph Fielding Smith/James E. Talmage Affair," in *The Search for Harmony: Essays on Science and Mormonism,* eds. Gene A. Sessions and Craig J. Oberg (Salt Lake City: Signature Books, 1993).

34. Millet, *What Happened to the Cross?*, 67.

Unlike beliefs and teachings, policy seems to have a stronger, more authoritative nature because it is usually incorporated into church governance through official instructional leadership handbooks and, in many cases, strict application. Policy may best be defined as procedural regulations that are contingent and not directly based in scripture or published revelations. Examples of policy that may at first seem doctrinal include the size of priesthood quorums, the wearing of white clothing and complete submersion during baptism, perfect word-for-word recital of sacramental prayers, the contemporary Word of Wisdom, and the specifics of temple rituals. Yet like beliefs and official teachings, it seems that policy is not co-extensive with doctrine in LDS discourse. For example, church president David O. McKay reportedly argued that the ban prohibiting those of African descent from ordination to the priesthood was policy and not doctrine.[35]

So what does distinguish policy from doctrine? Consider the following statements:

1. Photographs should not be taken of baptismal ordinances.
2. A new convert should be dressed in white for baptism.
3. Men of African descent should not be ordained into the priesthood.
4. A deacons quorum should be composed of twelve or less deacons.

The first of these is policy according to the current *Church Handbook of Instructions*, but it does not seem to be something that most Saints consider a teaching or a doctrine of the church. The second statement is also policy, and it is fair to say that it is taught by the church. However, many Saints would probably consider it problematic to call it doctrine as it seems to be a largely symbolic convention that is not necessary; if a situation arose where securing white clothing would not be possible, most Saints would see no problem with baptizing the new convert in whatever they could find—even blue jeans and a Metallica t-shirt. The third statement becomes interesting for a few reasons. While it is not a statement that has application today in LDS beliefs, teachings, or doctrine, in 1960 it was widely discussed and written about. It was certainly policy at the time, but did it rise to the level of doctrine? While President McKay said privately it was not,

---

35. See Gregory A. Prince and Wm. Robert Wright, *David O. McKay and the Rise of Modern Mormonism* (Salt Lake City: University of Utah Press, 2005), 75.

other LDS leaders at the same time (such as Bruce R. McConkie and Joseph Fielding Smith) taught that it was.[36] Perhaps their belief in the nature of the policy led them to distinguish it from or attribute it to church doctrine—as the former believed that the ban could and would be lifted, while the latter believed it to be divinely mandated until at least the Millennium.[37]

Finally, many Latter-day Saints would more likely claim the last statement to be doctrine because it is a policy that is taught by the church and is contained in the LDS scriptures (D&C 107:85). However, some may still have reservations about calling the size of priesthood quorums doctrine because it may seem to them to be an arbitrary number that could be changed by revelation (or counsel) to accommodate a growing, culturally changing church. From an examination of these statements, it seems clear then that something that is a policy is not necessarily a doctrine; and for many Latter-day Saints, one of the distinguishing marks between the two is that the former is a contingent regulation that may or may not be divinely instituted, while the latter is something that is necessary and cannot be changed. Furthermore, while a believing Saint may adhere to the policies of the church, not only may she feel that they are contingent, but she may also disagree with the policy and believe it ought to change. This was, in fact, the view of many Saints regarding the priesthood/temple ban before it was lifted in 1978.[38]

If beliefs, teachings, and policies are not necessarily doctrine, then what is a doctrine? Like teachings and policies, a doctrine must have some sort of official support. While determining what official support consists of is problematic, we can reasonably maintain that speculations, theories, and even revelations of lay members would not be considered doctrine. And as discussed earlier, even that which is officially taught by the church is not necessarily considered doctrine either. However, unlike beliefs, teachings, and policies, which are not

---

36. Joseph Fielding Smith, *Doctrines of Salvation*, vol. 1, ed. Bruce. R. McConkie (Salt Lake City: Bookcraft, 1964), 61, 66.

37. Prince and Wright, *David O. McKay*, 79–80; Joseph Fielding Smith, *Answers to Gospel Questions*, vol. 2 (Salt Lake City: Deseret Book Co., 1958), 188.

38. For example, see Hugh B. Brown's disagreement with the priesthood ban in Edwin B. Firmage, ed., *An Abundant Life: The Memoirs of Hugh B. Brown* (Salt Lake City: Signature Books, 1988), 129, 142–43.

purported necessarily to be true or correct, doctrine does seem to have this quality. This is especially evident in LDS general conference addresses and teachings from church leaders where "doctrine" is used almost always in conjunction with "truth."[39] For example, in the April 2008 general conference, Elder Richard B. Wirthlin urged Latter-day Saints who had strayed from the church for various reasons to return. He added to this, however, "To those who have strayed because of doctrinal concerns, we cannot apologize for the truth."[40] Making this same relationship of truth and doctrine, Millet appeals to "true doctrine" when discussing his authoritative model.[41]

Though there is a relationship between truth and doctrine, the mere truth of a statement is not sufficient for it to be considered doctrine in ordinary LDS discourse. As Oman points out,

> [T]here are issues about which Church Doctrine is silent. For example, I take it to be fairly uncontroversial that there is no Church Doctrine on the precise location of Williamsburg, Virginia. ... No one could plausibly argue, however, that because of this, no statement about the location of Williamsburg, Virginia ... could be true or false. The statement that "Williamsburg, Virginia, is located on the banks of the Potomac River" is clearly false, the silence of Church Doctrine notwithstanding. Nor does it make sense of our ordinary usage of the term Church Doctrine to say, "It is Church Doctrine that Williamsburg, Virginia, is on the York–James Peninsula."[42]

Furthermore, just because a statement about a religious matter happens to be true, its truthfulness is likewise not a sufficient condition for being doctrine. For example, it may be the case that the mortal Jesus was actually married or that Earth was created fewer than 13,000 years

---

39. Compare to Armand L. Mauss, "Fading of the Pharaoh's Curse, " in *Neither White nor Black: Mormon Scholars Confront the Race Issue in a Universal Truth*, eds. Lester E. Bush and Armand L. Mauss (Midvale, Utah: Signature Books, 1984), 173–75. Mauss provides four categories of doctrine: official teachings and policy fall under the categories of canonical and official doctrines. (Beliefs would fall under the categories of authoritative and popular doctrines.) His definition of doctrine, I believe, fails to recognize ordinary usage within the LDS Church that equates doctrine with truth. For Mauss, his definition of doctrine is "an operational construct, not a theological one, not synonymous with 'truth' in an ultimate, objective sense" (173).

40. Richard B. Wirthlin, "Concern for the One," *Ensign*, May 2008, 18.

41. Millet, "What Do We Really Believe?" 265, 273, 278.

42. Oman, "Jurisprudence and the Problem of Church Doctrine," 5.

ago. Even if those were true unknown to us, that would not be sufficient for them to be doctrine. Like the location of the Potomac River, church doctrine is silent on these matters.

The role that truth plays in determining doctrine is then not to say that the actual truth of something makes it doctrine; rather, it is the claim of truth within an *official context* that makes it doctrine. Despite the fact of the matter, it would be odd for a church leader to say during general conference, "X is a doctrine, but it is not true" or "X is a doctrine, but it may not be true." When something is declared to be a doctrine, it is assumed that an implicit endorsement of its truth accompanies it.[43] What distinguishes a doctrine from a belief, teaching, or policy is that while the latter may be given or made with a presumption that it may not actually be true or correct, a doctrine is something that is officially considered and assumed to be true.

DOCTRINE AND TRUTH

While discussing his method of determining doctrine, Millet acknowledges that difficulties arise when approaching controversial LDS teachings of the past that are no longer taught today when it is clear that "someone in the past *has* spoken on these matters, *has* put forward ideas that are out of harmony with what we know and teach today."[44] Millet recognizes that the "hard issues" arise when Latter-day Saints are confronted with teachings that were presented as doctrine by previous leaders of the church (such as Brigham Young's Adam–God teaching). He asks, "Well then, what *else* did this Church leader teach that is not considered doctrine today? How can we confidently accept anything else he taught? What other directions taken or procedures pursued by the Church in an earlier time do we not follow in our day?"[45] Millet believes that his authoritative model, with an emphasis on contemporary teachings, is able to address these hard issues because modern church leaders have corrected the errors of the past by either directly replacing or indirectly abandoning those former teachings. Other teachings of Brigham Young can be known to be true because they are still taught

---

43. A search of the last thirty-seven years of general conference sermons on the church's website in 2008 resulted in over 800 returns that mention doctrine in conjunction with it being true.
44. Millet, "What Do We Really Believe?" 271.
45. Millet, "What Do We Really Believe?" 272.

today. What Millet may overlook is that there are even harder issues that arise when past teachings are put into a context of modern revelation, changing teachings, and truth claims that doctrines make. While the hard issues for Latter-day Saints may concern the rest of Brigham Young's teachings, the harder issues in light of these past teachings may ask *what it means* for something to be true in today's LDS Church. If leaders of the past could be mistaken in their teachings, what in principle would prevent the teachings of current leaders from being mistaken? These questions have largely been ignored by LDS thinkers.

While Oman argues that truth is not co-extensive with doctrine, he does not go as far as to say that LDS doctrines are nonetheless true. He does, however, defend himself from the accusation that he is claiming that the truths of the doctrines should be contested. He writes, "It is important to understand that when I say that certain aspects of Church Doctrine are inherently contestable, I am not talking about disagreements over whether Church Doctrine is true or whether it should be followed."[46] One reason why truth and doctrine become problematic together is that in ordinary LDS discourse "truth" is predominantly used along with a correspondence theory of truth. According to this theory, a statement is considered true if it accurately represents the facts of the world. For example, the statement "Salt Lake City is the capital of Utah" is true according to this theory if it happens to be the case that Salt Lake City *actually* is the capital of Utah. This correspondence theory seems to be what then-Elder Dallin H. Oaks appeals to in his April 2008 general conference talk when he says, "A testimony of the gospel is a personal witness ... that certain facts of eternal significance are true and that we know them to be true."[47] Not only do most Latter-day Saints hold to a correspondence theory of truth, but many Saints and church leaders frequently appeal to doctrine as being "absolute truth" that is even more accurate in its truth claims than science. Elder Richard G. Scott, a former nuclear engineer, said of the scientific method, "It has two limitations. First, we never can be sure we have identified absolute truth, though we often draw nearer and nearer to it. Second, sometimes, no matter how earnestly we apply the

---

46. Oman, "Jurisprudence and the Problem of Doctrine," 14.
47. Dallin H. Oaks, "Testimony," *Ensign,* May 2008, 26.

method, we can get the wrong answer."[48] Theories of truth that depart from correspondence are usually condemned as relative and signs of a deteriorating society. Exemplifying this notion of absolute truth being superior to a relative truth, Elder Dieter F. Uchtdorf said in a general conference of the church,

> When we bear testimony, we declare the absolute truth of the gospel message. In a time when many perceive truth as relative, a declaration of absolute truth is not very popular, nor does it seem politically correct or opportune. Testimonies [tell] of things how "they really are" … Satan wouldn't mind if we declared the message of our faith and gospel doctrine as negotiable according to circumstances. Our firm conviction of gospel truth is an anchor in our lives; it is steady and reliable as the North Star.[49]

The conundrum lies in trying to fit this correspondence theory of truth into the broader context of modern revelation and changing teachings within the church. This becomes clear if we apply either the interpretive or authoritative model of determining doctrine. If we were to begin with Oman's interpretive model, we would first have to find a "brute fact" of doctrine, which itself would require Millet's authoritative model to define. However, because the authoritative model depends on contemporary sources to determine doctrine, the question of temporal relativity emerges. For example, if we applied Millet's authoritative model in 1852, we would see that Adam–God was taught by the president of the church, taught by his counselors, published in official church publications, had consistent "sticking power" at the time, and was apparently taught as part of the temple endowment ceremony.[50] By Millet's criteria, Adam–God was a true doctrine in 1852. However in 2020, if we applied this same criteria, we would see that Adam–God is not only no longer taught by church leaders, but is condemned as false doctrine;[51] Adam–God is not published in any official church curriculum, and its "sticking power" has long since been unstuck. So by these same criteria, in 2020 Adam–God is a false doctrine. Other examples

---

48. Richard G. Scott, "Truth: The Foundation for Righteous Decisions," *Ensign*, Nov. 2007, 91.

49. Dieter F. Uchtdorf, "The Power of a Personal Testimony," *Ensign*, Nov. 2006, 38.

50. See David John Buerger, "The Adam–God Doctrine," *Dialogue: A Journal of Mormon Thought* 15, 1 (1982): 14–58.

51. For example, see Bruce R. McConkie, "The Seven Deadly Heresies," *BYU Devotional Speeches of the Year, 1980* (Provo, Utah: BYU Press, 1981), 78.

of where a change in "true doctrine" appears to occur include the age of the Earth, the state of life before the Fall of Adam,[52] the immorality of birth control,[53] the perpetuation of the priesthood ban, and theories for the ban.[54] At various times in the past, if Millet's criteria are applied, we would get a different "true doctrine" than that which would be received today. Furthermore, many of these doctrines of the past were not considered tangential beliefs, but were taught along with the injunction that adhering to them was essential for salvation. Thus they were not just "true doctrine" in times past, but were "true saving doctrine" that are now considered false, non-doctrinal, even apostate.

One may respond that the reason for the changes in what counted as true doctrine is that they were true for the people at the time they were given and taught, but are no longer true for Saints today. For example, a Latter-day Saint may argue that the use of birth control was, in fact, a sinful practice until the mid-twentieth century, but that it is no longer the case. This, however, is problematic because (1) the temporal relativity of doctrine has been frequently condemned by LDS leaders; and (2) many of these doctrines refer to historical facts that do not change. For example, the statement "George Washington was the first president of the United States" refers to a historical fact of the late eighteenth century. This fact cannot change. Similarly, either God the Father took on mortality as Adam or he did not. Either the Earth is less than 13,000 years old or not.

---

52. For example, see Joseph Fielding Smith's appeals to authority, scripture, etc., as he argues for a young earth and a rejection of death prior to the fall as church doctrine in *Man, His Origin and Destiny* (Salt Lake City: Deseret Book, 1954). Compare with Morris S. Petersen, "Earth," in *Encyclopedia of Mormonism*, 4 vols. (New York: Macmillan Publishing Co., 1992), 2:431–33.

53. For example, see LDS Church President Joseph F. Smith in the June 1917 *Relief Society Magazine*: "I regret, I think it is a crying evil, that there should exist a sentiment or a feeling among any members of the Church to curtail the birth of their children. I think that is a crime whenever it occurs, where husband and wife are in possession of health and vigor and are free from impurities that would be entailed upon their posterity. I believe that where people undertake to curtail or prevent the birth of their children that they are going to reap disappointment by and by. I have no hesitancy in saying that I believe this is one of the greatest crimes in the world today, this evil practice." Cited in Lester Bush, "Birth Control Among the Mormons: Introduction to an Insistent Question," *Dialogue: A Journal of Mormon Thought* 10, 2 (Autumn 1976): 22. Compare to "Birth Control" in the 2004 church-produced *True to the Faith* (Salt Lake City: Intellectual Reserve, 2004) which states that the decisions for birth control "are between the [married couple] and the Lord" (26).

54. See the latter discussion concerning the ban.

These challenges exist not only for Millet's and Oman's models of determining doctrine; they lie at the heart of LDS concepts of doctrine, truth, and modern revelatory authority. If a church leader at T^1 (time one) were understood to teach true doctrine, and if a later church leader at T^2 (time two) were to preach a revelation that supersedes or contradicts those of the previous leader, then theoretically any true doctrine at T^1 could become false doctrine at T^2. Similarly, any false doctrine condemned at T^1 could, in principle, be overturned and considered true doctrine at T^2.

A useful example of this problem may be found in John Lewis Lund's 1967 *The Church and the Negro*:

> Brigham Young revealed that the Negroes will not receive the Priesthood until a great while after the advent of Jesus Christ, whose coming will usher in a millennium of peace. ...
>
> *In view of what President Young and others have said, it would be foolish indeed to give anyone the false idea that a new revelation is immediately forthcoming on the issue of the Negroes receiving the Priesthood.* If the prophet of God were to receive a revelation tomorrow giving the Negroes the Priesthood it would be certainly be accepted regardless of what Brigham Young or any other previous prophet has said. This is because the words of the living oracles relate more specifically to the era in which we live. ...
>
> Mormons view a prophet as God's literal mouthpiece on earth. ... The faithful Latter-day Saint accepts the prophet's words as God's will. Prophets do not inspire God; God inspires prophets.[55]

For Lund, the doctrines taught by Brigham Young and other church leaders would have precluded the idea of a later revelation giving blacks the priesthood before the Second Coming. Such an idea would be "foolish" and "false" because that revelation would contradict the teachings of Young and others that were presumed to be true and representative of God's will. Both could not be true because either the priesthood would not be given to black Saints before the Second Coming or it would be. Despite this, Lund is open to the idea that a new revelation might come that would be equally true and representative of God's will. This should, of course, raise the question as to how statements by Young should be understood were the priesthood ban to be lifted prior

---

55. John Lewis Lund, *The Church and the Negro: A Discussion of Mormons, Negroes and the Priesthood* (Glendale, California: Paramount Publishers, 1967), 45, emphasis added.

to the Millennium (as occurred eleven years later). Can a Latter-day Saint accept both as being absolutely true doctrine? It seems that the later revelation would show that the prior teachings by Brigham Young and other church leaders were, in fact, false. Elder Bruce R. McConkie addressed this very issue when he said,

> Forget everything that I have said, or what President Brigham Young or President George Q. Cannon or whomsoever has said in days past that is contrary to the present revelation. We spoke with a limited understanding and without the light and knowledge that now has come into the world.
>
> We get our truth and our light line upon line and precept upon precept. We have now had added a new flood of intelligence and light on this particular subject, and it erases all the darkness and all the views and all the thoughts of the past. They don't matter any more.[56]

According to Millet, the hard issue for Latter-day Saints deals with the remainder of Young's past teachings. However, this also reveals harder issues of why a Latter-day Saint should accept the teachings of a modern leader as true doctrine when they apparently contradict the doctrines of other leaders of the past. If a church leader of the past could be wrong about X, why should a church leader of the present be trusted about Y? Such problems cannot simply be dismissed as being unrelated to salvation—many of the doctrines that are no longer taught today (such as the sin of birth control, the requirement of plural marriage, and the condemnation of organic evolution) were once taught as being essential for salvation.[57]

These problems not only concern simple beliefs, but have practical and moral implications. If, for example, person A taught that (a) plural marriage would no longer be practiced by the church in twenty years, he would have been considered as espousing false doctrine and subject to church discipline. At the same time, if person B believed and taught that (b) the church would continue to practice plural marriage into the

---

56. Bruce R. McConkie, "All Are Alike unto God," address given at the Church Education System Religious Educators Symposium on August 18, 1978.

57. For birth control as a sin, see note 53 above. For a belief in the doctrine of polygamy being essential for salvation see Brigham Young, Aug. 19, 1866, *Journal of Discourses*, 11:269, where Young states that "[t]he only men who become Gods, even the Sons of God, are those who enter into polygamy." For a condemnation of evolution as essential for salvation, see Smith, *Doctrines of Salvation*, 1:93, where Joseph Fielding Smith argues that a belief in evolution entails a denial of the atonement. See also, McConkie, "The Seven Deadly Heresies."

twentieth century, he would have been considered as affirming true doctrine. Yet in 1900 we would see that person A who may have been excommunicated for his belief was now holding a true doctrine and that person B a false one. Likewise, a person today who believes and teaches something that is considered as false doctrine by the church and is disciplined could theoretically have her beliefs validated at some point in the future. For example, while the church urged members in California to support a constitutional amendment banning same-sex marriages,[58] a Latter-day Saint could believe and argue (based on the historical fact that church leaders have sometimes been wrong) that the push against same-sex marriages by church leaders may also be wrong. And while public criticism of the church's opposition to same-sex marriage may incur informal or formal discipline, it is conceivable that continuing revelation by a future church leader, no matter how foolish and false it may seem in light of current teachings, may vindicate that person.

Finally, one may argue that the truthfulness of a doctrinal teaching is only secondary to a Latter-day Saint's *believing and following* the current teachings of church leaders, regardless of their truth or falsity. But this seems to ignore the way in which truth has been understood from the church's founding. It would also appear to challenge the faith claims that lie at the foundation of the church—as the truthfulness of the LDS faith claims play a very important role in the religious discourse.

IS IT CHURCH DOCTRINE THAT CHURCH DOCTRINE IS TRUE?

In follow-ups to their respective essays, Millet stresses that "doctrine means teaching,"[59] and Oman takes things a slight step back and says that "church doctrine is a standard for teaching."[60] These are, of course, straightforward definitions of the term and are perhaps the appropriate uses when responding to observers who simply want a list of the contemporary LDS Church's teachings. Thus, if a simple list of teachings were all that was being delineated, then no real justification would be needed other than an appeal to common sense

---

58. "LDS Church Backs Marriage Measure on California Ballot," *Deseret News*, June 24, 2008.
59. Robert L. Millet, "Defining Doctrine: A Response to Loyd Ericson," *Element: The Journal of the Society for Mormon Philosophy and Theology* 5, 1 (Spring 2009): 1.
60. Nathan B. Oman, "Truth, Doctrine, and Authority," *Element: The Journal of the Society for Mormon Philosophy and Theology* 5, 1 (Spring 2009): 9.

and common usage—or, as Millet puts, we could simply appeal to "a description of present Church practice,"[61] which Oman calls "sensible rules of thumb for discovering church doctrine."[62] In light of such a view, Oman's theory of doctrine as authority offers a plausible theoretical basis for the practice.

With the perspective of doctrine as teachings, the question "What is LDS doctrine?" would be analogous to the hypothetical question "What does Professor Xavier teach at the School for Gifted Youngsters?" Like Millet's criteria, in order to give a careful description of what Professor X teaches, we would simply need to listen to Professor X's lectures, read his syllabus and self-authored course manual,[63] and participate in his lab activities. We would, of course, also have to be careful to note when Professor X is speaking off-the-cuff and offering his opinion, exclude what he says among friends at an after-school party, and check to see if he is continuing to teach what he had taught in previous semesters. Furthermore, because Professor X is both highly knowledgeable in his field and a bit hard-nosed in his self-assurance, Oman's theory of doctrine and authority can adequately describe the relationship between Professor X's teachings and his students. Just as "the concept of authority … is not so demanding that church doctrine must be identical with the truth," a similar concept of professor-student authority does not demand that Professor X's teachings be identical with the truth. Even though it is possible that some of his teachings may be wrong, students "are justified in letting the authority of [his teachings] override their own … best judgments so long as they believe that [Professor X], like a doctor, enjoys an epistemological advantage."[64] Furthermore, regardless of whether Professor X is right or wrong on a particular matter, the authority of his teachings requires that students

---

61. Millet, "Defining Doctrine," 1.

62. Oman, "Truth," 10.

63. While the corollaries of Professor X's lectures, syllabi, etc., to Millet's criteria may be clear, I specifically chose "self-authored manuals" to be a corollary to church-authored manuals. Just as it would be incorrect to state that Professor X teaches the particular things in a text he uses for a course, it would be incorrect to say that the contemporary LDS Church teaches everything found in the LDS scriptures (see my example above with the Word of Wisdom). Because scripture needs to be interpreted, it seems that there will always be a layer of interpretation (perhaps through a church manual or statement from church leaders) that would always separate the church's teachings from scripture.

64. Oman, "Truth," 13.

affirm his teachings in tests and quizzes and not publicly contradict him in class in order to receive passing grades.

If church doctrine were merely just a set of official teachings, then I would join with Oman in stating that church doctrine has no direct relation to truth and is primarily about authority. I could also join Millet in saying that the best way to know what is and is not contemporary church doctrine is simply to look at the criteria in his doctrinal parameters. The problem, however, is that, within the Latter-day Saint tradition, doctrine is more than just a list of official teachings. As Millet puts it in his original essay: "There is power in doctrine, power in the word, power to heal the wounded soul, power to transform human behavior."[65] Millet is not alone in defining doctrine as such, and by both Millet's and Oman's models for defining doctrine, it seems to be a clear and unambiguous doctrine that doctrine is more than mere teachings. The church-produced teaching manuals constantly encourage teachers and students to testify of the truthfulness and power of church doctrine.[66] A quick search on the church's website brings up hundreds of example from general conference talks from just the last couple decades that define and use the word "doctrine" in a manner that denotes truth and power, not merely teachings. In one talk alone, then-Elder Henry B. Eyring uses the word forty-five times with this meaning.[67] In fact, given its occurrence and use in contemporary church-produced manuals, general conferences, church statements,[68] and scripture, there is perhaps no doctrine of the church more pronounced than the doctrine that church doctrine is true.

This should hopefully make clear what is perhaps the greatest challenge to defining church doctrine. The challenges are not simply in defining the contemporary teachings of the LDS Church. Rather, they are the challenges of Latter-day Saints defining church doctrine for those within the tradition. Without recognizing the heavy emphasis

65. Millet, "What Do We Really Believe?" 265.

66. See for example, "Lesson 3: The Teacher's Divine Commission," in *Teaching, No Greater Call: A Resource Guide for Gospel Teaching* (Salt Lake City: Church of Jesus Christ of Latter-day Saints, 1999), 8–10.

67. Henry B. Eyring, "The Power of Teaching Doctrine," *Ensign*, May 1999, 73.

68. For example, the church's official statement on doctrine states that "members are encouraged to independently strive to receive their own spiritual confirmation of the truthfulness of Church doctrine." *LDS Newsroom* "Approaching Mormon Doctrine."

in church doctrine about church doctrine's truthfulness, the challenge of defining church doctrine becomes as interesting and simplistic as a student trying to find out what she needs to study for Professor X's midterm exam. The challenge arises not when one wishes to know what the LDS Church teaches in its manuals and how members are to relate to those teachings, but when Latter-day Saints try to ascertain what the doctrines of truth and power are—that the church has a primary (though perhaps not exclusive) claim on truth is, after all, one of the foundational doctrines of the restoration. If it is the case, as Millet and Oman agree, that the doctrines of the church can and do change, and if the doctrines of the restored church are true, then how should Latter-day Saints understand the truthfulness of these changing doctrines?[69] How do we make sense of a new true doctrine of the restoration contradicting a discontinued true doctrine of the restoration? Is truth relative? Does truth change with time? Is the Mormon corpus of true church doctrine smaller than we might initially think—and, if so, what are those doctrines and how do we determine which are true and which are not?

Or, is the church doctrine of church doctrine's truthfulness not true?

---

69. See, for example, Charles R. Harrell, *"This Is My Doctrine": The Development of Mormon Theology* (Salt Lake City: Greg Kofford Books, 2011).

TWO

LDS THEOLOGY AND THE OMNIS
THE DANGERS OF THEOLOGICAL SPECULATION

DAVID H. BAILEY

Engaging in doctrinal speculation and then later adopting these speculations as religious dogma is as old as recorded history.

One example is the adoption of the traditional geocentric cosmology of antiquity into the doctrinal system of the early Christian church. Early theologians found support for this world view in the numerous biblical references to the "four corners," "foundations," "pillars" and "ends" of the earth, and in passages describing the earth as fixed and immovable, with the sun, stars, and planets moving on heavenly spheres around the earth.[1] As a result, this geocentric cosmology became part of traditional Christian dogma, in spite of the fact that these ancient poetic passages were never intended to be read as authoritative, precise statements of scientific fact in our modern sense, and in spite of the fact that even in medieval times the scholarly world, at least, recognized that some aspects of this cosmology (e.g., a flat earth) were not factual. In the sixteenth century, Catholic officials declared Galileo's writings on Copernicus's heliocentric theory to be incompatible with official church doctrine.[2] Martin Luther, for whom the Bible was the infallible word of God, rejected the Copernican theory, in part, because the Bible records Joshua commanding the sun, not the earth, to stand still (Josh. 10:12–13).[3]

Another example is the doctrine of Mary. In the first few decades after Jesus Christ, early theologians who had formulated the doctrine of original sin were concerned that Jesus could have inherited Adam's sin

---

1. For examples, see 1 Sam. 2:8; 2 Sam. 22:16; Job 28:24; 38:4; Ps. 75:3; Isa. 11:12; 48:13; Jer. 31:37; Heb. 1:10; Rev. 7:1; Ps. 93:1; 104:5; 104:19; Eccl. 1:5; Job 9:6–7; Isa. 38:7–8; and Amos 8:9.

2. Will and Ariel Durant, *The Story of Civilization*, 11 vols. (New York: Simon and Schuster, 1935–75), 7:600–12. Ariel Durant is listed as co-author on vols. 7–11.

3. Durant, *Story of Civilization*, 6:858.

from Mary. Thus they taught that Mary was and remained a virgin, in spite of biblical references to Jesus' four brothers and two or more sisters (see Matt. 13:55–56; Mark 3:31, 6:3; John 1:45, 6:42; Rom. 1:3; Gal. 4:4.) Some later theologians even taught that Mary became a postpartum virgin, fearing that she may have retained physical evidence of her delivery. In the nineteenth century, once scientific evidence came to light indicating that both the male and female contribute genetic information (meaning that women, in the Catholic view, also transmit the sin of Adam), Catholic theologians promoted the doctrine that Mary was immaculately conceived and, further, that she was taken bodily—"assumed"—into heaven. In short, what started out with good intention to resolve a point of theology eventually mushroomed into a system of doctrines that many today, even in the Catholic and Protestant worlds, now recognize as both dubious and baroque.[4]

A third example is the doctrine of predestination. It is well known that early Christian theologians were heavily influenced by Greek-Platonic philosophy, which viewed qualities or aspects of this world as mere shadows of "ideals" existing in the unseen world. Thus even by the year 413 CE, God's omniscience was taken for granted in the writings of Augustine, who argued that since God sees the future in all details, future events are irrevocably predestined.[5] During the Middle Ages, Augustine's predestination was de-emphasized in Catholic thought, but in 1525, Martin Luther, citing Augustine, argued that since God is omniscient, everything must happen as he has foreseen it, so that all events, through all time, have been predetermined in God's mind and are forever fated to be. Citing the writings of Paul for additional support, Luther concluded that by divine predestination the elect are chosen for eternal happiness, the rest are graceless and damned to everlasting hell, and that humankind is as "unfree as a block of wood, a rock, a lump of clay, or a pillar of salt" (Rom. 9:18, Eph. 1:3–7).[6]

In 1535, John Calvin took these doctrines even further, conceding that although predestination—the notion that God has determined

4. John Shelby Spong, *A New Christianity for a New World* (New York: Harper Collins, 2002), 111–12.

5. St. Augustine, *The City of God*, in Mortimer J. Adler, ed., *Great Books of the Western World*, 60 vols. (Chicago: Encyclopedia Britannica, 1990), Vol. 16, Book 5, Chap. 9; see also Durant, *Story of Civilization*, 4:68.

6. Durant, *Story of Civilization*, 6:375.

the eternal fate of billions of souls—is a "horrible decree," its purpose is to promote our admiration of God's glory. As Calvin explained, "No one can deny that God foreknew the future final fate of man before He created him, and that He foreknew it because it was appointed by his own decree."[7] In other words, whereas Luther had argued that the future is determined because God has foreseen it and his foresight cannot be falsified, Calvin taught that God foresees the future *because* he has willed and determined it to be so. Historian Will Durant observed that Calvin ignored Christ's conception of God as a loving and merciful father, as well as numerous biblical passages that assure humanity's freedom to mold its own destiny (see 2 Pet. 3:9; 1 Tim. 2:4; 1 John 2:2; 4:14; and others.). Instead, Calvin developed the thought of his predecessors to "ruinously logical conclusions." Durant summarized Calvin's career harshly: "We shall always find it hard to love the man who darkened the human soul with the most absurd and blasphemous conception of God in all the long and honored history of nonsense."[8]

Unfortunately, members of the Church of Jesus Christ of Latter-day Saints cannot take much comfort in the above examples, because LDS history has also been characterized by a certain amount of free-wheeling doctrinal speculation. Some well-known examples include: (a) Adam was the father of Jesus;[9] (b) certain sins require one's blood to be shed in retribution;[10] (c) practicing polygamy is essential for exaltation;[11] (d) certain racial groups were "less valiant" in the pre-mortal existence;[12] (e) the six periods of creation each lasted a literal 1,000 years;[13] (f) the Book of Mormon is the history of the *entire* ancient western hemisphere;[14] and (g) humankind will never succeed in space travel.[15]

7. *Story of Civilization*, 464.

8. *Story of Civilization*, 465, 490.

9. Brigham Young, *Journal of Discourses*, 26 vols. (London: LDS Booksellers Depot, 1854–86), 1:50–51 (Apr. 9, 1852).

10. Brigham Young, *Journal of Discourses*, 4:53–54 (Sept. 21, 1856).

11. Brigham Young, *Journal of Discourses*, 11:269 (Aug. 19, 1866); Joseph F. Smith, in 20:28 (July 7, 1878).

12. Bruce R. McConkie, *Mormon Doctrine*, 2nd ed. (Salt Lake City: Bookcraft, 1966), 527.

13. *Mormon Doctrine*, 255.

14. Spencer W. Kimball, "Of Royal Blood," *Ensign*, July 1971, 7; Mark E. Petersen, *LDS Conference Report* (Salt Lake City: Church of Jesus Christ of Latter-day Saints, Apr. 1953), 81.

15. Joseph Fielding Smith, *Answers to Gospel Questions*, 5 vols. (Salt Lake City: Deseret Book Co., 1966), 2:191; also Joseph Fielding Smith, Letter to Orville Gunter, May 7, 1958, photocopy in my possession.

One common thread in these and other examples is the attempt to justify, by doctrinal exposition, notions that have already been widely assumed in the religious movement. Another common thread is the usage of quasi-axiomatic reasoning to press questionable premises to logical extremes. But perhaps the most pervasive underlying thread is the perennial desire for "answers," even in cases where ultimate answers cannot be provided. According to the Apostle Paul, the early Christians, not content with "sound doctrine," had developed "itching ears" (Titus 4:3). Sadly, "itching ears" are characteristic of religious movements in almost any era, including the LDS movement today.

THE OMNI DOCTRINES

The terms *omnipotent, omniscient, omnipresent* and *omnibenevolent* play a central role in the definition of God for traditional Christian faiths, although they are used more often today by conservative and evangelical denominations. Some Latter-day Saints also use these terms, particularly the first two. Nonetheless, it is a curious fact that these words, with the exception of "omnipotent" in one poetic verse in Revelation (19:6), do *not* appear in the Bible. Instead, these terms and related absolutist doctrines were formulated with the creeds of early Christianity during the first few centuries after Jesus, when much of Christian theology was recast in terms of Greek metaphysics. As mentioned, the literal omniscience of God was already taken for granted by the time Augustine wrote *City of God* in 413 CE. By 1265, God's omnipotence, omniscience, and omnipresence were featured as fundamental doctrines in Thomas Aquinas' *Summa Theologica*.[16]

Biblical support for these doctrines is mixed. In the Hebrew Bible one finds numerous passages extolling the great power, knowledge, and wisdom of God. But the compassionate and flexible natures of God are also portrayed. The Hebrew Bible describes God as having second thoughts about his creation in light of human wickedness at the time of Noah; willing to negotiate step-by-step with Abraham over the fate of Sodom and Gomorrah; and instructing the Israelites that they should no longer consider children guilty because of the sins of their parents or ancestors (Gen. 6:5–6; 18:23–33; Eze. 18:1–32). This latter teaching, in

---

16. Thomas Aquinas, *Summa Theologica*, in Adler, *Great Books*, vol. 17: part 1, chaps. 7–14.

Ezekiel, is in contrast to passages such as in Deuteronomy, where persons of illegitimate birth are banned from the congregation of the Lord "even to the tenth generation" and where persons of Ammonite or Moabite ancestry are banned "for ever" (Deut. 23:2–4; Ruth 1:16–2:23).[17]

In the New Testament, there is no hint of such absolutist theology in Jesus' teachings. Instead, Jesus focused on righteous, humble, and unselfish living, as exemplified by the Sermon on the Mount and numerous parables. Jesus described God as his "father." He reduced the Mosaic law to two principles: love God and love your neighbor as yourself. He mentioned only simple criteria for discipleship: "continue in my word" and "love one another" (Matt. 6:9; 7:21; Mark 14:36; Luke 10:21; 22:42; John 5:17; Matt. 22:39; John 8:31; 13:35). The Apostle Paul mentioned predestination in two passages, as noted above, but again his focus was on the basic principles of Christianity and salvation, as exemplified by his "faith, hope, and charity" sermon (1 Cor. 13:1–13). In any event, nowhere in the New Testament is there any suggestion that affirmation of a rigid, absolutist "creed" is required for salvation, much less affirmation of the omni doctrines that later became central to Christian theology.

Most Latter-day Saints today use the omni terms informally—the equivalent of referring to God poetically as "Almighty." But some LDS writers use the terms more formally as statements of theological fact. For example, one LDS scholar, responding to criticisms that the Latter-day Saints are not really Christian, wrote, "God is omniscient, omnipotent, omnipresent, infinite, eternal and unchangeable."[18] Another LDS writer, after documenting how the simple primitive Christian concept of God changed under the influence of Greek philosophy in the first few centuries after Jesus, nonetheless stated that God is omnipotent and omniscient.[19]

According to O. Kendall White, the omni doctrines in today's LDS discourse are characteristic of what he terms "Mormon neo-orthodoxy," namely, an increasing emphasis on the greatness and absoluteness of

17. Ironically, according to the Hebrew Bible, King David's great-grandmother, Ruth, was Moabite.

18. Craig L. Blomberg, Stephen E. Robinson, *How Wide the Divide? A Mormon and an Evangelical in Conversation* (Downers Grove, Illinois: InterVarsity Press, 1997), 59, 72.

19. Richard R. Hopkins, *How Greek Philosophy Corrupted the Christian Concept of God* (Bountiful, Utah: Horizon Publishers, 1998), 309–11.

God, the inscrutability of his ways, the contrasting depravity of humankind, a stronger emphasis on salvation by grace, the need for unquestioning faith, and a minimization of human free will.[20] More recently LDS sociologist Armand Mauss analyzed these same developments and concluded that since the middle of the twentieth century, the LDS Church has in many respects moved toward convergence with evangelical Protestantism, partly under external pressures and partly because of internal forces.[21]

I often wonder if modern-day Saints who teach and use the omni terms fully appreciate their meaning and import, especially as they have been understood by the Christian world and by the evangelical Protestant world today. While a comprehensive study of the omni doctrines is beyond the scope of this essay, we may get the flavor of this absolutist theology from the website of a large conservative Protestant organization: "[T]he God of biblical Christianity is at least (1) personal and incorporeal (without physical parts), (2) the Creator and sustainer of everything else that exists, (3) omnipotent (all-powerful), (4) omniscient (all-knowing), (5) omnipresent (everywhere present), (6) immutable (unchanging) and eternal, and (7) necessary and the only God that exists."[22]

This website then elaborates further on the implications of these omni doctrines:

> Unlike humans, God is not uniquely associated with one physical entity (i.e., a body) … unlike a god who forms the universe out of preexistent matter, the God of the Bible created the universe *ex nihilo* (out of nothing). Consequently, it is on God alone that everything in the universe, indeed, the universe itself, depends for its existence. … Omnipotence literally means "all-powerful." When we speak of God as omnipotent, this should be understood to mean that God can do anything that is consistent with being a personal, incorporeal, omniscient, omnipresent, immutable, wholly good, and necessary Creator. … God is all-knowing, and His all-knowingness encompasses the *past, present, and future*. He has absolute

---

20. O. Kendall White Jr., *Mormon Neo-Orthodoxy: A Crisis Theology* (Salt Lake City: Signature Books, 1987), 89–137.

21. Armand L. Mauss, *The Angel and the Beehive: The Mormon Struggle with Assimilation* (Urbana: University of Illinois Press, 1994), 177–92.

22. North American Mission Board, "The Mormon Concept of God," www.namb.net/apologetics-blog/the-mormon-concept-of-god, accessed May 9, 2019.

and total knowledge. ... Since God is not limited by a spatiotemporal body, knows everything immediately without benefit of sensory organs, and sustains the existence of all that exists, it follows that He is in some sense present everywhere. When a Christian says that God is immutable and eternal, he or she is saying that God is *unchanging*. ... There never was a time when God was not God. ... Moreover, since everything that exists depends on God, and God is unchanging and eternal, it follows that God cannot *not* exist. In other words, He is a *necessary* being, whereas everything else is contingent (or dependent on God for its existence).

For many conservative Protestant denominations, a corollary of the omnipotence and omniscience of God is that the Bible, as God's word, is both *complete* and *inerrant*. There is no possibility that the Bible is mistaken on any significant point of history or doctrine; no further revelation is possible; and scientific and secular research cannot uncover any important fundamental truths except those already in the Bible: "Holy Scripture ... is of infallible divine authority in all matters upon which it touches. ... Scripture is without error or fault in all its teaching ... We further deny that any normative revelation has been given since the completion of the New Testament writings."[23]

EARLY LDS DOCTRINE AND THE OMNIS

The omnis, as these terms are widely understood in the conservative Christian world today, correspond to theological notions that most Latter-day Saints would not find acceptable. First, Joseph Smith and other LDS leaders have taught that God is not incorporeal but has a literal physical existence within space and time. Second, Doctrine and Covenants 93:29–33 states that the "elements" are eternal, not created by God, and that the "souls" of humankind are also eternal and thus not contingent upon God. And in 1844 Joseph Smith rejected the doctrine of creation *ex nihilo*: "Learned Docters tell us God created the heavens & earth out of nothing[.] they account it blasphemy to contradict the idea—they will call you a fool—you ask them why they say dont the bible say he created the world & they infer that it must be out of nothing[.] The word create came from the word Barau[.] dont mean so—it means

---

23. "Chicago Statement on Biblical Inerrancy," www.carm.org/creeds/chicago.htm, accessed May 9, 2019.

to organize—same as a man would use to build a ship."[24] Third, Joseph Smith and other leaders have asserted that the heavens are open and that anyone may receive inspiration and revelation from on high (see A-F 9).

In his 1844 King Follett discourse, Joseph Smith elaborated on these ideas, rejecting the traditional Christian notion that God is on a different plane of existence from humans. Instead, humans, at least in intelligence, have the same potential as God: "You have got to learn how to make yourselves Gods in order to save yourselves and be kings and priests to God, the same as all Gods have done—by going from a small capacity to a great capacity, from a small degree to another, from grace to grace, until the resurrection of the dead, from exaltation to exaltation. ... Intelligence is eternal and exists upon a self-existent principle. It is a spirit from age to age and there is no creation about it. The first principles of man are self-existent with God."[25]

Although Protestants and Catholics do not accept God's physical existence, Joseph Smith seems to have anticipated the thinking of modern theologians who recognize that the notion of the utter depravity of humankind, compared to the boundless omnipotence of God, denies human achievements in charity, science, art, and literature. Anglican bishop and theologian John Shelby Spong, for example, laments the "enormous chasm between the human and the divine" in traditional Christian thought, "a chasm so broad and so deep that we have almost come to think of human and divine as opposites."[26]

Joseph Smith also rejected the doctrine of predestination. He argued that unconditional election of individuals to eternal life was not taught by the ancient apostles. He acknowledged that individuals might be pre-ordained for salvation, but God "passes over no man's sins, but visits them with correction, and if His children will not repent of their sins He will discard them."[27] In the 1950s, LDS Church President David O. McKay noted that Joseph Smith had rejected the doctrine of predestination a century prior.[28]

---

24. Joseph Smith, sermon, Apr. 7, 1844, reported by William Clayton, *Joseph Smith Papers*, www.josephsmithpapers.org, accessed July 29, 2020.

25. Stan Larson, "The King Follett Discourse: A Newly Amalgamated Text," *BYU Studies* 18, 2 (Winter 1978): 198–208.

26. Spong, *New Christianity*, 151.

27. Joseph Smith, *Times and Seasons* 2, 15 (June 1, 1841): 429–30.

28. David O. McKay, *Gospel Ideals* (Salt Lake City: Bookcraft, 1960), 25–26.

In a larger sense, Joseph Smith rejected all traditional creeds, stemming back to his first vision in 1820, where he learned that creeds were an "abomination" (JS-H 1:19). In 1843, in response to a question from a local political official, he declared: "the most prominent points of difference in sentiment between the Latter Day Saints & Sectarians viz: the latter are all circumscribed by some peculiar creed which deprived its members of the right of believing anything not contained in it; whereas the Latter Day Saints have no creed, but are ready to believe <u>all true principals</u> existing, as they are made manifest to us from time to time."[29]

On another occasion, Joseph recorded his disapproval of a disciplinary council that had accused an elderly member of preaching false doctrine: "I never thought it was right to call up a man and try him because he erred in doctrine, it looks too much like [another denomination] and not like Latter day Saintism. [Some other denominations] have creeds which a man must believe or be kicked out of their church. I want the liberty of believing as I please, it feels so good not to be trameled. It dont prove that a man is not a good man, because he errs in doctrine."[30]

Here again we see overtones of modern religious thought, which recognizes both the futility of attempting to encapsulate God in a creed as well as the potential for abuse in imposing creeds and other inflexible doctrinal tenets on others. Spong, for instance, wrote:

> In the Christian West today, we are far too sophisticated to erect idols of wood or stone and call them our gods. We know that such an activity no longer has credibility. In our intellectual arrogance, however, we Westerners—especially the Christian theologians among us—have time after time erected idols out of our words and then claimed for those words the ability to define the holy God. We have also burned at the stake people who refused to acknowledge the claim that God and our definitions of God were one and the same. Truth now demands that we surrender these distorting identifications forever.[31]

After Joseph Smith's death, many LDS leaders continued in this open-ended tradition, avoiding traditional rigid dogmas in general and the

---

29. William Clayton, journal, January 1, 1843, in James B. Allen, *No Toil nor Labor Fear: The Story of William Clayton* (Provo: Brigham Young University Press, 2002), 387

30. Sermon, Apr. 8, 1843, reported by William Clayton, *Joseph Smith Papers*.

31. Spong, *New Christianity*, 60–61.

omnis in particular. Brigham H. Roberts, in his *The Mormon Doctrine of Deity*, pointed out in detail how the LDS Church's "finitistic" theology, which rejects the omnis, avoids many of the pitfalls of traditional Christianity.[32] Brigham Young emphasized that there is "no such thing" as a miracle, in the sense of God's acting supernaturally outside space and time.[33] James E. Talmage agreed: "Miracles are commonly regarded as occurrences in opposition to the laws of nature. Such a conception is plainly erroneous, for the laws of nature are inviolable. However, as human understanding of these laws is at best but imperfect, events strictly in accordance with natural law may appear contrary thereto. The entire constitution of nature is founded on system and order."[34]

There have been some instances in LDS literature where the omnis have been taught, both implicitly and explicitly. In 1853, Orson Pratt taught that God was omniscient, so that God could not increase in intelligence. But Brigham Young declared these teachings to be "false."[35] Wilford Woodruff agreed: "If there was a point where man in his progression could not proceed any further, the very idea would throw a gloom over every intelligent and reflecting mind. God himself is still increasing and progressing in knowledge, power and dominion, and will do so world without end."[36]

In the twentieth century, however, James E. Talmage affirmed the omnis in his book *The Articles of Faith*, although he did not provide much scriptural support.[37] Later, Bruce R. McConkie affirmed the omnis in his *Mormon Doctrine*, citing as his source this passage from Joseph Smith's *Lectures on Faith*: "We here observe that God is the only

32. Brigham H. Roberts, *The Mormon Doctrine of Deity* (1903; repub. Bountiful, Utah: Horizon Publishers, 1982), 95–114.

33. Brigham Young, *Journal of Discourses*, 13:140–41 (July 11, 1869).

34. James E. Talmage, *The Articles of Faith* (1899; repub. Salt Lake City: Deseret Book Co., 1966), 220. This is reminiscent of contemporary Catholic theologian John F. Haught, who wrote: "Too often we have understood the conception of God as 'all-mighty' in a way that leads to theological contradictions, many of which have been pointed out quite rightly by scientific skeptics. Our view however, is that God's 'power' (which means 'capacity to influence') is more effectively manifested in a humble 'letting be' of a self-organizing universe than in any direct display of divine magicianship." Haught, *Science and Religion: From Conflict to Conversation* (New York: Paulist Press, 1995), 161.

35. James R. Clark, ed., *Messages of the First Presidency of the Church of Jesus Christ of Latter-day Saints*, 6 vols. (Salt Lake City: Bookcraft, 1965–75), 2:214–23.

36. Wilford Woodruff, *Journal of Discourses*, 6:120 (Dec. 6, 1857).

37. Talmage, *Articles of Faith*, 42–44.

supreme governor and independent being in whom all fullness and perfection dwell; who is omnipotent, omnipresent and omniscient; without beginning of days or end of life."[38]

However, historians now recognize that Joseph Smith did not write *Lectures on Faith*. More likely Sidney Rigdon, one of Joseph Smith's colleagues, was the author, particularly for the Second Lecture which presents the omni doctrines.[39] In part because of the authorship question, and also because of the presence of some questionable doctrines, *Lectures* was dropped from the LDS canon in 1920.[40] In any event, the question of who authored *Lectures* is largely academic, because it is clear from other sources (notably the King Follett discourse) that Joseph Smith distanced himself from the traditional omni doctrines of orthodox Christianity.

PHILOSOPHICAL AND SCIENTIFIC DIFFICULTIES

Scholars and theologians have recognized for centuries that there are numerous philosophical and scientific difficulties with the omni doctrines. There is not room here to analyze these complex issues in detail, but here is a brief summary of the difficulties:

1. If God is all-powerful and all-good, and if he created all things, then what are we to make of Satan or of evil in general?[41]

2. If God is all-powerful, and if he has acted in the world throughout history, why does he permit human suffering, disease, and premature death? For example, why did God permit the September 11 terrorists to kill thousands of God-fearing people from numerous religious faiths? This is the age-old "theodicy" (problem of evil) question.

3. If God possesses all knowledge and can see into the future with complete fidelity, then what of human free will? How do we escape the conclusion that we are mere robots, acting out a course that was irrevocably set in motion eons ago? More to the point, what justification

---

38. Joseph Smith, *Lectures on Faith* (1835; repub. Salt Lake City: Deseret Book Co., 1985), 13.

39. Kent Robson, "Omnis on the Horizon," *Sunstone*, 8, 4 (1983): 21–24.

40. Richard S. Van Wagoner, Steven C. Walker, and Allen D. Roberts, "The Lectures on Faith: A Case Study in Decanonization," *Dialogue: A Journal of Mormon Thought* 20, 3 (Fall 1987): 71–77.

41. As the ancient Greek philosopher Epicurus is reputed to have written, "Then whence cometh evil?" In Lucius Caecilius Firmianus Lactantius, *Divinae Institutiones* (c. 318), 7:494.

is there for punishing humans for misdeeds or, for that matter, for rewarding them for righteous living?

4. If God is omnipotent in the strong sense, and if God supernaturally intervenes in the world about us, then how do we explain scientific laws, where we see principles obeyed with extreme precision and unfailing consistency? And how is it that humans can uncover these laws?

With regards to item 3, some theologians, beginning with Augustine, have argued that God's absolute foreknowledge does not imply that God is responsible for what happens. But if the future can be foreseen and/or predicted with complete fidelity by any means, even by a hypothetical supercomputer, then we must necessarily conclude that only one future course is possible. In that event, free will is at best an illusion—we are indeed acting out a course that was defined eons ago. It only compounds these difficulties to assert further that it is God who possesses this absolute foreknowledge and who set the system into motion.

The notion that the future can be perfectly predicted goes back at least to Pierre-Simon Laplace, who wrote in 1812: "An intelligence knowing all the forces acting in nature at a given instant, as well as the momentary positions of all things in the universe, would be able to comprehend in one single formula the motions of the largest bodies as well as of the lightest atoms in the world, provided that its intellect were sufficiently powerful to subject all data to analysis; to it nothing would be uncertain, the future as well as the past would be present to its eyes."[42]

This notion, called by some the "clockwork universe" or the "Laplacean computer," was destroyed by twentieth-century science. In particular, the uncertainty principle of quantum mechanics showed that the very information needed to make such predictions, namely the unlimited-precision measurement of the current state of a physical system, is unattainable, not due to limitations of measurement technology, but instead as a fundamental characteristic of the universe we inhabit. Some have questioned whether quantum mechanical laws can have any macro-scale impact worth taking seriously. But consider for example the moment when the genetic molecules from two

---

42. Durant and Durant, *Story of Civilization*, 9:548.

human beings unite to form a new individual. Even a slight disturbance to such delicate processes, such as a chance encounter with a cosmic ray, can have drastic, long-term consequences. Indeed, recent research in the field of chaotic processes shows that this magnification of microscopic effects is more the rule than the exception in real-world physical processes.[43]

This does not mean that any prediction of the future is impossible. Present-day supercomputers are able to predict local weather fairly well up to about ten days out and are also used to predict long-term climate patterns such as global temperature trends.[44] But while general trends of future events can be anticipated, beyond a certain point the details of these processes cannot be foreseen.

MODERN LDS ANALYSIS

As mentioned, issues related to the omni doctrines have been studied by several LDS scholars, beginning with B. H. Roberts and his book *The Mormon Doctrine of Deity.* In his *The Theological Foundations of the Mormon Religion,* Sterling M. McMurrin notes, "Mormon theologians have moved somewhat ambiguously between the emotionally satisfying absolutism of traditional theism and the radical finitism logically demanded by their denial of creation and encouraged by the pragmatic character of their daily faith. Here they have often failed to recognize the strength of their own position and have, therefore, neglected to grasp and appreciate the full meaning of its implications."[45]

In 1975, in an analysis of LDS theology, Truman Madsen quotes Anglican theologian Edmond B. LaCherbonnier as observing, "Mormons also conceive God as temporal, not eternal in the sense of timeless. This idea of a timeless eternity is incompatible with an acting God, for it would be static, lifeless, impotent. If God is an agent, then he must be temporal, for timeless action is a contradiction in terms."[46]

---

43. Steven H. Strogatz, *Nonlinear Dynamics and Chaos: With Applications to Physics, Biology, Chemistry, and Engineering* (Boca Raton, Florida: CRC Press, 2000).

44. J. E. Kay et. al, "The Community Earth System Model (CESM) Large Ensemble Project," *Bulletin of the American Meteorological Society,* Aug. 2015, 1333–49.

45. Sterling M. McMurrin, *The Theological Foundations of the Mormon Religion* (Salt Lake City: University of Utah Press, 1965), 29.

46. Truman G. Madsen, ed., *Reflections on Mormonism, Judaeo-Christian Parallels* (Provo, Utah: BYU Press, 1978), 157. Also quoted in Robson, 1989 (see note 47).

Another contemporary LDS study is a 1989 article by Kent Robson.[47] On the issue of God's foreknowledge and human free agency, Robson concludes: "The issue is this: as Mormons we believe in freedom and free agency. In order for me to have freedom, I must have alternatives in my future that are truly *open* and not just *appear* to be open. ... [If] God knows my every specific act, then I have no *real and meaningful* freedom."[48] Other contemporary LDS references include a 1999 article and a 2001 book by Blake Ostler,[49] and a 2000 article by Kelli Potter.[50] These authors discuss in detail issues such as free agency and the problem of evil.

Perhaps the most eloquent treatment of these issues in recent LDS scholarly literature is Eugene England's posthumously published essay, "The Weeping God of Mormonism."[51] The title comes from the Book of Moses 7:28–41 (Pearl of Great Price):

> And it came to pass that the God of heaven looked upon the residue of the people, and he wept; and Enoch bore record of it, saying: How is it that the heavens weep, and shed forth their tears as the rain upon the mountains? And Enoch said unto the Lord: How is it that thou canst weep, seeing thou art holy, and from all eternity to all eternity? ... The Lord said unto Enoch: Behold these thy brethren; they are the workmanship of mine own hands, and I gave unto them their knowledge, in the day I created them; and in the Garden of Eden, gave I unto man his agency; And unto thy brethren have I said, and also given commandment, that they should love one another, and that they should choose me, their Father; but behold, they are without affection, and they hate their own blood; ... And it came to pass that the Lord spake unto Enoch, and told Enoch all the

47. Kent E. Robson, "Omnipotence, Omnipresence, and Omniscience in Mormon Theology," in Gary James Bergera, ed., *Line Upon Line: Essays on Mormon Doctrine* (Salt Lake City: Signature Books, 1989).

48. Robson, "Omnipotence," 71.

49. Blake T. Ostler, "Mormonism and Determinism," *Dialogue: A Journal of Mormon Thought*, 32, 4 (Winter 1999): 43–75; Blake T. Ostler, *Exploring Mormon Thought: The Attributes of God* (Draper, Utah: Greg Kofford Books, 2001).

50. Kelli Potter, "Finitism and the Problem of Evil," *Dialogue: A Journal of Mormon Thought*, 33, 4 (Winter 2000): 83–96.

51. Eugene England, "The Weeping God of Mormonism," *Dialogue: A Journal of Mormon Thought*, 35, 1 (Spring 2002): 63–80. However, inspection of the Bible revision manuscripts indicates that Joseph Smith portrayed Enoch and the heavens weeping, rather than God. See Colby Townsend, "Returning to the Sources: Integrating Textual Criticism in the Study of Early Mormon Texts and History," *Intermountain West Journal of Religious Studies* 10, 1 (2019): 77–79.

doings of the children of men; wherefore Enoch knew, and looked upon their wickedness, and their misery, and wept and stretched forth his arms, and his heart swelled wide as eternity; and his bowels yearned; and all eternity shook.

This passage affirms that the agency that God has given to humankind is fundamental and cannot be abrogated. Partly for this reason, God's power to remove evil and sin is limited. So God weeps with Enoch over the suffering that sometimes results. England notes that this passage represents a theodicy which, if not unique to Mormonism, may at least be unique among large, growing churches: "It is also, I believe, a theodicy that makes a crucial contribution to Mormonism's emergence as a mature, compassionate world religion, one that is able to contribute in important ways to God's efforts to save all his children not only through conversion but through sharing our revealed insights into the nature of God, in dialogue with others."[52]

Articles such as those mentioned above are not read widely in the LDS Church. Nonetheless, some rank-and-file Saints appear to have at least a fair understanding of these topics, even if they often do not appreciate the full doctrinal implications. For example, many Saints respond to difficulty No. 1 above (the existence of evil) by arguing that Satan lived in the pre-mortal world and, like us, had an eternal existence independent from God. This is actually a rather effective response. But note that this argument implicitly rejects the traditional Christian omni doctrine that God is the only uncreated and non-contingent being.

Saints typically respond to difficulty No. 2 (human suffering) either by assigning these calamities to Satan or by appealing, as England did in the "Weeping God of Mormonism," to the indispensable nature of human free agency. Note that appeals to free agency beg the fundamental question of why free agency is indispensable. Again, many Saints would argue that free agency is a fundamental law to which even God is subject or, at least, that he obeys based some higher principle. This notion is implicit in Moses 7, which England highlighted. But note

---

52. England, "Weeping God," 64. England's essay is a classic of LDS scholarship. For the recommendation that England's essay should be required to counter the trend of the omnis being advocated in some quarters of the church, see Brian Ferguson, "A 'Traditional Mormon' Thanks Gene," *Dialogue: A Journal of Mormon Thought*, 35, 3 (Fall 2002): v–vi.

that this response also implicitly rejects the traditional omni doctrine that God's omnipotence places him above any other law or principle.

Some modern-day Saints respond to question No. 3 (free agency and God's foreknowledge) by arguing that God's foreknowledge does not necessarily preclude human free agency. But others, such as McMurrin and Robson, are not persuaded by these arguments and, in any event, are not content with the conclusion that free agency is an illusion. There are no easy answers here, but, as we have seen, modern science provides some useful perspectives, suggesting that some specifics cannot be precisely foreseen, even if the overall course of human affairs proceeds as anticipated. In any event, most Saints are aware that the traditional Christian notion of predestination has been rejected by the church.

With regards to question No. 4 (scientific law and God's omnipotence), on the plus side many Saints have excelled in scientific professions, and church leadership has in recent years attempted to steer clear of most scientific controversies. On the minus side, many Saints continue to cling to the traditional world view that dismisses key scientific precepts (e.g., biological evolution and old-earth geology) as mere "theories" of the secular world. It is also common to hear LDS accounts of answers to prayers in which it is taken for granted, to paraphrase Ambrose Bierce, that God has annulled the laws of the universe on behalf of a single petitioner, who by his/her own confession is usually unworthy.[53]

The solution here is clear. Once one acknowledges that God works mostly, if not entirely, within the realm of natural law, as numerous LDS authorities and others have written, and not utterly beyond natural law or by capriciously setting aside natural law, then the philosophical basis for a "war" between modern science and religion dissolves. This principle is also in keeping with the precept that God allows free agency to operate largely without interference. This is a major and little-appreciated advantage of rejecting omni doctrines.

One important note is to observe, as a consequence of certain modern scientific findings (see above), that a God who works within the realm of natural law is not condemned to irrelevance. As physicist

53. Ambrose Bierce, *The Devil's Dictionary* (1911; repub. Oxford: Oxford University Press, 1998), s.v., "pray," www.sunsite.berkeley.edu/Literature/Bierce/DevilsDictionary, accessed May 9, 2019.

LDS THEOLOGY AND THE OMNIS

and Protestant theologian John Polkinghorne has written, "The dead hand of the Laplacean calculator, totally in control of the sterile history of his mechanical universe, has been relaxed. In its place is a more open picture, capable of sustaining motivated conjectures that can accommodate human agency and divine action within the same overall account. Modern science, properly understood in no way condemns God, at best, to the role of a Deistic Absentee landlord, but it allows us to conceive of the Creator's continuing providential activity and costly loving care for creation."[54]

In this regard, Brigham Young, James Talmage, and other LDS writers who have taught that there is no such a thing as a "miracle," and that behind every act of God is a rational, natural explanation, are in accord with modern thinking. This principle has also been taught more recently by LDS Apostle M. Russell Ballard: "'If there is a God,' the empathetic observer might wonder, 'how could He allow such things to happen?' The answer isn't easy, but it isn't that complicated, either. God has put His plan into motion. It proceeds through natural laws—which are, in fact, God's laws. And because they are His, He is bound by them, as we are."[55]

In summary, a reasonable response to each of the omni issues listed above is to qualify the notions of omnipotence and omniscience, or in other words to place reasonable, common-sense limitations on the interpretation of these terms. What most Latter-day Saints do not realize is that these "reasonable limitations" are inconsistent with the absolutist nature of the omni doctrines. No one knows the full resolution of these questions (such as what is the real meaning of free agency), but they should not be crucial, burning issues. Again, this is an important and largely unappreciated advantage of rejecting the traditional omni creeds.

THE PRINCIPLE OF PROGRESS

It is unfortunate, in a way, that some LDS writers have ventured into absolutist omni doctrines, since LDS theology already possesses a sharply contrasting doctrinal innovation: the "law of eternal

---

54. John Polkinghorne, *Belief in God in an Age of Science* (New Haven, Connecticut: Yale University Press, 1998), 75.

55. M. Russell Ballard, *Our Search for Happiness* (Salt Lake City: Deseret Book Co., 2001), 76.

43

progression." This doctrine asserts that humans have boundless potential, approaching that of God himself. A connected principle is the LDS Ninth Article of Faith: "We believe in all that God has revealed, all that he does now reveal, and we believe he will yet reveal many great and important things pertaining to the Kingdom of God." This language mirrors the definition of the "idea of progress" as given by twentieth-century American sociologist Robert Nisbet: "Mankind has advanced in the past, ... is now advancing, and will continue to advance through the foreseeable future."[56]

The principle of progress is well grounded in Judeo-Christian thought. Whereas most non-Christian ancient religions believed in an endless course of recurrent cycle, Judaism proposed a "linear" or "progressive" history, as can be seen in the Hebrew Bible account of the creation of the earth (order out of chaos); in the promise to Abraham that his seed would prosper; in the account of Moses and the children of Israel migrating to the promised land; and, finally, in their anticipation of a messiah who would reign in glory. Christianity further developed this tradition of progressive history by identifying Christ as the Messiah, by naming his advent as the "meridian of time," by teaching a higher law that superseded the Law of Moses, by predicting a future second coming of Christ, and by describing a heaven where the righteous dead will be resurrected.[57]

In the twentieth century, British philosopher Alfred North Whitehead noted that modern science, as it developed in the West, was based on the faith that as we progress in knowledge, "at the base of things we shall not find mere arbitrary mystery. ... When we compare this tone of thought in Europe with the attitude of other civilisations when left to themselves, there seems but one source for its origin. It must come from the medieval insistence on the rationality of God."[58]

The idea of progress was promoted by the controversial French theologian Pierre Teilhard de Chardin, who argued that human progress

56. Robert Nisbet, *History of the Idea of Progress* (1980; repub. Piscataway, New Jersey: Transaction Publishers, 1993), 4–5. See also David H. Bailey, "Mormonism and the Idea of Progress," *Dialogue: A Journal of Mormon Thought*, 33, 4 (Winter 2000): 69–82.

57. Mircea Eliade, *The Myth of the Eternal Return* (Princeton, New Jersey: Princeton University Press, 1971), 115.

58. Alfred North Whitehead, *Science and the Modern World* (New York: Macmillan, 1939), 17–19, 27.

was inexorable, virtually mandated by the laws of the universe, and that humans have virtually unlimited potential. He further saw the idea of progress as the one theme that could re-unify science and religion: "To incorporate the progress of the world in our picture of the kingdom of God ... would immediately and radically put an end to the internal conflict from which we are suffering."[59]

The law of eternal progression, both in the sense of human progression to divine levels and the sense of progress in knowledge and society, has been taught in the LDS Church throughout its history. James Talmage, while elaborating on the law of eternal progression in the first edition of his book *The Articles of Faith*, asserted that progression was possible after death not only within one kingdom of glory, but also between kingdoms.[60] John A. Widtsoe explained, "Progress ... is a process of adding to that which we now possess, by the elimination of errors, by the actual accretion of new truth, and by the development of greater self-mastery. ... It is a steady approach to the likeness of God."[61] Brigham H. Roberts taught that "the world's best hope is the world's continued progress in knowledge of the truth."[62]

More recently, Hugh B. Brown, a counselor in the First Presidency, wrote, "We should be in the forefront of learning in all fields, for revelation does not come only through the prophet of God nor only directly from heaven in visions or dreams. Revelation may come in the laboratory, out of the test tube, out of the thinking mind and the inquiring soul, out of search and research and prayer and inspiration."[63]

David O. McKay, while discussing Darwin's "beautiful" theory of evolution, argued that evolution may be seen in a progressive light, as suggesting that humankind is destined to progress towards eternal life: "Why should man come so far if he is destined to go no farther? A creature which has traveled such distances and fought such battles and

---

59. Pierre Teilhard de Chardin, *Toward the Future*, trans. Rene Hague (London: Collins, 1975), 96. De Chardin's views were censured by the Catholic church.

60. Talmage, *Articles of Faith*, 421; Thomas G. Alexander, "The Reconstruction of Mormon Doctrine: From Joseph Smith to Progressive Theology," *Sunstone*, July 1980, 24–33.

61. John A. Widtsoe, *Evidences and Reconciliations* (Salt Lake City: Bookcraft, 1943), 179.

62. Brigham H. Roberts, *The Truth, the Way, the Life: An Elementary Treatise on Theology*, ed. Stan Larson (Salt Lake City: Smith Research Associates, 1994), 16.

63. Hugh B. Brown, "A Final Testimony," in Edwin Firmage, ed., *An Abundant Life: The Memoirs of Hugh B. Brown* (Salt Lake City: Signature Books, 1988), 139.

won such victories deserves, one is compelled to say, to conquer death and rob the grave of its victory."[64]

Apostle and LDS Church President Gordon B. Hinckley openly celebrated the progress of the twentieth century:

> But in a larger sense this has been the best of all centuries. In the long history of the earth there has been nothing like it. The life expectancy of man has been extended by more than 25 years. Think of it. It is a miracle. The fruits of science have been manifest everywhere. By and large, we live longer, we live better. This is an age of greater understanding and knowledge. We live in a world of great diversity. As we learn more of one another, our appreciation grows. This has been an age of enlightenment. The miracles of modern medicine, of travel, of communication are almost beyond belief. All of this has opened new opportunities for us which we must grasp and use for the advancement of the Lord's work.[65]

Theologically speaking, it is clear that the law of eternal progression is a clear departure from the omni doctrines. To begin with, the notion that humans can progress to godhood, however one wishes to view this notion, effectively shatters the unbridgeable gulf between God and humanity that is implicit in the omni doctrines. The law of eternal progression also conflicts with absolutist omni doctrines that have little or no room for new discoveries in science or, for that matter, for social progress or achievements in the arts and the humanities.

There is no question that in spite of some lingering problems, our time is an era of unparalleled progress: (a) worldwide life expectancy has increased from age twenty-nine as recently as 1880 to age seventy-one today, in part, due to economic advances and also to the conquering of numerous deadly, debilitating medical conditions;[66] (b) worldwide literacy has increased from 20 percent in the 1800s to 83 percent today;[67] (c) the number worldwide living in extreme poverty has dropped from

---

64. David O. McKay, "A Message for LDS College Youth" (Provo, Utah: BYU Extension Publications), Oct. 8, 1952, 6–7. See also *Conference Reports* (Salt Lake City: Church of Jesus Christ of Latter-day Saints, Apr. 1968), 92. Here McKay quotes "Raymond F. West," but the statement originated with Pastor Charles Edward Jefferson, giving the Raymond F. West Memorial Lecture on Immortality.

65. Gordon B. Hinckley, *LDS Conference Reports* (Salt Lake City: Church of Jesus Christ of Latter-day Saints, Apr. 1999), 116.

66. Steven Pinker, *Enlightenment Now: The Case for Reason, Science, Humanism, and Progress* (New York: Viking, 2018), 54, 64–67.

67. Pinker, *Enlightenment Now*, 236.

90 percent in the 1800s to fewer than 10 percent today, and every day that number drops by 137,000;[68] (d) women worldwide have achieved full parity with men in primary, secondary, and tertiary education;[69] (e) the US violent crime rate is down by half since 1991, and the robbery rate is down by nearly two-thirds; crime has also declined in other major nations;[70] (f) since 1950, annual wartime battle deaths have dropped by a factor of eighteen;[71] (g) rates of abortion, teenage births, and teenage sex are declining;[72] and (h) within the last hundred years scientific research has uncovered the laws of relativity and quantum mechanics, unraveled the structure of DNA, measured the accelerating expansion of the universe, discovered thousands of planets outside the solar system, and placed a mobile phone with astounding capabilities in the hands of 70 percent of the world population.[73]

None of this is a license for complacency, because numerous challenges remain, notably global warming, species destruction, economic inequality, famine, bigotry, materialism, and war. But human progress

68. Pinker, *Enlightenment Now*, 89.

69. Pinker, *Enlightenment Now*, 240.

70. "Crime in the United States, 2017," FBI, Sept. 2018, www.ucr.fbi.gov/crime-in-the-u.s/2017/crime-in-the-u.s.-2017/tables/table-1, accessed May 9, 2019; compare to 1991 data here: www.ucr.fbi.gov/crime-in-the-u.s/2010/crime-in-the-u.s.-2010/tables/10tbl01.xls, accessed May 9, 2019; UK and Europe: "Where Have All the Burglars Gone," *Economist*, July 20, 2013, www.economist.com/news/briefing/21582041-rich-world-seeing-less-and-less-crime-even-face-high-unemployment-and-economic, accessed May 9, 2019.

71. Pinker, *Enlightenment Now*, 159–60.

72. Tara C. Jataloui et. al, "Abortion Surveillance—United States, 2015," Centers for Disease Control and Prevention (CDC), Nov. 23, 2018, www.cdc.gov/mmwr/volumes/67/ss/ss6713a1.htm, accessed May 9, 2019; Brady E. Hamilton et. al, "Births: Provisional Data for 2018," CDC, June 2019, www.cdc.gov/nchs/data/vsrr/vsrr-007-508.pdf,, accessed May 9, 2019; "Youth Risk Behavior Survey: Data Summary and Trends Report, 2007–2017," CDC, undated, www.cdc.gov/healthyyouth/data/yrbs/pdf/trendsreport.pdf, accessed May 9, 2019.

73. Albert Einstein, "On the Electrodynamics of Moving Bodies," *Annalen der Physik* 17 (1905): 891–921; John von Neumann, *Mathematical Foundations of Quantum Mechanics* (Berlin: Springer, 1932; trans. Princeton, New Jersey: Princeton University Press, 1955); James D. Watson and Francis H. C. Crick, "Molecular Structure of Nucleic Acids," *Nature,* Apr. 25, 1953, 737–38; Adam G. Riess et al. (1998), "Observational Evidence from Supernovae for an Accelerating Universe and a Cosmological Constant," *Astronomical Journal* 116 (1998): 1009–38; Kenneth Chang, "Seven Earth-size Planets Orbit Dwarf Star, NASA and European Astronomers Say," *New York Times*, Feb. 22, 2017, www.nytimes.com/2017/02/22/science/trappist-1-exoplanets-nasa.html, accessed May 9, 2019; Rayna Hollander, "Two-thirds of the World's Population Are Now Connected by Mobile Devices," *Business Insider*, Sept. 19, 2017, www.businessinsider.com/world-population-mobile-devices-2017-9, accessed May 9, 2019.

is real. Thus any movement, religious or secular, that fails to recognize and celebrate this progress is doomed. The LDS movement's embrace of progress has a promising future, provided that its adherents recognize the importance of this principle and avoid retreating into traditional, outmoded, progress-denying absolutist dogmas.

CONCLUSION

The traditional Christian notion, taught widely even today, of an omnipotent, omniscient, and omnipresent deity is not only problematic from a number of philosophical and scientific points of view, but goes against certain fundamental tenets that have been taught in the LDS movement from its inception. It is unfortunate that these doctrines are still being taught by some in the LDS Church today. Why follow other religious movements down a theological path that has proven to be problematic and, indeed, which many would argue has been refuted by modern science and day-to-day lived experience?

At the very least, Latter-day Saints should place limits on the omni doctrines, clarifying that these doctrines: (1) do not place God beyond space and time as the sole uncreated entity; (2) do not relegate humanity to a depraved status, utterly distinct in nature from God; (3) do not require that God's ways be viewed as inscrutable and incomprehensible; (4) do not abrogate or trivialize human free agency; (5) do not require that God violates natural law; and, perhaps most importantly, (6) do not deny the principle of progress. It is also essential that Latter-day Saints avoid attempting to deduce, by technical arguments reminiscent of medieval scholastics, doctrines based on literal interpretations of the omnis.

One important reason to reject or limit the omni doctrines is that they conflict with what may be the most original doctrine of LDS theology: the "law of eternal progression," a principle nearly synonymous with the "idea of progress" championed by secular writers. Along this, it follows from the creedless nature of the LDS religion and the Ninth Article of Faith that Latter-day Saints should never presume that any precept is forever unchangeable or unchallengeable.

Some may say that modern conservative LDS discourse, which includes the omnis and other doctrinal excursions, should be countered by a liberal, progressive discourse, with a similarly elaborate theology.

But the lesson of history is that there is danger in any form of theological speculation or dogmatism, whether it be "liberal" or "conservative." In too many cases, well-meaning speculation in one era becomes a theological quagmire in another era, both in Christian history in general and in LDS history in particular.

There is also a practical benefit to steering clear of theological speculation. When someone teaches a questionable doctrinal notion in a church setting, experience shows that engaging in a public debate with such a person is typically more divisive than convincing. In contrast, it is less likely to give offense to merely point out that the notion in question represents a significant excursion from basic principles of salvation and thus should be avoided.

Finally, the LDS movement has an admirable tradition (even if not always followed consistently) of being a practical, reasonable religion. Church members would be well advised to maintain a simple doctrinal foundation, avoiding theological excursions, and focusing on charitable living—serving the poor and needy, helping one another through difficult times, raising compassionate youth of integrity.

Indeed, a focus on people is one arena where all the church can unite—liberals and conservatives, young and old, newly baptized and life-long members, foreign converts and five-generation pioneer descendants. It is also an arena where thinking Latter-day Saints can participate with full intellectual honesty.

THREE

CRAWLING OUT OF THE PRIMORDIAL SOUP
A STEP TOWARD THE EMERGENCE OF AN LDS
THEOLOGY COMPATIBLE WITH ORGANIC EVOLUTION

STEVEN L. PECK

Evolution is a messy process. In his provocatively titled essay "Narnia's Aslan, Earth's Darwin, and Heaven's God," evangelical Christian Wesley J. Wildman details some of the waste and brutality of natural selection that are inevitable accompaniments of evolution. He then poses a stark challenge: "Surely such a loving, personal Deity would have created in another way, a way that involved less trial and error, fewer false starts, fewer mindless species extinctions, fewer pointless cruelties, and less reliance on predation to sort out the fit from the unfit." By way of conclusion, he issues the far-from-rhetorical question: "What sort of God could, would, and did create the world through evolution?"[1] Wildman's question suggests that evolution has striking implications for theology—including, I would add, LDS theology.

And, in fact, what might it mean that God "used" evolution to create life's diversity? Was this a choice for God among other alternatives? Do Wildman's pessimistic conclusions hold for Mormonism? Does evolution imply a noninterventionist deity? Are there more optimistic views possible, some of which may actually suggest that evolution enhances and expands our view of God? Are adjustments necessary to our key doctrines of the Creation, Fall, and Atonement to accommodate an evolutionary perspective? And why should we make this accommodation? What is lost and what is gained if our faith community fully and without compromise embraces evolution? There *are* deep and unavoidable theological implications for incorporating into

---

1. Wesley J. Wildman, "Narnia's Aslan, Earth's Darwin, and Heaven's God," *Dialogue: A Journal of Mormon Thought* 43, 1 (Spring 2010): 210–17.

our theology the belief that natural selection structured the way life evolved on our planet.

I would like to sketch some of these implications. By this I mean rough out some of the potential problems and perplexities that need to be sorted through in embracing a fully compatible perspective between evolution through natural selection and the LDS faith. In this conspectus, I hope to gesture to possible solutions to the perplexities that merging evolution and theology may bring to LDS thought. There are many sticking points, and I mean only to make a beginning and to seed conversation. I make no claims that the results are either complete or thorough, but I hope that making such a start will be useful.

Another potential difficulty is that some of the proposed solutions to the identified problems cannot be sorted out except through further revelation. Since Latter-day Saints fully anticipate the bestowal of further light and knowledge, the current incompleteness should neither surprise nor disturb. Ruminations such as these might serve as a catalyst for the kinds of questions that must be asked before revelation can be given. In scriptural and LDS history, questions are well known to have opened every major revelation from the first vision of Joseph Smith to the 1978 revelation on priesthood ordination and temple admission regardless of skin color. Questions such as those orbiting a reconciliation of evolution and LDS faith are difficult and will sometimes remain without answers, yet that does not mean we should not ask them. Elie Wiesel captures this need nicely in a conversation with a friend:

> "Man comes closer to God through the questions he asks Him, he liked to say. Therein lies true dialogue. Man asks and God replies. But we don't understand His replies. We cannot understand them. Because they dwell in the depths of our souls and remain there until we die. The real answers, Eliezer, you will find only within yourself."
>
> "And why do you pray, Moishe?" I asked him.
>
> "I pray to the God within me for the strength to ask Him the real questions."[2]

For the purposes of this essay, I assume that evolution through natural selection is a true description of how life arose on this planet and that life on Earth has emerged through a completely Darwinian

---

2. Elie Wiesel, *Night*, trans. Marion Wiesel (New York: Hill and Wang, 2006), 5.

process (throughout this essay, *Darwinian* refers to evolution through natural selection). Much has been written on the nature of the evidence supporting these claims, including the evidence found in the fossil record, comparative anatomy, geological stratigraphic analysis, DNA molecular studies, the physics of radiometric data, and so on, and I do not here debate the nature of the evidence nor the conclusions drawn from inferences made from that evidence. Here I accept them as accurate according to current understandings in contemporary evolutionary science. The LDS tradition also has a rich history of attempts at legitimizing and reconciling evolutionary science with the faith and tracing views of evolution within Mormonism, historically and contemporaneously.[3] This project is different in that I assume from the outset that evolution through natural selection has been established as true (and I use that word very deliberately) and that there is a legitimate, faithful response both to doctrine and to our best understanding of how life on Earth unfolds.

Because evolution through natural selection is thought to be a universal principle[4] or physical algorithm,[5] let me briefly give the necessary

---

3. See, for example, the following articles in *Dialogue: A Journal of Mormon Thought*: Duane E. Jeffery, "Seers, Savants, and Evolution: The Uncomfortable Interface," 8, 3 (Autumn 1973): 41–75; Michael R. Ash, "The Mormon Myth of Evil Evolution," 35, 4 (Winter 2002): 19–38; David H. Bailey, "Mormonism and the New Creationism," 35, 4 (Winter 2002): 39–59; and David H. Bailey, "Scientific Foundations of Mormon Theology," 21, 2 (Summer 1988): 61–79. See also Trent D. Stephens and D. Jeffrey Meldrum, *Evolution and Mormonism: A Quest for Understanding* (Salt Lake City: Signature Books, 2001); William E. Evenson, "Evolution," *Encyclopedia of Mormonism*, 4 vols. (New York: Macmillan, 1992), 2:478; Eldon J. Gardner, "Organic Evolution and the Bible," in *The Search for Harmony: Essays on Science and Mormonism*, ed. Gene A. Sessions and Craig J. Oberg (Salt Lake City: Signature Books, 1993); William E. Evenson and Duane E. Jeffery, *Mormonism and Evolution: The Authoritative LDS Statements* (Salt Lake City: Greg Kofford Books, 2005); Howard C. Stutz, *"Let the Earth Bring Forth": Evolution and Scripture* (Draper, Utah: Greg Kofford Books, 2011). More recently, a "Gospel Topics" essay on LDS.org approvingly cited highly technical evolutionary theory in defense of the Book of Mormon. See "Book of Mormon and DNA Studies," *Gospel Topics Essays*, www.churchofjesuschrist.org/study/manual/gospel-topics-essays/book-of-mormon-and-dna-studies.

4. Christian Illies, "Darwin's A Priori Insight," in *Darwin and Philosophy*, ed. Vittorio Hösle and Christian Illies (Notre Dame, Indiana.: University of Notre Dame Press, 2005), 58–82.

5. Daniel C. Dennett, *Darwin's Dangerous Idea: Evolution and the Meanings of Life* (New York: Simon and Schuster, 1996). For an interesting rebuttal to Dennett's description of Darwin's idea as dangerous, see Conor Cunningham, *Darwin's Pious Idea: Why the Ultra-Darwinists and Creationists Both Get It Wrong* (Grand Rapids, Michigan: Wm. B. Eerdmans, 2010).

ingredients for its operation and tease apart why natural selection creates tension for LDS theology.

Evolution by natural selection requires three elements: (1) variation in traits, including a source of novel variation; (2) selection on trait differences based on the environment in which relevant entities are embedded; and (3) offspring able to inherit trait differences from their parents. Often a fourth element, embedded in the above conditions, is made explicit: (4) time.

If these conditions are in place, natural selection will enhance how well the object fits local environmental circumstances. This adaptation will occur whether those entities are chemicals, organisms, or digital computer programs. Within the philosophy of biology, this phenomenon is referred to as an a priori principle rather than a cause. The task, then, of the empirical scientist is to show that a particular kind of entity is just the sort of thing to which these four principles apply. I focus on the evolution of organisms on Earth because it is our best and clearest example.

These principles have theological implications. First, note that this process is competitive. Some of the organisms are selected at the expense of others. There are clear winners and losers. Second, the variation is random with respect to what will be successful and unsuccessful. The organisms are confronted with both the requirements for survival and the local environment in which they find themselves. These factors create a direction in selection: toward better fit, or a closer adaptive alignment, with that environment. Evolution is then determined by which traits succeed in a given local environment and which do not. There is no grand overall direction toward which it moves, no master plan which it fulfills. The evolutionary process is blind variation in traits being chosen at a specific location and time that results in some organisms being more successful in producing the next surviving generation than others in the local environment in which they are reproducing.

Third, these competitive bouts to acquire the resources the organism needs to survive (mates, food, territory, etc.) are played out in units of the energy required to survive. Over time, these energy exchanges create a positive feedback loop. The organisms that are able to capture the most energy and employ it for successful survival are most likely to replace other entities in the next generation by entities with traits like their own. Two basic strategies have been especially useful in survival: (1) using chemical changes induced by the energy of sunlight or heat to create energy in more usable forms to maintain the organism's structure and function, and (2) stealing this energy from those who create it or from others who have stolen it. Most plants are good examples of the first strategy; cattle and puma are examples of the second.

Empirical observations on how evolution has played out to date on Earth depict a process that is enormously creative, patulous (spreading widely from a center), complex, and diverse. All of these characteristics increase through time as the history of life on Earth unfolds. This increase, scientists believe, occurs because evolving organisms tend to transform their environment. These modifications change the selective regime in which organisms are embedded, and these changes cause even more complexity. This pattern of increased environmental complexity is called niche construction in evolutionary biology.[6] For example, when life forms moved from Earth's early oceans to land, plants opened new niches. These vegetative incursions created new habitats as plants competed for limited resources and diversified over time to capture those limited resources. Next, insects began exploiting these plants, which further changed the environment, allowing a greater diversification of habitats. Amphibians then exploited both of these new feeding opportunities, followed in turn by reptiles, then birds, and then mammals. Each of these waves of diversity opened new niches and habitats, creating further occasions for exploiting the competitive interactions of organisms and increasing habitat diversity, organism complexity, and the amount of creativity in the way that species of organisms change into more diverse and varied forms in the universe.

This narrative is the standard, empirically based, scientific explanation of every example of structured life on Earth. God enters this story (or fails to do so) with no necessary explanatory power. God has long been used as an explanation for otherwise puzzling aspects of life on Earth and its abundant and obviously designed features. For example, Xenophon's Socrates pointed out in the fourth century BCE that nature's numerous designed aspects suggest a designer: "Again, the incisors

---

6. Kevin N. Laland, John Odling-Smee, Marcus W. Feldman, and Jeremy Kendal, "Conceptual Barriers to Progress within Evolutionary Biology," *Foundations of Science* 14, 3 (Aug. 2009): 195–216.

of all creatures are adapted for cutting, the molars for receiving food from them and grinding it. And again, the mouth through which the food they want goes in, is set near the eyes and nostrils; but since what goes out is unpleasant, the ducts through which it passes are turned away and removed as far as possible from the organs of sense. With such signs of forethought in these arrangements, can you doubt whether they are the works of chance or design?" Aristodemus, Socrates's interlocutor, answers: "No, of course not. When I regard them in this light they do look very like the handiwork of a wise and loving creator."[7]

The argument that design implies an outside designer runs very deep, from antiquity up into the modern period. William Paley developed its most carefully articulated expression in his *Natural Theology* (1802). In it he famously argues that, were you to find a watch on the beach, you would never attempt to claim that it had been produced by natural processes. Its very existence implies a watchmaker.[8] Darwin had read Paley thoroughly and understood that any explanation of the origin of life on Earth must include an explanation of design. Evolution by natural selection does so. Despite unscientific attempts to deny this achievement—for example, by the Discovery Institute's cleverly conceived intelligent design movement[9]—most scientists agree that evolution provides a sufficient explanation of design. In fact, the Darwinian conclusion that design is not evidence of a designer has been one of evolution theory's most threatening aspects to a belief in deity/designer.

What are the implications of design-without-a-designer for theology? More specifically, what are the implications for LDS thought and philosophy? To explore this question in detail, I draw on distinctions in theological outlooks made by Niels Gregersen, University of Copenhagen professor of theology.[10] He identifies five theological responses

7. Xenophon, *Memorabilia*, trans. E. C. Marchant, Loeb Classical Library (Cambridge, Massachusetts: Harvard University Press, 1923), 57.

8. Interestingly, President Spencer W. Kimball played off this idea in "Absolute Truth," *Ensign*, Sept. 1978, 3.

9. Barbara Forrest, "The Wedge at Work: How Intelligent Design Creationism Is Wedging Its Way into the Cultural and Academic Mainstream," in *Intelligent Design Creationism and Its Critics: Philosophical, Theological, and Scientific Perspectives*, ed. Robert T. Pennock (Cambridge, Massachusetts: MIT Press, 2001), 5–53.

10. Niels Henrik Gregersen, "Emergence: What Is at Stake for Religious Reflection?" in *The Re-Emergence of Emergence: The Emergentist Hypothesis from Science to Religion*, ed. Philip Clayton and Paul Davies (Oxford: Oxford University Press, 2006), 279–322.

to the idea of "emergence" that serve elegantly to partition the space of responses to evolution. Emergence is the idea that properties of a complex system may arise that are unpredictable or unanticipated from a reductive description of lower-level processes. Emergent properties are generally explainable by the lower-level processes but rely on complex, local interactions. A classic example is a snowflake, the existence of which would have been hard to predict just from the properties of freezing water, but which is explicable in terms of those same properties.

I find these five responses useful for exploring evolution theologically because, in part, evolution and emergence are twin concepts that play in, about, and through each other in integrated ways and are part and parcel of the complexity that needs a theological response. These responses are equally useful in illuminating aspects of LDS theology.

GREGERSEN'S FIVE THEOLOGICAL RESPONSES

The five perspectives or responses are (1) flat religious naturalism, (2) evolving theistic naturalism, (3) atemporal theism, (4) temporal theism, and (5) eschatological theism. I consider each perspective in turn; but, interestingly, all are possible responses in LDS thought, although admittedly sometimes with a bit of twisting and hammering. Before beginning, however, a couple of clarifications are necessary to draw attention to certain aspects of LDS theology that need special consideration as we assess the possibility of Darwin-compatible Mormon theism. Moreover, none of these models embraces a cheap fundamentalist creationism, by which I mean a view in which creation consists of sudden legerdemain-like wand waving. All five perspectives try to explain emergence in terms of the full complexity of the evolutionary story as detailed in the observable physical record and currently accepted as standard by scientists.

A difficulty that makes this project of bringing together evolution and LDS theology tough slogging is that, within LDS thinking, what we mean by a "physical universe" is often muddled. Mormonism displays a kind of expansive physicalism suggesting that the universe in toto is a farrago of matter of one kind or another (D&C 131:7), that part of it ("spirit matter") remains undetectable by our perceptual apparatuses and instrumentation, while we have phenomenological or manipulative access to only the less "fine" or less "pure" part. This materiality includes gods, spirits, intelligences, and so on, and may exist in extraspatial or temporal dimensions (or both); but the universe does, presumably, still follow laws of some kind. All matter is subject to God's manipulation, thanks to his greater knowledge and influence. This theological description imposes a kind of dualism in which some aspects of the universe are available to us and others are not. Lacking reliable epistemic access to the "spirit matter" part of this world, this concept remains outside our scientific theories and practices, even though it may play a role in a deeper physical reality.[11]

Second, in Mormon thought God is embodied. It is not completely clear what this means,[12] but it implies that at least in some sense God has a biology. What such a biology might entail, however, is speculative, but at least two key doctrines are contingent on the concept: (1) the literal physical son-father relationship of Jesus Christ to God the Father, and (2) the human capacity for a bodily theosis,[13] which recapitulates God's developmental process, if not completely in scope, at least in such a way that it can be considered human beings' movement toward becoming godlike.[14] I am clearly riding roughshod over some controversial ideas about which much ink has been spilled and in which more nuance and refinement could be considered; but among average LDS Church members whom I know, the claim "As

11. Kent C. Condie, "Premortal Spirits: Implications for Cloning, Abortion, Evolution, and Extinction," *Dialogue: A Journal of Mormon Thought* 39, 1 (Spring 2006): 35–56.

12. James E. Faulconer, "Divine Embodiment and Transcendence: Propaedeutic Thoughts and Questions," *Element: A Journal of Mormon Philosophy and Theology* 1 (Spring 2005), www.smpt.org/docs/faulconer_element1-1.html.

13. *Theosis* is the term most often used within Eastern Orthodox Christianity to describe the process of attaining union with God including a certain likeness. This term and others like it (*deification, divination*) do not map perfectly onto LDS conceptions of "becoming like God" or "exaltation." For one discussion on this topic, see Jordan Vajda, "Partakers of the Divine Nature: A Comparative Analysis of Patristic and Mormon Doctrines of Divinization," *FARMS Occasional Papers* 3 (2002).

14. When asked if Mormons believed that God was once a man, LDS Church President Gordon B. Hinckley responded: "I wouldn't say that. There was a couplet coined, 'As man is, God once was. As God is, man may become.' Now that's more of a couplet than anything else. That gets into some pretty deep theology that we don't know very much about" (quoted in Don Lattin, "Musings of the Main Mormon," *San Francisco Chronicle*, Apr. 13, 1997, www.sfgate.com/cgi-bin/article.cgi?file=/chronicle/archive/1997/04/13/SC36289). President Hinckley seems to have been referring primarily to the question of God's past rather than humanity's future. See Blair Hodges, "Did President Hinckley downplay deification?" *By Common Consent* (blog), Jan. 2, 2012, www.bycommonconsent.com/2012/01/02/did-president-hinckley-downplay-deification.

man is, God once was; as God is, man may become" is considered neither surprising nor controversial.

Flat Religious Naturalism

In Gregersen's partitioning of religious space by emergence, the first category is flat religious naturalism. In this view, the natural world is all there is—nothing beyond the physical reality accessible to current and future science. This view, though denying anything supernatural, leaves open the possibility that other substances might be discovered. For example, dark matter would be fully acceptable in flat naturalism because it can be inferred through human observation at galactic scales. But the idea that God might use supernatural means or substances (including a soul or Descartes's *res cogitans*) to accomplish his goals or purposes is dismissed.

While this perspective might seem to be the basic grounding of a strict materialism, it still acknowledges the sacred nature of the universe.[15] An encounter with God is therefore not one of personal relationship, transcendence, or eminence, but rather one of mystery. God in this view is just nature and its processes, and the proper response is awe. Nature is, in fact, divine. This view resonates well with certain forms of Buddhism and other forms of nontheistic religion.

While at first glance it seems unlikely that Mormonism could be situated along this axis, Mormonism does in some sense embrace a mystery about fundamental questions that have occupied creedal Western religions. These questions focus on God's nature, attributes, and powers. For example, in this view, the laws that frame and structure the matter from which all things, including God, are constituted are not created by God, but are self-existent with him. Matter, intelligence, and the laws that govern their interaction are self-existent and uncreated—with some resulting confusion in the way Mormons talk about God. For example, some speak as if God created the laws of the universe and buy into anthropic arguments about God's fine-tuning the universe as the lawgiver, then fall into talking about God using natural, albeit possibly higher, laws to organize the universe from unorganized matter.[16]

15. Ursula Goodenough, "The Sacred Depths of Nature: Excerpts," *Zygon: Journal of Religion and Science* 35 (Sept. 2000): 567–86.
16. These ideas are found in Joseph Smith's King Follett discourse. See "Mormon Literature Sampler: The King Follett Discourse," mldb.byu.edu/follett.htm.

Theologically, Mormonism offers the following intriguing revelation on matter:

> There is no such thing as immaterial matter. All spirit is matter, but it is more fine or pure, and can only be discerned by purer eyes; we cannot see it; but when our bodies are purified we shall see that it is all matter. (D&C 131:7–8.)

If we carry this statement a little farther, matter could be broadly conceived to include God, spirits, and intelligence as part of the "finer" or "purer" matter thought to make up the extended universe. In this context, flat religious naturalism might be conceivable in the LDS faith, as it has few answers to questions about why the universe exists as it does and embraces the idea that its constituent substances are eternal. This matter includes the intelligences that eventually became God by taking on his mantle. Therefore, mystery and awe at this scale may be the only appropriate response.

Evolving Theistic Naturalism

Evolving theistic naturalism is the perspective that God has emerged from the natural world and is a quality of nature itself. Nature has moved forward in increasing complexity, and part of this complexity is God. Just as consciousness emerges from neural complexity in materialist explanations of consciousness, God emerges from the complexity of the entire universe. Obviously, in this view God is not prior to the universe, nor does he act as its creator in the traditional sense.

Mormonism does not accommodate this view very well. Seeing God as *just* an emergent property of the natural universe does not seem to fit within the spectrum of proposed LDS theologies.

Atemporal Theism

This view is the classic post-Plotinian view of God that includes the divine attributes of omnipresence, omnipotence, and omniscience. According to this view, God exists outside of time, is the rational ground of all being, and has created the universe and its laws, fine-tuning it for human life. Atemporal theism assumes that God is "outside of" time and that, in some sense, the past, present, and future are all "present" before God. An implication of this view is that God cannot be affected by the world, thus emphasizing his transcendence. This view is compatible both with evolution and with creationism, which posits that the world was created suddenly in all its complexity. This view of God seems to impose a strict determinism on the final teleological goal of the creation (which, again from God's perspective, occurs as a simultaneous "now"). God, in this view, is unchangeable. Human freedom may be possible, but such assertions are often incoherent since God knows what we will choose and sees our exact future resulting from those choices.

Mormon belief systems seem varied (or generally confused) on this point. LDS theologian Blake Ostler makes the point that Joseph Smith's doctrines, developed in Nauvoo, Illinois (1839–44), do not allow this view of God, but it is not uncommon to find discourse that assumes this view.[17]

Yet because of the Plotinianization by conservative Christianizing influences, Mormonism has maintained a relationship with this view.

Temporal Theism

Taking the form of process theology, the theological possibilities of temporal theism have received a friendly reception among many LDS thinkers.[18] In this view, God has a core identity that makes him God but influences, and is influenced by, temporal changes. In addition, the future is open. While it may be possible that God understands and can "see" all logical possibilities, those potentialities are realized only in some actual futures. Furthermore, those futures' realizations depend on the actions of free agents, which may include fundamental particles (e.g., atoms) and their associations.

This viewpoint seems most open to theistic Darwinism by providing an opening for God to be part of the unfolding universe. This view continues to be the most promising way to harmonize the two fields and is the perspective largely embraced by Catholic scholars Pierre Teilhard de Chardin and John Haught (discussed below).

---

17. Blake T. Ostler, *Exploring Mormon Thought: The Attributes of God* (Salt Lake City: Greg Kofford Books, 2001), 359–60; and Neal A. Maxwell, "Patience," *Ensign*, Oct. 1980, 28.

18. James McLachlan, "Fragments for a Process Theology of Mormonism," *Element: A Journal of Mormon Philosophy and Theology* 1 (Fall 2005), www.smpt.org/element.html; Andrew Miles, "Toward a Mormon Metaphysics: Scripture, Process Theology, and the Mechanics of Faith," *Element: A Journal of Mormon Philosophy and Theology* 4 (Spring 2008); and Dan W. Wotherspoon, "Awakening Joseph Smith: Mormon Resources for a Postmodern Worldview" (PhD diss., Claremont Graduate University, 1996).

Eschatological Theism

The last model Gregersen explores is eschatological theism. In this perspective, emergent features in the world do not depend strictly on the past. The future is often determined by contingent events in the present that could have been otherwise had God not intervened. New futures hinge on small events that turn out to be major turning points (recall the proverb "For want of a nail the kingdom was lost"). Eschatological theism denies that future emergent events result exclusively from the operation of natural law; rather, God "pulls" the future into existence through such bifurcation and contingent points in history to achieve the ends that he is interested in bringing about. Thus he exercises influence on these events. As this argument goes, the future cannot be strictly determined through an analysis of the present state of things, and a future state can be understood only retrospectively by looking into the past. It is eschatological in the sense that God's purposes and aims can be understood only in retrospect: "The point here," explains Gregersen, "is that potentialities do not simply reside in the past configurations of matter; they result from interplay between creaturely potencies and the coming into being of the divine possibilities offered to the world. Accordingly, the past and the present must be seen in light of the future, rather than the future being explained out of the past or the present."[19]

This view is strongly interventionist. Contingent events in the past that were brought together were among the possibilities present at the time of the contingent event. This reading of the past, then, looks very similar to declaring that what happened was just God's will. So in practical terms, it is not clear how this point of view offers any advantage over looking at things from the viewpoint of atemporal theism. In both, God is clearly teleologically drawing things toward a future that he has determined.

However, from the LDS viewpoint that prophecy is an important part of how the world works, eschatological theism may be useful in showing how the specific prophecies found in the scriptures are brought to pass by God's intent—that they were pulled into the future by divine action.

---

19. Gregersen, "Emergence," 299.

All five of these viewpoints assume compatibility between theology and evolution. But Gregersen's perspectives are very general, and it will be useful to look at some specific responses from philosophers and theologians to problems of teleology and design.

THEOLOGICAL RESPONSES TO EVOLUTION

Since the moment Darwin's *On the Origin of Species* appeared in 1859, theologians have responded with attempts at both dismissal and reconciliation.[20] The latter have taken the form of everything from complete acceptance—simple variations on the theme of "That's just the way God did it!"—to deeper, more nuanced attempts at bringing the two ways of knowing—evolution and theology—together.

To get a sense of how LDS thinking may respond to the introduction of evolution into its theological concepts, it is useful to look at how other Christian groups have responded to the challenge.[21] Most efforts by Catholic and Protestant theologians have focused on three aspects, all of which are relevant to LDS responses to evolution: (1) teleology and divine purpose, with humans being an important goal toward which the universe is directed; (2) design and its implications about God's attributes; and (3) the presence of natural evil. All three topics orbit the question of how and to what extent God acts in the world. I discuss the third topic, natural evil, separately from the first two as part of the section titled "Mormon Evolutionary Theology" below.

Teleology and Divine Purpose

One of the most troubling aspects in reconciling Darwinism with the idea of a personal God is its relentless lack of direction—its

---

20. David N. Livingstone, "Evolution and Religion," in *Evolution: The First Four Billion Years*, ed. Michael Ruse and Joseph Travis (Cambridge, Massachusetts: Belknap, 2009), 348–69.

21. Many interesting responses to evolution from Jewish, Islamic, and Hindu sources posit a personal God who acts in the world. Buddhist responses are less troubled by evolution because of its inherent naturalism. I am not including them in my analysis because Christian responses make an interesting model for creating LDS-compatible theologies, both of which must include ideas of the fall and the atonement, which are not present in the same ways in non-Christian religions. Discussions of various other religious perspectives can be found in Philip Clayton, ed., *The Oxford Handbook of Religion and Science* (New York: Oxford University Press, 2008).

purposelessness on macroevolutionary scales.[22] Laypersons often interpret this lack of a "goal" as supporting the claim that evolution is a random process, but that is not quite right. Within a local environment, by random, variation inheritable traits (traits that occur through the genetic code) are selected disproportionally in such a way that those traits that provide the organism with some advantage in that environment tend to survive at higher rates. These traits are passed on to the next generation more frequently. So while there is no final goal toward which evolution tends, it is driven by selection within local environments. Nonetheless, it is correct to say that, over long time periods, evolution is not aiming at any particular direction or purpose.

One of the first philosophers to explore how certain features found in living organisms could arise evolutionarily without teleology was French philosopher Henri Bergson (1859–1941). He saw evolution moving toward intelligence, instinct, and complexity. Bergson couched this form of evolution in terms of an *élan vital*, a life force that pushed life (and its precursor elements prior to life) forward in time, resulting in differentiation over a span of time in which the past is "gathered into a present."[23]

Michael Vaughan, in presenting Bergson's work, explains this process as "the organized being's ability to organize the re-emergence of creative change through the structures that it creates."[24] This force is not seen as something "extra"—such as the vitalism[25] that Enlightenment thinkers posited to explain life—but is an inherent property of matter and assemblages of matter. Evolutionary change is seen as inventive and creative. Vaughan adds:

---

22. Creationists, including "intelligent design creationists," sometimes try to distinguish between micro- and macroevolutionary processes that biologists do not recognize. Macroevolution refers to the timescale at which evolutionary change is considered and is not a different kind of evolution, as is often implied by such groups. For example, it is not uncommon to find people who claim that they believe in microevolution (meaning something like the changes that might be found among different breeds of dogs) but not macroevolution. To a biologist that is the equivalent of claiming, "I believe in inches but not miles."

23. Gilles Deleuze, "Lecture Course on Chapter Three of Bergson's *Creative Evolution*," *SubStance: A Review of Theory and Literary Criticism* 36, 3 (2007): 72–90.

24. Michael Vaughan, "Introduction: Henri Bergson's *Creative Evolution*," *SubStance: A Review of Theory and Literary Criticism* 36, 3 (2007): 7–24.

25. Vitalism was an idea with ancient roots but became prominent during the Enlightenment (seventeenth-eighteenth centuries). It posited that life was made possible by a force not present in nonliving things.

The truth is that adaptation explains the sinuosities of the movement of evolution, but not its general directions, still less the movement itself. The road that leads to the town is obliged to follow the ups and downs of the hills; it adapts itself to the accidents of the ground; but the accidents of the ground are not the cause of the road, nor have they given it its direction. At every moment they furnish it with what is indispensable, namely, the soil on which it lies; but if we consider the whole of the road, instead of each of its parts, the accidents of the ground appear only as impediments or causes of delay, for the road aims simply at the town and would fain be a straight line. Just so as regards the evolution of life and the circumstances through which it passes—with this difference, that evolution does not mark out a solitary route, *that it takes directions without aiming at ends, and that it remains inventive even in its adaptations.*

But, if the evolution of life is something other than a series of adaptations to accidental circumstances, so also it is not the realization of a plan. A plan is given in advance. It is represented, or at least representable, before its realization. The complete execution of it may be put off to a distant future, or even indefinitely; but the idea is none the less formidable at the present time, in terms actually given. If, on the contrary, evolution is a creation unceasingly renewed, it creates, as it goes on, not only the forms of life, but the ideas that will enable the intellect to understand it, the terms which will serve to express it. That is to say that *its future overflows its present, and can not be sketched out therein in an idea.*[26]

Bergson thus opens the door for a theological response (although he was not a theist as such) that allows for direction in evolution without teleology, but that nonetheless moves to places of potential theological interest such as intelligence, complexity, and even consciousness.

Design and God's Implied Attributes

One of the first theologians to attempt to address these concerns was Jesuit paleontologist Pierre Teilhard de Chardin (1881–1955). His engagement with evolution was personally costly since his church put considerable institutional pressure on him for his insistence on a theological engagement with evolution. He saw the universe as moving toward greater and greater "seeing" and described humans as the highest expression of this ability. Each human being stands as one who can

---

26. Henri Bergson, *Creative Evolution*, trans. Arthur Mitchell (1907; repr., New York: Barnes and Noble, 2005), 68; emphasis mine.

"see" himself or herself in reflexive self-awareness. Therefore, the highest expression of life is found in this subjective experience. He breaks the history of the universe into "Pre-Life," "Life," and "Thought," the last of which he calls "the Noosphere." The emergence of consciousness characterizes the evolutionary stage of the Noosphere. It is important to keep in mind that this capacity for thought emerges from the universe through the progression of a flat ontology. Speaking of the universe, he wrote: "It is beginning to seem that there is definitely *more* in the molecule than the atom, *more* in the cell than in the molecule, *more* in the society than in the individual, and *more* in mathematical construction than in the calculations and theorems. We are now inclined to admit that at each further degree of combination *something* which is irreducible to isolated elements *emerges* in a new order."[27]

In Teilhard de Chardin's view, design is inherent in the evolutionary processes, which tend inexorably toward greater and greater complexity until consciousness arrives and finds its highest expression in humans. He also embraces a strong eschatology, which he calls the Omega Point. At this point, which occurs at the end of time, the universe preserves all that has happened, including all persons and their consciousness. In the final end of the universe, a universal consciousness will emerge. This consciousness is not God, but rather the final intent and purpose of God's creation. Teilhard de Chardin also recognizes the hard questions that arise through the brutality and wastefulness of the evolutionary process. He makes no effort or claims to understand these negative aspects but notes that such "evil" resembles "nothing so much as the way of the Cross."[28]

While his attempt to reconcile these disparate fields has not endured as a solution to the problem of an evolutionary theology, his efforts were significant in raising questions about how to embrace fully both evolution and theology in inventive and imaginative ways.

Since Teilhard de Chardin's effort, many theological efforts by both Catholics and Protestants have been situated in temporal theism. An especially promising area seems to be the process theology movement.[29]

---

27. Pierre Teilhard de Chardin, *The Phenomenon of Man*, trans. Bernard Wall (New York: Harper & Row, 1959), 268; emphasis in the original.

28. Teilhard de Chardin, *Phenomenon of Man*, 313.

29. See, for example, David R. Griffin, *Reenchantment without Supernaturalism: A Process Philosophy of Religion* (Cornell, New York: Cornell University Press, 2000); and Alfred North Whitehead, *Process and Reality*, corrected ed. (New York: Free Press, 1978).

In this panentheistic view, God is more than, but also present in, all matter. As mentioned earlier, current efforts to reconcile evolution and religion have found this a productive area of shared space.

Catholic theologian John Haught argues that, in this process theology view, God is present "deeply" in creation and influences evolutionary processes in ways that are not manipulations of matter in an interventionist sense. Rather, God is deeply present in the fabric of the universe in ways that are indistinguishable to science or other forms of human observation.[30] God's purposes unfold because they are deeply present in the created world; they appear to emerge in the universe's overall movements and processes, moving forward in creative and unexpected ways. Haught sees creation in terms of "promise" rather than "design." He argues that science can fully study the universe's ontology and that its observations will be valid and informative, but that God is working on a different level. His purposes will unfold as the universe unfolds, not only as an ordering and organizing influence but also as a source of novelty:

> Theologically speaking, process theology suggests that we should logically foresee rather than be surprised, that God's creation is not driven coercively, that it is widely experimental, and that it unfolds over the course of a considerable amount of time. To those who object that process theology is hereby illegitimately redefining the idea of God's power in order to contrive a fit with neo-Darwinian theory, the reply is simply that no other conception of power is more consistent with the quite orthodox religious belief that God is infinite love.[31]

Haught therefore sees creation, not as a one-time event, but as an ongoing process in which God is continuously present. This unfolding is not interventionist. God is not prodding creation when it gets off track. Rather, his presence permeates all aspects of the universe.

Anglican theologian and scientist Arthur Peacocke writes similarly that his own naturalistic theology "is also based on an evolutionary perspective of the cosmological and biological sciences. This view entails an understanding of creation by God as a continuous activity, so

---

30. John F. Haught, *Deeper than Darwin: The Prospect for Religion in the Age of Evolution* (Cambridge, Massachusetts: Westview Press, 2004).

31. John F. Haught, *God after Darwin: A Theology of Evolution* (Boulder, Colorado: Westview, 2000), 42.

that dynamic models and metaphors of divine creation and creativity become necessary. The work of God as Creator is regarded as manifest all the time in those very natural processes that are unveiled by the sciences in all their regularities."[32]

It is important to point out that although these views are naturalistic in that they do not accept miraculous interventions or divine guidance, they also embrace such basic Christian ideas and values as grace, incarnation, atonement, and resurrection, albeit with significant reinterpretations. For example, Karl Peters, professor emeritus of philosophy and religion at Rollins College, after describing a particularly meaningful interaction with his family, terms it a manifestation of grace in his life: "Reflecting on this event as a classical empiricist with a non-personal model of God as the creative process, I can see how the various elements that I have described—the family relationships, the beautiful weekend, the choir music, the setting of the service, the way it was conducted, my past experiences, my understanding of God as present when love is present—all came together serendipitously as an event of grace. I can think of the event as an example of serendipitous creativity—of God as the creative process—at work in my life."[33]

In addition to responses from process theologians, classic Trinitarian Christians have also responded to developing formal Christologies that embrace evolution through natural selection as creation. Celia Deane-Drummond, chair of theology and the biological sciences at the University of Chester in Great Britain, describes the work of creation as a "theo-drama" in which the freedom of creation emerges through actor-agents. These "actors" interact freely with one another, expressing individual choices and responses. She sees God's relationship with all of creation as an encounter. God, incarnated as Christ, enters the stage and becomes part of the play, an act that thereby affects the unfolding drama for all creation. Atonement and redemption are universal in scope, and humans have the greatest freedom to participate with Christ in redemption through his atonement. Her perspective specifically

---

32. Arthur Peacocke, "A Naturalistic Christian Faith for the Twenty-First Century: An Essay in Interpretation," in *All That Is: A Naturalistic Faith for the Twenty-First Century*, ed. Philip Clayton (Minneapolis, Minnesota: Fortress Press, 2007), 9.

33. Karl E. Peters, "Empirical Theology and a 'Naturalistic Christian Faith,'" in *All That Is: A Naturalistic Faith for the Twenty-First Century*, ed. Philip Clayton (Minneapolis, Minnesota: Fortress Press, 2007), 102.

incorporates ecological concerns into the drama, with humans being required to care for and assist Christ with the redemption of all creation. Her work is a profound reconfiguring of Christ and his mission in a Darwinian framework that may have relevance to Latter-day Saints, as may her view of a universal atonement.[34] She describes her task thus: "This is also how I have sought to present the challenge of relating Christology and evolution: Namely, it is a challenge that insists on retaining hope for the future but also probes our own identity as evolved human persons living in an evolved world."[35]

Theologies continue to engage fruitfully and meaningfully with evolutionary biology. This ongoing conversation is important because evolution by natural selection continues to play an important role in understanding the development of life on Earth in ways that impinge directly on the idea of creation. The theologies of many religions play a role in this conversation. For example, in a 1996 statement on evolution to the Pontifical Academy of Sciences, Pope John Paul II said: "New knowledge has led to the recognition of the theory of evolution as more than a hypothesis. It is indeed remarkable that this theory has been progressively accepted by researchers, following a series of discoveries in various fields of knowledge. The convergence, neither sought nor fabricated, of the results of work that was conducted independently is in itself a significant argument in favor of this theory."[36]

These examples show that evolution is being taken seriously as a subject for theological discourse outside Mormonism. All of these theological responses, however, usually assume classic Nicene conceptions of Deity. It is clear that process theology has been influential in framing a response to evolution. However, the LDS view of God is much different, and Catholic and process responses may not transfer adequately to Mormonism. For example, both Teilhard de Chardin and Haught assume God's omnipresence within all that exists (and beyond). While LDS thinkers would agree that God's influence is everywhere, his actual presence is constrained by his possession of a physical body. Also, these theologians assume the Trinitarian nature of God in a different

---

34. Celia Deane-Drummond, *Christ and Evolution: Wonder and Wisdom* (Minneapolis, Minnesota: Fortress Press, 2009).

35. Deane-Drummond, *Christ and Evolution*, 57.

36. Pope John Paul II, *Truth Cannot Contradict Truth*, address to the Pontifical Academy of Sciences, Oct. 22, 1996, www.newadvent.org/library/docs_jp02tc.htm.

way than Mormons do. Third, these responses differ from Mormon thought in their assumption that God is the author of the laws of the universe and that creation occurred ex nihilo. These differences have strong implications for the way that a Mormon theology of evolution must be constructed.

However, other aspects translate well from Catholic and process rapprochements between religion and evolution. The concept that God is affected by his creation and that agents have agency and thereby influence the direction in which the future unfolds are ideas that line up nicely (with some adaptation) into Mormon ideas, to which we now turn.

MORMON EVOLUTIONARY THEOLOGY

Before offering a few of my own speculations, it is important to point out that Latter-day Saints have held a variety of positions on the subject of evolution over the years. Such variety is a reminder that Latter-day Saints have long had a variety of options to consider.[37] One of the first Mormons to argue for an evolutionary-inclusive LDS theology was W. H Chamberlin. Chamberlin was part of the 1911 controversy at Brigham Young University when several scholars were dismissed because they were promoting evolution and modern biblical criticism.[38] In evolution, Chamberlin saw evidence for God's eminence in the world. In a paper to BYU students published in its newspaper, *White and Blue*, on February 14, 1911, he argued that evolution can never conflict with religion because they deal with different planes of influence and interest.[39] He clarified the eminence that he saw in nature in a *Deseret News* article a month later on March 10:

> Without penetrating beneath the surface of the vast ocean of life and experience science has been able to perform its well-known service for

37. One of the best, though often overlooked, extended analyses of Mormonism's adaptive relationship to the sciences is Erich Robert Paul's *Science, Religion, and Mormon Cosmology* (Urbana: University of Illinois Press, 1992).

38. Gary James Bergera, "The 1911 Evolution Controversy at Brigham Young University," in *Search for Harmony*, ed. Sessions and Oberg, 23–42; James M. McLachlan, "W. H. Chamberlin and the Quest for a Mormon Theology," *Dialogue: A Journal of Mormon Thought* 29, 4 (Winter 1996): 151–67; and James M. McLachlan, "The Modernism Controversy," in *Discourses in Mormon Theology: Philosophical and Theological Possibilities*, ed. James M. McLachlan and Loyd Ericson (Salt Lake City: Greg Kofford Books, 2007), 39–83.

39. William H. Chamberlin, "The Theory of Evolution as an Aid to Faith in God and in the Resurrection," *The White and Blue*, Feb. 14, 1911, 4.

mankind. The mighty deep itself suggests the magnitude of the blessing for man that will come from the religious man's identification of the power in and through Nature, creating and sustaining it with the Spirit of God and in his successful efforts to discover and conform to the laws that condition life in harmony with the Divine nature and will.[40]

However, Chamberlin's notion of eminence must be understood with reference to his approach to the material world. He embraced the idea of "spiritual realism"—a reaction to the naturalism of evolutionary thinker Herbert Spencer and the positivistic world view embraced by the Vienna Circle and a growing number of European contemporaries.[41] Spiritual realism was a form of idealism that described all of existence as flowing from "a society of minds." In that sense, it was "spiritual" and dependent on mind. W. H. Chamberlin's brother and biographer, Ralph Chamberlin, described it thus: "The Philosophy of Spiritual Realism holds that reality is spiritual. Mind is inherent in all Nature in the form of innumerable spiritual agents or selves, which are free causes."[42] W. H. Chamberlin posited that all "efficient" (meaning direct) causes reflected the reality of final causes arising in minds. He did not dispute the existence of an inorganic world prior to the appearance of life in the universe. However, the outflowing of existence from mind provides evidence for panpsychism (the idea that all matter has some kind of awareness). Ralph Chamberlin, explaining his brother's thought, said, "Matter is not inanimate, in the sense of inert, 'but an expression of activity,'" and continued, "The elements may be interpreted as uniform methods or expressions of an underlying activity and viewed as 'analogous to the habits as we know them in ourselves.'"[43]

Ralph Chamberlin further argued that the evolution of the entire universe, even prior to the development of life, was very similar to the way that an embryo develops, with many processes moving simultaneously toward the final goal of an individual organism: "Just as the developing embryo of the sea-urchin, or of any section of it,

40. Quoted in Ralph V. Chamberlin, *The Life and Philosophy of W. H. Chamberlin* (Salt Lake City: Deseret Book Co., 1925), 158.
41. McLachlan, "Modernism Controversy," 39–83.
42. Chamberlin, *Life and Philosophy of W. H. Chamberlin*, 320.
43. Chamberlin, *Life and Philosophy of W. H. Chamberlin*, 254. The embedded quotations are from an unpublished essay by W. H. Chamberlin, "Berkeley's Philosophy of Nature and Modern Theories of Evolution."

varies as a whole, and can be understood only as a reciprocally related set of movements working toward an end, giving the impression of being guided by a hidden pattern, so inorganic nature, prior to the organic evolution, varied in such a way as strongly to suggest a similar control."[44] He commented that life on Earth, viewed retrospectively, seemed to have followed a similar route to the ends toward which the universe is heading, as seen today in extant organisms. Quoting W. H., Ralph Chamberlin explained:

> In relation to our interests or needs, minds are the sole support of our experience of any and all objects of Nature, of their temporal and spatial relations, and especially of the causal interconnections which we discover as maintaining among the objects of Nature, and which we describe as the laws or uniformities of Nature. The minds that form that phase of life called environment embrace *a priori*, as living premises embrace a conclusion, the matter and energy by this environment. What man calls Nature is a symbol of the presence of mind.[45]

My reading of Chamberlin's thought is that the conditions in which God and a society of minds find themselves as individuals include both ourselves and all of matter that is spiritual (this is backwards from the way that most Mormons would construct the nature of matter, i.e., spirit *is* matter, rather than the other way around). In Chamberlin's antimaterialist view, God is conceived as the highest entity, the most knowledgeable and powerful, in a society of minds. Like us, he is a "thou" who, through this society, brings into being the world we see around us. That world is conditioned completely by the society of minds and their goals. As Ralph Chamberlin describes it, "The world is an active, living whole, an organic system of a higher order, a product and expression of a society of minds."[46]

Evolution here is seen as part of God's purposes being brought forth by this society of minds. Two aspects are important for my argument. First, this approach is deeply idealistic in the sense that there is no material world, only a spiritual world of mind. Second, it is deeply teleological. While it has echoes of Bergson's work with a universe

---

44. Chamberlin, *Life and Philosophy of W. H. Chamberlin*, quoting from W. H. Chamberlin, "Berkeley's Philosophy of Nature and Modern Theories of Evolution."
45. Chamberlin, *Life and Philosophy of W. H. Chamberlin*, 255.
46. Chamberlin, *Life and Philosophy of W. H. Chamberlin*, 322.

unfolding in ways that are creative, Chamberlin appears to see God's work moving forward in a way reminiscent of Haught's evolution in which the evolutionary process is inextricably embedded in the universe, except that he explains this depth as "mind" moving the evolutionary process forward.

While Chamberlin's work is friendly to evolution and Darwinism, it is so at the expense of a physical world, an approach that creates problems from a modern scientific perspective. In addition, it is much too teleological for modern scientific views of how evolution proceeds, which have now moved away from teleological explanations. However, on the positive side, this perspective also moves away from the hermeneutic of suspicion in which early LDS thought held much of evolutionary theory.

John A. Widtsoe, a chemist and LDS Church apostle, although sympathetic to ideas from biological evolution as he understood it, did not engage Darwinism directly. He merely noted in his book *Rational Theology* that "the exact process whereby man was placed upon the Earth was not known with certainty, nor is it vital to a clear understanding of the plan of salvation."[47] B. H. Roberts, the most theologically minded member of the Council of the Seventy, was friendly to evolutionary ideas but discounted the contemporaneous scientific version of Darwinism in favor of *panspermia*, meaning that organisms of various kinds lived elsewhere and moved to Earth by unspecified means. Through a vitalistic life force, they developed to their present state. After rejecting three types of evolution, which he called materialistic, agonistic, and theistic, he noted:

> The development theory of this chapter and work recognizes and starts with the eternity of life—the life force; and the eternity of some life forms, and the possibilities of these forms, perhaps in embryonic status, or in their simplest forms (save as to man) are transplanted to newly created worlds there to be developed each to its highest possibilities, by propagation, and yet within and under the great law of life of Genesis 1, viz., each "after," and within, "its kind" (Gen 1:11–12, 21, 24–25).[48]

The battle among LDS apostles Joseph Fielding Smith, James E.

47. John A. Widtsoe, *Rational Theology* (Salt Lake City: Signature Books, 1997), 46–47.
48. B. H. Roberts, *The Truth, the Way, the Life* (Provo, Utah: BYU Studies, 1996), 240.

Talmage, and B. H. Roberts (not an apostle) is well documented and need not be repeated here.[49] In short, when contemporary Christian creationism was introduced into Mormonism through Joseph Fielding Smith's reading of Seventh-day Adventist writer and PhD geologist George McCready Price's work,[50] engagement between Mormon theology and evolutionary theory slowed to a standstill. Evolutionary theology has been slow to make headway in mainstream Mormon thought, in part, perhaps, because of the controversy that emerged from this encounter and Smith's subsequent forceful (if not canonical) expression of his personal opinions.[51]

But it may be time to take some steps in this direction again. Creationist responses to the theory of evolution, which may have been understandable in the first half of the twentieth century, are becoming less and less tenable. I feel that it is important to begin to articulate an informed LDS theology that is friendlier to our current understanding of biological evolution.

A couple of points should be kept in mind. These are not statements of my belief. Rather, I offer them as toy models—ideas that we can play with to test their utility and durability. The problem of "unconceived alternatives" that has been articulated for science[52] carries even more weight in theological speculation, where a firm grasp of transcendental realities can be largely inaccessible or unavailable. This condition is especially true when both revelation and scriptures are underdetermined on the subject of how the creation actually happened. Currently, evidence from the natural world and its scientific interpretation are the only "revelation" we have for understanding that process. The scriptures may be read in literalistic ways that are unsympathetic to evolutionary views, for example, or sympathetically if read more metaphorically. Even so, we may have enough information on "the three pillars of eternity" (Creation, Fall, Atonement) to start working

49. Richard Sherlock, "'We Can See No Advantage to a Continuation of the Discussion': The Roberts/Smith/Talmage Affair," *Dialogue: A Journal of Mormon Thought* 13, 3 (Fall 1980): 63–78; and Jeffery, "Seers, Savants, and Evolution," 41–75.

50. Richard Sherlock, "A Turbulent Spectrum: Mormon Reactions to the Darwinist Legacy," in *Search for Harmony*, ed. Sessions and Oberg, 69.

51. For example, in books like *Man: His Origin and Destiny* (Salt Lake City: Deseret Book Co., 1954).

52. P. Kyle Stanford, *Exceeding Our Grasp: Science, History, and the Problem of Unconceived Alternatives* (Oxford: Oxford University Press, 2006).

toward some coherence in appraising the evidence of the natural world, especially since their associated controversies have been articulated in rather unbalanced and scientifically uninformed ways.[53]

What do we gain by taking Darwinian evolution seriously in LDS thought? First, we make available a conceptual space where, at a minimum, LDS theology does not oppose the most important theories of today's science. I recognize the fluid status of scientific thought and its strengths and weaknesses, but it appears that evolution, at least, will continue to be extremely influential in understanding how life developed on Earth. It is very unlikely that anything will replace evolution through natural selection as broadly conceived in the foreseeable future.

Second, evolution adds an interesting and informative dimension to several key doctrines. I offer some tentative steps on how evolution may inform and be made compatible with LDS theology. I repeat that these explorations serve as pump priming for more complete development. I also suggest where these ideas may be problematic or need further sorting out.

I want to speculate on reconciling the intersection between Mormon theology and Darwinian evolution in four areas—natural evil, design, embodiment, and teleology—and then speculate (wildly) on how these may be reconciled.

Natural Evil

The first major theological question raised by evolution involves the existence of natural evil. Several authors have opined that LDS views have solved the classic problem of evil. Arguments for this assertion range from the naive stance that God is not culpable for the evils of the world because Adam and Eve chose to disobey to more nuanced views. One of them is BYU philosopher David Paulsen's contention that Joseph Smith rescues the theodicy problem. His theology suggests a god who is subject to certain natural laws: "Elsewhere Joseph taught that there are also 'laws of eternal and self-existent principles—normative structures of some kind, I take it, that constitute things as they

53. The phrase "the three pillars of eternity" is borrowed from Bruce R. McConkie, "The Three Pillars of Eternity," BYU devotional address, Feb. 17, 1981, www.speeches.byu.edu/?act=viewitem&id=598.

75

(eternally) are. What are possible instances of such laws or principles?'"[54] Paulsen argues that Joseph Smith gives three conditions under which God does not or cannot prevent evils: (1) unpreventable absolutely, (2) preventable by God but not absolutely, and (3) not preventable without preventing some greater good or causing some greater evil.[55]

If God did use such a method as natural selection, it would make sense that this method was the natural law that Paulsen describes as necessary—necessary because natural selection is a horrifying process, as Wildman reminds us. It is hard to imagine that evolution by natural selection is a reasonable choice for creation if other methods were available. Phillip Kitcher, philosophy professor at Columbia University, writes of the problem that evolution poses to theology:

> Many people have been troubled by human suffering, and that of other sentient creatures, and have wondered how those pains are compatible with the designs of an all-powerful and loving God. Darwin's account of the history of life greatly enlarges the scale on which suffering takes place. Through millions of years, billions of animals experience vast amounts of pain, supposedly so that, after an enormous number of extinctions of entire species, on the tip of one twig of the evolutionary tree, there may emerge a species with the special properties that make us able to worship the Creator.[56]

This level of suffering and cruelty is problematic for most kinds of natural theology. Kitcher therefore uses the presence of these kinds of natural evil and their extent to dismiss theological claims about a loving god. He adds:

> Our conception of a providential Creator must suppose that He has constructed a shaggy-dog story, a history of life that consists of a three-billion-year curtain-raiser to the main event, in which millions of sentient beings suffer, often acutely, and that the suffering is not a byproduct but constitutive of the script the Creator has chosen to write.
>
> To contend that species have been individually created with the vestiges of their predecessors, with the junk that accumulates in the history of life is to suppose that Intelligence—or the Creator—operates by whimsy. The

---

54. David L. Paulsen, "Joseph Smith and the Problem of Evil," *BYU Studies* 39, 1 (2000): 53–65. He is quoting from Joseph Fielding Smith, comp., *Teachings of the Prophet Joseph Smith* (Salt Lake City: Deseret Book Co., 1974), 181.

55. Smith, *Teachings of the Prophet Joseph Smith*, 60.

56. Phillip Kitcher, *Living with Darwin: Evolution, Design, and the Future of Faith* (Oxford: Oxford University Press, 2007), 123.

trouble is that the charge doesn't go away when the action of the Creator is made more remote. For a history of life dominated by natural selection is extremely hard to understand in providential terms. ... There is nothing kindly or providential about any of this, and it seems breathtakingly wasteful and inefficient. Indeed, if we imagine a human observer presiding over a miniaturized version of the whole show, peering down on his "creation," it is extremely hard to equip the face with a kindly expression.[57]

If natural selection were a natural law necessary for the creation of a diverse and fully functioning universe, then Paulsen's analysis of how LDS theology escapes the problem of evil would seem to make sense. In fact, if less cruel methods were available and God did not use them, then theologians must adduce (presumably very tricky) arguments about how this method can be reconciled with attributes of love and kindness.

Mormon doctrines of Creation and Fall may (with some adventuresome speculation) also provide a rescue for the deep problem that Kitcher identifies. Mormon theology contains an inherent dualism positing that a spiritual aspect of existence mediates the consciousness of humans, plants, animals, and, indeed, Earth itself. We have very limited details about how these spirit and material worlds interface with each other; however, taking evolution as a given natural law offers some possibilities for making the unimaginable cruelty of life, the Creation, and the Fall at least coherent.

Biology has long since abandoned vitalism, and modern biologists see no necessary reason to view organisms as anything more than biological machines. However, one of the acknowledged hard problems in the philosophy of mind is the idea of subjective consciousness. Such consciousness seems to extend beyond the usual kinds of explanatory gaps that science fills. Philosopher of science Colin McGinn believes that a biological explanation of consciousness is forever beyond the purview of science because, no matter how completely we understand the correlations made by science between brain states and consciousness, consciousness, with its qualitative feel, can be experienced and recognized only from within subjective experience.[58] Granted, we must be

---

57. Kitcher, *Living with Darwin*, 124.
58. Colin McGinn, *The Mysterious Flame: Conscious Minds in a Material World* (New York: Basic Books, 1999).

careful in claiming that science will never figure out such and such a problem, a claim that sets up a "God of the Gaps" dilemma, which scientific advances repeatedly undermine. Still, providing scientific access to personal subjectivity does seem to be an inherently intractable problem. We can imagine a world unfolding strictly according to the forces of natural selection in which organisms are nothing more than biological machines—Cartesian wet robots, if you will. A Mormon-type creation, then, would be the union of these creatures (including a human body) with spirit material that allows these machines to become sentient and experiential beings. Such a union would link a consciousness-bestowing element to the material aspects of the world.

Speculating even farther afield, we could conceive of the Fall, less literally, as likewise a process of a spiritual and material coming together. This view smacks more of a kind of Gnosticism or Platonism, but even so may be worth exploring. Adam and Eve, in this view, would be the first of Heavenly Father's spirit children to be linked to one of these biological machines, with the traditional animating creation taking place as a union between spirit and evolved material. As a result of this union, all humans and all creatures participate in the Fall—as a fall into materiality. In some sense, perhaps the participants even choose their participation. Continuing this line of thought, we see that Christ must then, as LDS thought commonly holds, redeem all creation.[59] Rather than causing a fall as a necessary imposition on all sentient creatures, Adam and Eve open the possibility of a participatory fall, during which conscious experience enters the world.

In this view, the natural evils of the living world did not begin until the Fall and form part of the price of experience, not only for humans but for all creatures. Humans participate as God's children (as per LDS theology), but their role is more to act with Christ in bringing redemption to the world of experiencing beings. Christ's atonement becomes truly universal, opening the opportunity for both the resurrection and the permanent bringing together of the spiritual and the material. This step joins experience and material existence. I argue that Mormonism, in this way, provides an answer that escapes natural theology and the deeper problem of evil, while making Christ's atonement truly universal. This

59. Sheila Taylor, "The Hope for Universal Salvation," *Element: A Journal of Mormon Philosophy and Theology* 2 (Fall 2006).

approach also allows a reconciliation with traditional views of Adam and Eve as real living persons—the first instance of sentience and the literal spirit children of God (agreed, we don't know what that means exactly). This approach also provides something vital to the world through the Fall since, in a very technical sense, there was no death before the Fall.

This kind of evolutionary-based view of the Fall also releases God from naive views that he is culpable for it. There is something inherently troubling about God's setting up Adam to fail and fall. By analogy, it is as if I blame a mouse killed in my mousetrap for its desire for cheese rather than blaming myself for having baited and placed the trap.

However, this approach also has troubling aspects. If we remove God's consciousness-inducing spirit children from the biotic world, then, logically, we have to accept that beings like Neanderthals had no consciousness. Since it is well established that many early hominins had religious practices, created art, and made intricate tools, it is hard to argue that they had no vestiges of phenomenal consciousness. This idea is also highly dualistic, but in very Mormon rather than Cartesian ways.

Design

How important to our theology is the idea that God is the designer in creation? Natural theology, starting with Augustine, has made the design and complexity of the universe one of the evidences of God through creation. These early theologies even held that God's attributes could be read from the features of the natural world. As underscored by Xenophon's claim that "signs of forethought" in Nature attest design (quoted earlier), this move to see design as evidence of Deity's involvement in creation obviously predates Christian theological speculation. Currently, we know that the natural law of evolution through natural selection[60] fully explains the complexity of life on Earth (and presumably life elsewhere). Therefore, the question logically follows: Are the arguments for God from design necessary or important to a Mormon theology? Christian theologians and apologists have spilled significant quantities of ink over design, but why this question matters deserves some examination. For example, in relation to the embodiment of God, did he design his body?

---

60. Illies, "Darwin's a Priori Insight," 59, holds that evolution is in fact one of nature's principles and is a priori true.

It seems circular to make Paleyesque arguments for design that do not mesh well with some of Mormonism's foundational tenets, especially since arguments from design had become problematic long before Darwin. Scottish philosopher David Hume pointed out that design implies nothing about a designer and speculated that the designer of the universe could have been anything from an evil demon to a largely incompetent committee.[61] (The many blunders and inefficiencies found among Earth's organisms were apparent even in Hume's time, the eighteenth century.) If God's embodiment implies some sort of biology, then the design comes from elsewhere. LDS thinkers have speculated since the time of Joseph Smith and Orson Pratt that God works within natural law. If this principle includes evolution through natural selection, it seems that attempts to distance ourselves theologically from evolution could be a grave error. Thus, if we interpret the theory of evolution in a Mormon framework, it constitutes a potentially helpful and perhaps even necessary explanation for an embodied God, rather than merely posing problems for natural theology.

Embodiment

We believe that, in some sense, we were created in the bodily image of God. We use scriptures like the Book of Mormon's Ether 3:6, where the brother of Jared sees the Lord's finger, which was "as the finger of a man," to orient this belief. We also believe that "the Father has a body of flesh and bones as tangible as man's; the Son also" (D&C 130:22). These scriptures present problems for a non-teleological process such as evolution by natural selection—but perhaps not as many problems as we might first think. Evolutionary biologist Simon Conway Morris argues that, given the vastness of the universe and the limited number of solutions to the biological engineering problems of surviving in a planetary ecosystem, humans, or something like them, might be an inevitable evolutionary product.[62]

For example, reptile ichthyosaurs, mammal dolphins, and fish all have evolved very similar shapes to solve the problem of moving

---

61. David Hume, *Dialogues Concerning Natural Religion* (Mineola, New York: Dover, 2006), 35–38.

62. Simon Conway Morris, *Life's Solution: Inevitable Humans in a Lonely Universe* (Cambridge, England: Cambridge University Press, 2003).

gracefully in oceans. These evolutionary convergences can take on very specific biological forms. Sabertooth cat-like predators who fed on large grassland mammals evolved as both marsupials (mammals with a pouch, like kangaroos and wallabies) and as mammals with placentas (e.g., bats, horses, and lions). Both marsupial and placental sabertooths were very similar in shape, ecological niche, and size. Both evolved from small rat or small opossum-like precursors. The universe is unimaginably large. Why? Allowing evolution to flower into something human-like could be one of the reasons. James E. Faulconer asks an intriguing question about God's embodiment:

> The bodies of flesh and bone with which I am familiar do not shine, have blood, cannot hover, can be wounded and die, must move through contiguous points of time-space. In short, they are not at all like the bodies of the Father and the Son. So what does it mean to say that the Father and the Son have bodies? In fact, does it mean anything at all? When I use the word "body" in any other context, I never refer to something that shines, can hover, is immortal, and moves through space seemingly without being troubled by walls and doors. Given the vast difference between what we mean by the word "body" in every other case and that to which the word refers in this case, one can legitimately ask whether the word "body" has the same meaning in this case that it has in the others.[63]

One could also legitimately ask: Is God a *Homo sapiens*? Is God a mammal? Scientists have speculated on what a bipedal hominid evolved from avian precursors might look like. Would it have leftover structures like a pygostyle (a reduced fusion of vertebrae) instead of a tail? Slime molds can take very complex shapes in some of their life history stages. Can we imagine a human body that evolved from slime molds on another planet? It seems that many of our human features are part and parcel of our being mammals. Could being a mammal be a contingent feature of our evolution rather than an eternal part of our resurrected bodies? I do not have any answers to these questions, but they do not seem to be so problematic that they cannot be answered in ways that allow evolution as the mechanism of creation. These sorts of considerations significantly reduce problems of teleology, or God's presumed purpose for human beings.

---

63. Faulconer, "Divine Embodiment and Transcendence," 1.

Teleology

If God, of necessity, used evolution to achieve his purposes, what does that say about his being able to act in the world? I need to add a cautionary note here. When I say God *uses* evolution, I recognize that, in talking about a creator, it is possible that words like *allows* or *provides a space for* may be more appropriate. Nevertheless, if we embrace an evolutionary perspective, God's intervention, our petitionary prayer, and divine action to bring about his purposes become thorny issues. A nice thing about the magical view of creation is that it is no problem at all to imagine God intervening in the world. Why use evolution through natural selection in a nonteleological fashion if waving a magic wand was possible? In fact, if God can and sometimes does intervene, then why doesn't he do it all the time? Why *didn't* he do it during the Creation? This question opens an intriguing possibility: the necessary place of consciousness in divine interventions.

In Mormon thought, getting a physical body is important. Obviously, having a body means that we become part of the material world, as Faulconer speculates: "Our experience of the body, the only standard we have for understanding embodiment, suggests that to say that God has a body is to say that his omniscience and omnipotence must be understood in ways quite different from traditional Christianity because embodiment implies situated openness to a world. In other words, divine embodiment also implies that God is affected by the world and by persons in his world."[64]

So there seems to be something deeply important about physicality and spirit coming together. Could it be that the physical world can be manipulated only through consciousness-mediated direct action? Or through this kind of body that unites spirit and physical matter? When I read the scriptures, I see a god who makes arrangements for irreplaceable records to be kept, preserved, and maintained through conscious effort. He implies that, if they are not, this knowledge will be lost and not brought back through his intervention. I see the Lamanites languishing in unbelief until the sons of Mosiah are inspired to go among them. Angels bear messages to other consciousnesses but do not seem to manipulate the world in interventionist ways. Almost all

---

64. Faulconer, "Divine Embodiment and Transcendence," 18.

of the scriptures may be reinterpreted as acts of consciousness acting in the world. Christ's miracles, especially his resurrection, seem to be an exception, but much of how God works in the world seems to be that he communicates to and through conscious beings who then use their agency to act. Stories of people inspired to stop and help a widow take on new meaning if God cannot help the widow without us.

SPECULATIVE CONCLUSIONS

Evolution may bear on theology in other areas, and entire discourses could be developed on each of these topics. For example, studies on motherhood from the animal kingdom are providing great insights into the nature of motherhood in human beings.[65] Or consider the work of Joan Roughgarden, a biologist at Stanford University, who recently argued for a new model of evolution based not on selfish genetic forces (Richard Dawkins's "selfish gene" model) but on models of cooperation among creatures in a gendered and sexual context.[66] Her ideas on co-operation are a nice model for the kinds of human and perhaps divine society that Mormon theology posits—free agent interaction as part of a society of gendered minds. This area is new biological research, but it seems more promising than the selfish-gene model because it seems more attuned to the kinds of societies that we see forming in the natural world and that Mormon conceptions of theosis also model and predict.

Evolutionary views of creation also steer us into a deeper engagement with the natural world, as we see ourselves quite literally connected to the creatures and ecologies around us. The idea that our world emerged from deep time through natural selection implies that the wonderful diversity we see around us is contingent, unique, and precious. This evolutionary stance provides arguments for better stewardship of the natural environ-ment because its current state took an enormous length of time. Not only are the creatures of the earth here for us, but we are here for them. A Darwinian-influenced theology argues that care for creation becomes an important aspect of God's grace to the natural world through us.

A melding of evolution and theology also introduces another area

---

65. Sarah Blaffer Hardy, *Mother Nature: Maternal Instincts and How They Shape the Human Species* (New York: Ballantine Books, 1999).

66. Joan Roughgarden, *Evolution's Rainbow: Diversity, Gender, and Sexuality in Nature and Humans* (Berkeley: University of California Press, 2004); and *The Genial Gene: Decon-structing Darwinian Selfishness* (Berkeley: University of California Press, 2009).

important in Mormon thought. Perhaps the LDS conception of theosis and the path that leads to exaltation suggests a Darwinian selection process in which elements of trial, testing, and proving are inherent parts of progression through the first and second estates of premortal and mortal existence. Could natural selection drive emergence forward in an eternal context as well? Are classically conceived intelligences the sorts of entities subject to natural selection? Abraham 3:21–25 describes intelligences as varying in traits relevant for theosis such as intelligence, righteousness, obedience, and so on. (Recall that variation is the first condition necessary for natural selection to function.) Thinking of Christ as God's son means that we know at least one case in which traits were in some senses inherited—and heritability is the second condition necessary for natural selection. But how broadly this principle applies is, obviously, speculative. Lastly, these traits get selected—the third condition necessary for natural selection. Not only might evolution be the principle behind the beauty, wonder, and diversity of life in the universe, but it may also drive the selection processes that help produce our eternal destiny.

For me, evolution is an empowering idea. Linking it to our theology provides answers to several perplexing questions. It suggests that there is something wonderfully important about embodiment and why physical access to the universe is so important. Our doctrines, informed by evolution, answer questions about why such a cruel and wasteful process was chosen for creation and resituate the problem of evil. I find easy adaptations to our most important and profound doctrines. I see no reason why Latter-day Saints cannot, fully and without apology, embrace Darwinian evolution. As Darwin concluded in his magnificent *On the Origin of Species*: "There is grandeur in this view of life, with its several powers, having been originally breathed into a few forms or into one; and that, whilst this planet has gone cycling on according to the fixed law of gravity, from so simple a beginning endless forms most beautiful and most wonderful have been, and are being, evolved."[67]

---

67. Charles Darwin, *On the Origin of Species: The Illustrated Edition* (New York: Sterling Publishing, 2008), 513.

FOUR

"TO DESTROY THE AGENCY OF MAN"
THE WAR IN HEAVEN IN LDS THOUGHT

BOYD PETERSEN

"New light is occasionally bursting in to our minds, of the sacred scriptures, for which I am truly thankful," exulted W. W. Phelps in a June 1835 letter to Oliver Cowdery. "We shall by and bye learn that we were with God in another world, before the foundation of the world, and had our agency: that we came into this world and have our agency, in order that we may prepare ourselves for a kingdom of glory."[1] Phelps went on to declare that ministering angels were once mortal prophets who lived on Earth; that marriage may continue after mortality in the heavens; and that Adam's pre-mortal identity was Michael, the archangel who fought in the war in heaven.

Joseph Smith's 1830 translation of the King James Bible (from which the Book of Moses was drawn) had included four verses describing a celestial conflict where Satan put forward a plan to prohibit human agency and guarantee universal salvation. Jesus countered with God's own plan that allowed choice and provided atonement for sin, but could not ensure salvation for all. Five years later, Smith was translating the Egyptian papyri that would become the Book of Abraham. Included in the revelation was a description of a pre-mortal council where one "like unto God" proposed: "We will go down, for there is space there, and we will take of these materials, and we will make an earth whereon these may dwell" (Abr. 3:24). Latter-day Saints have traditionally assumed that Christ is the one "like unto God" who gives voice to these words; however, it is just as likely that the verse applies to Michael, who would come to be seen as a co-creator of the earth

---

1. "Letter No. 8," *Latter-Day Saints' Messenger and Advocate* 1, 9 (June 1835): 30, www.contentdm.lib.byu.edu/cdm/ref/collection/NCMP1820-1846/id/7160.

in the ritual drama Smith would reveal later in Nauvoo, Illinois. In Hebrew, the name Michael means "who is like God," something Smith likely knew even though his lessons in Hebrew would not begin until fall 1835. And in the ritual drama Smith would later create with the narrative of the Creation and Fall, Michael plays the role of co-creator with Jehovah of the earth and all that is in it.[2]

The war in heaven narrative became central to LDS thought and identity. By looking at the specific ways the war in heaven is used in LDS discourse, we can see how this narrative is shaped by its readers, how it comes to reflect those readers' anxieties and desires, and how it, in turn, creates a community of believers tethered to cosmic history. To do this, I propose to borrow from (and slightly modify) the four medieval categories of biblical hermeneutics. In this fourfold system, the first level of interpretation was the literal level (or *sensus historicus*), with no underlying meaning. The tropological level (the *sensus tropologicus* or *sensus moralis*) identified a moral message from the scriptural passage. The allegorical level (or *sensus allegoricus*) was the symbolic meaning, most often used to read the Hebrew Bible typologically as prophecy of the events and figures of the New Testament. Finally, the anagogical level (*sensus anagogicus*) revealed the deeper, immediate, often mystical nature of the passage, usually prophesying some future reality.

I use this interpretive lens, not to force LDS interpretation into some outdated frame of reference, but because I believe LDS interpretations fit remarkably well into this framework. In other words, the Latter-day Saints tend to employ scripture, or at least the war in heaven narrative, in ways similar to those employed by medieval Christians. It

---

2. William Clayton kept a record of the first ordinances performed in the Nauvoo temple. On December 10, 1845, he wrote that "H. C. Kimball presides as Eloheem, Orson Hyde as Jehovah and George A. Smith as Michael and N[ewell]. K. Whitney as the serpent," and on December 11, he added, "A little before six we commenced taking them through the ceremonies, Heber C. Kimball acting as Eloheem, George A. Smith as Jehovah, Orson Hyde as Michael, W. W. Phelps as the serpent. We were also assisted by P. P. Pratt." George D. Smith, ed., *An Intimate Chronicle: The Journals of William Clayton* (Salt Lake: Signature Books, 1995), 204, 207. The first exposé to document Michael's playing a role in the creation is Catherine Lewis's *Narrative of Some of the Proceedings of the Mormons; Giving an Account of Their Iniquities with Particulars Concerning the Training of the Indians by Them, Description of the Endowment, Plurality of Wives, &c, &c.* (Lynn, Massachusetts: n.p., 1848), 8. Lewis went through the Nauvoo temple endowment ceremony just after Joseph Smith's martyrdom. While both of these accounts are from after Smith's death, it is likely little was changed except for the fact that these ceremonies were performed in the temple rather than above the Red Brick Store.

is important, however, to understand that these levels of interpretation are not mutually exclusive; an individual can and often does invoke multiple levels of meaning in one discourse. In LDS thought, the war in heaven has been read as a literal premortal event; as a moral message to orient lives; as an allegory to explain current events; and as an illustration of a prophetic future for Christ's church. The narrative explains past, present, and future, and knits the individual LDS life into the fabric of sacred history.

In this essay, I first focus on the historical antecedents of the war in heaven, the origins and evolution of the narrative in Western religious traditions. Second, I explore the development of the narrative in LDS thought and its literal level of interpretation. Third, I discuss the tropological level, the moral messages pulled from the text. Fourth, I examine in some detail the allegorical level, the metaphoric interpretations of the text to explain current events. I focus much of the paper on this level, since it most vividly illustrates the LDS world view engaging with increasing conflicts about agency. Finally, I conclude with a brief look at the anagogical level—how the narrative is used to portray future prophetic events of church history.

ORIGINS AND EVOLUTION OF THE WAR IN HEAVEN

The idea of a war in heaven is rooted in the biblical story of fallen angels (Gen. 6); a reinterpretation of Isaiah 14; and the apocalyptic writings of John (Rev. 12). An enigmatic passage in Genesis describes the "sons of God," divine messengers who were sent down to watch over humanity. They were attracted to the human "daughters of men" and transgressed the boundaries God set between them. The offspring of these unions were a celestial-human hybrid that became known as *nephilim* or "fallen ones," translated in the King James Version as "giants." Developed in post-biblical Judaism (particularly the Enoch literature), the *nephilim* become monstrous creations that, as Elaine Pagels puts it, "took over the earth and polluted it."[3]

Around the same time, legends about a high-ranking angel who was

---

3. Elaine Pagels, *The Origin of Satan* (New York: Random House, 1995), 49. See also James R. Davila, "Melchizedek, Michael, and the War in Heaven," *Society of Biblical Literature 1996 Seminar Papers* 35 (1996): 259–72. A dated but informative survey of the war in heaven legend from antiquity through the Protestant Reformation is Bernard J. Bamberger, *Fallen Angels: The Soldiers of Satan's Realm* (Philadelphia: Jewish Publication Society, 1952).

cast out of heaven for insubordination were combined with a passage in Isaiah that speaks of the fall of a great prince whose name is translated in Latin as Lucifer (Isa. 14). The apocryphal Latin narrative *Vita Adae et Evae* (Life of Adam and Eve) further develops the narrative of angelic rebellion. The *Vita* speaks of God's calling the angels together following Adam's creation to admire and "worship the image of God," the first human. Satan refuses, stating, "I do not worship Adam. ... I will not worship one inferior and subsequent to me. I am prior to him in creation, before he was made, I was already made. He ought to worship me." The angel Michael threatens Satan, forcefully urging him to comply. Satan arrogantly replies, "I will set my throne above the stars of heaven and will be like the Most High."[4] With the hosts of angels who follow him, Satan is cast out of heaven onto the earth.

In Luke 10:18, Jesus says, "I beheld Satan as lightning fall from heaven." Later still, the eschatological Revelation of John tells of a "war in heaven" where "Michael and his angels fought against the dragon" and "the great dragon was cast out, that old serpent, called the Devil, and Satan, which deceiveth the whole world" (Rev. 12:7–9). Despite the past tense of this passage, it was originally read as a prophecy of the last days, the narrator presumably using past tense to record what he had seen in his vision. However, the similarity between this end-of-times conflict and the beginning-of-times conflict found in the *Vita Adae et Evae* caused the two stories to be linked in the minds of readers. As Frederick Holweck wrote in the *Catholic Encyclopedia*, "St. John speaks of the great conflict at the end of time, which reflects also the battle in heaven at the beginning of time."[5] The idea that a third of the angels was expelled with Satan comes from Revelation 12:4, which speaks of the dragon's tail casting a third of the stars of heaven to the earth, before the start of the "war in heaven."

The narrative crosses into Islam, where the Qur'an tells of the fallen angel Iblis who refused to bow down before Adam, stating, "I am better than him. You created me from fire and created him from clay." God casts Iblis out of heaven, warning, "Whoever follows you among them—I

---

4. M. D. Johnson, trans., "The Life of Adam and Eve" [Vita], *The Old Testament Pseudepigrapha*, ed. James H. Charlesworth, 2 vols. (New York: Doubleday, 1985), 2:262.

5. Frederick Holweck, "St. Michael the Archangel," *Catholic Encyclopedia*, 15 vols. (New York: Robert Appleton Company, 1911), 10:276, www.newadvent.org/cathen/10275b.htm.

will surely fill Hell with you, all together." On Earth, Iblis tempts Adam and Eve and all their posterity (Sura 7:10–20; also 38:65–88).

Despite the lack of any coherent biblical account, the war in heaven as a trope became central to Christian thought. Speculation about the war in heaven appears throughout the writings of the Christian Church Fathers. Origen believed that the fall of Lucifer and the rebel angels effected the creation of the physical world, a cosmic fall into physicality.[6] In *The City of God*, Augustine refers to the fall of Lucifer as the beginning of sin and expounds on the origin and status of the fallen angels. He also speculates that humans were created to fill the hole left in heaven by the banishment of the fallen angels—how "from this mortal race" God would "collect, as now He does, a people so numerous, that He thus fills up and repairs the blank made by the fallen angels, and that thus that beloved heavenly city is not defrauded of the full number of its citizens, but perhaps may even rejoice in a still more overflowing population."[7] This replacement theory is continued by Pope Gregory the Great (ca. 540–604) and eventually makes its way into the Old English poem *Genesis A,* where humanity is created to occupy the fallen angels' vacant "thrones, rich in glorious wealth, thriving with gifts, bright and fruitful, in the kingdom of God."[8]

The narrative was further developed in medieval mystery plays, with elaborate mechanical set-pieces called Hell-Mouths, complete with flash-pots, flame and variously colored smoke, into which Lucifer and the fallen angels are cast. The fifteenth-century York cycle of

6. See P. Tzamalikikos, *Origen: Cosmology and Ontology of Time* (Leiden: Brill, 2006), esp. Chap. 3, "The Fall and the Creation of the World."

7. St. Augustine, *The City of God*, trans. Marcus Dods, George Wilson, and J. J. Smith (Peabody, Massachusetts: Hendrickson, 2009), Bk. 22, chap. 1, 732. See also Bk. 3, chap. 5, p. 70; Bk. 10, chap. 24–25, p. 295; Bk. 11, chap. 13 and 15, pp. 321–23; Bk. 12, chap. 9, p. 350; Bk. 14, chap. 11 and 13, pp. 413, 416; Bk. 15, chap. 23, p. 462; Bk 16, cha.p 17, p. 489; Bk. 21, chap. 25, p. 720; and Bk. 22, chap. 1, pp. 731–32. Augustine takes up the replacement theory again in his *Enchiridion on Faith, Hope and Love,* trans. Thomas S. Hibbs (Washington, DC: Regnery, 2002), Bk. 29, p. 36.

8. Dorothy Haines, "Vacancies in Heaven: The Doctrine of Replacement and *Genesis A,*" *Notes and Queries* 44, 2 (June 1997): 150–53. See also David F. Johnson, "The Fall of Lucifer in *Genesis A* and Two Anglo-Latin Royal Charters," *Journal of English and Germanic Philology* 97, 4 (Oct. 1998): 500–21; Thomas D. Hill, "The Fall of Satan in the Old English, *Christ and Satan,*" *Journal of English and German Philology* 76, 3 (July 1977): 315–25; and Michael Fox, "Ælfric on the Creation and Fall of the Angels," *Anglo-Saxon England* 31 (2002): 175–200. My thanks to Dr. Miranda Wilcox for suggesting Old English source materials and Dr. Zina Petersen for advice on medieval sources.

plays depicts the sin of Lucifer as pride, his angelic hosts falling spontaneously rather than being cast out by God; it also recalls Augustine's replacement theory with God creating humans to take the place of the fallen angels.[9] The replacement theory reappears in the Arthurian poem *Joseph d'Arimathie* written by Robert de Boron, a French poet of the late twelfth and early thirteenth centuries. Robert writes that, when God cast out the angels, "for three days and three nights they rained down, so that never fell a heavier rain, nor one which harmed us more." Robert postulates that the result of this "rain" was three classes of fallen angels residing in three different locations: one class landed in hell, where they torture lost souls; another class landed on Earth, where they torment and tempt humanity; and another class remain in the sky, where they are able to assume different appearances and get humans to turn from virtue.[10] In his Arthurian epic *Parzival*, Wolfram von Eschenbach writes of fence-sitting angels, "those who did not stand on either side when Lucifer and *Trinitas* began to do battle," who were cast down to earth where they were imprisoned in the holy grail (which Wolfram imagines to be a stone with mystical powers).[11]

The most prominent account of the war in heaven was written not as scripture, but as an epic poem in 1667 by John Milton. In *Paradise Lost*, Milton fused the Christian version of the narrative with scenes of classical epic warfare. In Milton's version, Satan is never commanded to worship Adam (as in the apocryphal *Life of Adam and Eve*); still, the sins for which he is expelled from heaven are pride and jealousy.[12] It is

---

9. Richard Beadle and Pamela King, eds., *York Mystery Plays: A Selection in Modern Spelling* (Oxford, England: Oxford University Press, 1984), 1–7.

10. The quotation is from the English prose translation of *Joseph of Arimathea: A Romance of the Grail*, trans. Jean Rogers (London: Rudolf Steiner, 1990), 35–36. The original medieval French version written in octosyllabic couplets is in Robert de Boron, *Joseph d'Arimathie: A Critical Edition of the Verse and Prose Versions*, ed. Richard O'Gorman (Toronto: Pontifical Institute of Mediaeval Studies, 1995), 216–21.

11. Wolfram von Eschenbach, *Parzival*, ed. and trans. André LeFevre, *The German Library* (New York: Continuum, 2003), 125.

12. The reception of Milton's poem was mixed. In his *History of Sin and Heresie Attempted* (1698), Charles Leslie found Milton's account of the war in heaven wrongheaded for having "dress'd Angels in Armour, and put Swords and Guns into their Hands, to form romantick Battles in the Plains of Heaven." He felt that "if Mr. Milton had made the cause of [angelic] discontent to have been the incarnation of Christ ... his contexture [sic] had been nearer to the truth," in *The Theological Works of The Rev. Charles Leslie* (Oxford, England: Oxford University Press, 1832), 7:439–40, www.books.google.com. See also William Poole's "The Early Reception of Paradise Lost," *Literature Compass* 1 (2004): 1–13.

impossible to overstate the influence of Milton's *Paradise Lost* on subsequent generations. By the middle of the eighteenth century, Milton's *Paradise Lost* came to be, as Perry Miller has described it, "not so much a secondary Book of Genesis as a substitute for the original."[13]

When John Dryden asked Milton if he could turn his blank-verse epic into a sacred opera, Milton replied, "Certainly, you may tag my verses, if you will." The result, in heroic couplets, was *The State of Innocence and Fall of Men*, published in 1674, the year Milton died. Sadly, no music was ever composed for the libretto and the play was never performed. Perhaps it was never intended to be performed since the elaborate stage directions called for a "Lake of Brimstone or rolling Fire; the Earth of a burnt Colour," and "the rebellious Angels, wheeling in Air, and seeming transfixed with Thunderbolts: The bottom of the Stage being opened, receiv[ing] the Angels, who fall out of sight."[14] Nevertheless, it became during Dryden's lifetime, one of his most widely read dramas.

Some sixty years after Milton, American minister Jonathan Edwards repeated the Miltonian myth in a series of 1733 sermons: "Satan and his angels rebelled against God in heaven, and proudly presumed to try their strength with his. And when God, by his almighty power, overcame the strength of Satan, and sent him like lightning from heaven to hell with all his army; [sic] Satan still hoped to get the victory by subtilty." Edwards concluded: "God, therefore, has shown his great wisdom in overthrowing Satan's design."[15] Then, some sixty years later, Thomas Paine attacked the logic of this narrative in his 1794, *The Age of Reason*, a vigorous defense of Deism. Paine ridiculed the "Christian Mythologists" who believe "in an insurrection and a battle in Heaven, in which none of the combatants could be either killed or wounded."[16]

In the visual arts, depictions of the war in heaven appear in frescos, sculpture, stained glass, etchings, and paintings from at least the

---

13. Perry Miller, *Errand into the Wilderness* (New York: Harper, 1956), 220. Miller further notes that "the effect of Milton upon American 'primitive' painting of the late eighteenth and early nineteenth centuries is especially striking" (220).

14. *The Works of John Dryden: Plays Amboyna, The State of Innocence, Aureng-Zebe*, ed. Vinton A. Dearling, Vol. 12 (Berkeley: University of California Press, 1995), 97.

15. Jonathan Edwards, *The Works of President Edwards*, 10 vols. (New York: Carvill, 1830), 7:87, www.books.google.com.

16. Thomas Paine, *The Age of Reason: Being an Investigation of True and Fabulous Theology*, 1794 (Boston: Josiah P. Mendum, 1852), 14, www.books.google.com.

middle ages on. In 1498, Albrecht Dürer produced the woodcut *St. Michael Fighting the Dragon*, a theme repeated by painters like Raphael (1503), Guido Reni (1636), Sebastiano Ricci (1720), and Johann Georg Unruhe (1793). A statue representing St. Michael fighting the dragon adorns the spire of the eleventh-century Romanesque chapel on Mont St. Michel in Normandy, France. The fall of the rebel angels is depicted in the fifteenth-century illuminated *Les Très Riches Heures du Duc de Berry*, as well as in paintings by Hieronymus Bosch (1500), Pieter Bruegel I (1562), and Peter Paul Rubens (1620). Testifying of Milton's enduring importance, three illustrated editions of *Paradise Lost* appeared in the nineteenth century, one by William Blake (1807), one by John Martin (1827), and one by Gustave Doré (1866). All contain depictions of the fall of Satan and his legions.

LITERAL LEVEL

Uniquely LDS versions of the story emerged soon after the church's founding in 1830. Retained in the LDS narrative is the idea of a pre-mortal conflict, Satan's fall, and the associated banishment of one-third of the hosts of heaven. However, several new concepts also emerge. In Joseph Smith's inspired translation of the opening chapters of Genesis (dictated in 1830 and later canonized as the Book of Moses in the Pearl of Great Price), the war in heaven was caused by a conflict about agency. Satan proposed "to redeem all mankind, that one soul shall not be lost." However, the price of such salvation would be "destroy[ing] the agency of man, which ... the Lord God, had given him" (Moses 4:1–3). The scripture transforms the war from a military battle into a conflict of ideas about salvation: Satan attempting to save all but circumscribing agency, God allowing failure and defending agency. That same year, Smith produced the revelation that is now LDS Doctrine and Covenants 29, in which Satan rebels, stating, "Give me thine honor, which is my power; and also a third part of the hosts of heaven turned he away from me because of their agency" (v. 36).

In 1832, Smith and Sidney Rigdon's grand vision recorded in Doctrine and Covenants 76 included a glimpse of the war in heaven. New to this revelation is the idea that the war continues to be waged on this earth, though with different stakes, and that "those who know [God's] power, and have been made partakers thereof, and suffered themselves through the power of the devil to be overcome, and to deny the truth and defy my power" become sons of perdition "doomed to suffer the wrath of God" for eternity (vv. 25–38). Finally, in 1835, Smith produced a translation of some Egyptian papyri "purporting to be the writings of Abraham, while he was in Egypt." This text tells of a council in heaven where the pre-mortal souls or "intelligences"—including many who were "noble and great"—assembled to hear of the earth's creation. There Satan competed with Jesus to be the redeemer of humankind. When his prideful offer was rejected, he "kept not his first estate; and, at that day, many followed after him" (Abr. 3:28).[17]

Smith later elaborated on the topic in his King Follett sermon, April 7, 1844: "The contention in heaven was—Jesus said there would be certain souls that would not be saved; and the Devil said he could save them all, and laid his plans before the grand council, who gave their vote in favor of Jesus Christ. So the Devil rose up in rebellion against God, and was cast down, with all who put up their heads [sic] for him."[18] The account of the speech recorded in the *History of the Church* was an amalgamation of four accounts by Willard Richards, Wilford Woodruff, Thomas Bullock, and William Clayton. However, a retrospective summary of the sermon recorded by George Laub makes it clear that Smith's discourse, like Doctrine and Covenants 76, placed the war in heaven in the context of the unpardonable sin. In Laub's account, Jesus proposed that "he could save all those who did not sin against the Holy Ghost & they would obey the laws that was given," while Satan countered that he "can save all Even those who Sined against the Holy Ghost." Laub's version adds that Satan "accused

17. Brent L. Top, "War in Heaven," *Encyclopedia of Mormonism*, 4 vols. (New York: Macmillan, 1992), 4:1546–47. For a synopsis of early accounts of the war in heaven from an LDS perspective, see Stephen Ricks and Daniel Peterson, "The War in Heaven: A Comparison of Interpretations," *Tangents III* (Spring 1975): 99–105.

18. Joseph Smith Jr. et al., *History of the Church of Jesus Christ of Latter-day Saints,* ed. B. H. Roberts, 2d ed. rev. (6 vols., 1902–12, Vol. 7, 1932; rpt. Salt Lake City: Deseret Book Co., 1980), 5:327–37. See also Joseph Smith, Apr. 6, 1844, *Journal of Discourses,* 26 vols. (London and Liverpool: LDS Booksellers Depot, 1855–86), 6:8–9; Joseph Fielding Smith, comp. and ed., *Teachings of the Prophet Joseph Smith* (1938; Salt Lake City: Deseret Book Co., 1976 printing), 357; Andrew F. Ehat and Lyndon W. Cook, eds., *The Words of Joseph Smith: The Contemporary Accounts of the Nauvoo Discourses of the Prophet Joseph* (Salt Lake: Bookcraft, 1980), with the versions recorded by Richards, 342; Woodruff, 347; Bullock, 353; and Clayton, 361.

his brethren and was h[u]rled from the council for striving to break the law emediately and there was a warfare with Saten."[19]

Despite Smith's intriguing hint linking the war in heaven and the sons of perdition in Doctrine and Covenants 76 and the King Follett sermon, the nature of the premortal conflict has primarily been seen in LDS theology as a an ongoing battle between good and evil.[20] Most early LDS interpretations suggest that Lucifer's proposal entailed a kind of unlimited universal salvation.[21] For example, W. W. Phelps wrote in 1844 that "Lucifer lost his [first estate] by offering to save men in their sins."[22] Today, however, most Latter-day Saints understand his proposal to have been to curtail human choice, to require righteousness. As LDS Apostle James E. Talmage wrote in his officially sanctioned book *Jesus the Christ*, which was published in 1915: "all would be safely conducted through the career of mortality, bereft of freedom to act and agency to choose, so circumscribed that they would be compelled to do right—that not one soul would be lost."[23]

Elder Dallin H. Oaks's 2016 view of Satan's plan incorporates both contemporary and early LDS approaches: "Satan's proposal would have ensured perfect equality: it would 'redeem all mankind,' that not one soul would be lost. There would be no agency or choice by anyone and, therefore, no need for opposition. There would be no test, no failure, and no success. There would be no growth to attain the purpose the Father desired for His children."[24] By speaking of "perfect equality," Oaks appears to link Satan's proposal to a kind of universalist salvation; by referring to "no agency or choice," he may, however, be in line with contemporary views that Satan's plan would require righteousness and curtail free will.

Two other recent publications should be noted. In a 2008 article published in *Element*, the journal of the Society for Mormon

19. Eugene England, ed., "George Laub's Nauvoo Journal," *BYU Studies* 18, 2 (Winter 1978): 22–23.

20. Terryl L. Givens, *Wrestling the Angel: The Foundations of Mormon Thought: Cosmos, God, Humanity* (New York: Oxford University Press, 2015), 130–35.

21. See ibid., 132–35.

22. W. W. Phelps, "The Answer," *Times and Seasons* 5, 24 (Jan. 1, 1845): 4–6, in Givens, *Wrestling*, 134.

23. James E. Talmage, *Jesus the Christ: A Study of the Messiah and his Mission according to Holy Scriptures Both Ancient and Modern* (Salt Lake: Deseret News Press, 1915), 8.

24. Dallin H. Oaks, "Opposition in All Things," LDS General Conference Address, Apr. 2016, www.churchofjesuschrist.org/study/ensign/2016/05/sunday-afternoon-session/opposition-in-all-things?lang=eng.

Philosophy and Theology, Jeffrey M. Bradshaw and Ronan J. Head proposed that the conflict of the war in heaven was that Satan offered a form of universal redemption without the possibility of exaltation or deification.[25] And, influenced by early LDS models of the war in heaven, Terryl Givens proposes that, since agency is an eternal aspect of human intelligences, Satan could not limit agency. Rather, his strategy was to limit the consequences of using that agency. The conflict continues, as Givens notes, in "the tendency of a decadent culture … always to obscure or deny the connection between choice and consequence."[26]

The LDS narrative also changes the outcome of the war in heaven from the traditional Christian model. As. Givens has summarized: "The righteous partisans of Christ earn the reward of mortal embodiment and progression; those in league with Satan become the fallen angels doomed to nonphysicality."[27] Unlike Origen, LDS thought sees the physical world as a reward for those who opposed Satan, rather than an unfortunate cosmic fall.

Early references to the war in heaven were often quite speculative and focused on things that now seem quaint or inconsequentially tangential, such as the demographics and prosopography of heaven and hell. For example, Orson Pratt proposed that there were prior rebellions in heaven since "God has always been at work," and he attempted to calculate exactly how many spirits were cast out with Satan. "Their numbers, probably, cannot be less than … one hundred thousand millions of rebellious spirits or devils who were cast out from Heaven and banished to this creation."[28] Wilford Woodruff, engaging in his own mathematical inquiry, concluded that "one hundred million devils" were cast out of heaven, with "a hundred [assigned] to every man, woman and child that breathes the breath of life."[29] Brigham Young

---

25. Jeffrey M. Bradshaw and Ronan J. Head, "Mormonism's Satan and the Tree of Life," *Element* 4, 2 (Fall 2008): 1–50.

26. Terryl L. Givens, "'Moral, Responsible, and Free,' Or What God Do We Worship?" Speech to the J. Reuben Clark Law Society Meeting, Phoenix Arizona, Mar. 7, 2010, 10, www.static1.squarespace.com/static/597de9b0914e6bed5fd41726/t/59da992da9db09b4b 05207bb/1507498288431/Moral%2C+Responsible%2C+and+Free-+Duck+Version.pdf.

27. Terryl Givens, *When Souls Had Wings: Premortal Existence in Mormon Thought* (New York: Oxford University Press, 2010), 216.

28. Orson Pratt, July 18, 1880, *Journal of Discourses*, 21:287–88; Dec. 19, 1869, 13:63.

29. Wilford Woodruff, June 6, 1880, *Journal of Discourses*, 21:125–26, and Sept. 12, 1875, 18:115.

suggested that the premortal division took place only among spirit beings, not resurrected beings, and speculated that a "portion of grace allotted to those rebellious characters" prevented them from being returned to their "native element."[30] Jedediah M. Grant, one of Young's counselors, posited that, when Satan was cast out, he was given a "mission" to tempt mortal souls.[31] John Taylor hypothesized that Satan "probably intended to make men atone for their own acts" through "the shedding of their own blood as an atonement for their sins."[32]

Latter-day Saints thus do not regard the war in heaven as a symbolic fable but have, from the beginning, read it as a reality of cosmic history. And in light of increasing concerns about social mores, warfare, communism, and progressive politics, the frequency of citations to the war in heaven has increased. One can observe this trend by looking at the number of instances in which general authorities have spoken directly or indirectly of a war in heaven in general conference, as recorded in the *Journal of Discourses* (1855–86), *Collected Discourses* (1886–98), *Conference Reports*, and the *Ensign* (1971–present). In their analysis of rhetorical themes in LDS general conference sermons from 1830 to 1979, Gordon and Gary Shepherd outlined five periods of developing theology and changes in emphasis. I have attempted a similar analysis of how the war in heaven trope has been used in general conference sermons, adding two more periods. Such attempts suffer from a significant limitation: as the Shepherds note, conference records are incomplete during the nineteenth century, especially during the church's first decade.[33] Even if, due to the sketchy data, we consider the numbers found in Periods 1 and 2 (see Figure 1) with extreme caution, a strong trend toward increased references is readily apparent in general conference addresses. These results can be compared with results found by searching the term "war in heaven" in the *Corpus of LDS General Conference Talks*, a database of discourses from

30. Brigham Young, Apr. 8, 1871, *Journal of Discourses*, 14:93–94; and Mar. 16, 1856, 3:256. Young taught that those who left the gospel, particularly those identified as Sons of Perdition, would be "disorganized," lose their identity, and have their spirit matter returned to its "native element" to be recycled to create other souls. (See, for example, Brigham Young, June 27, 1858, *Journal of Discourses*, 7:57.)

31. Jedediah M. Grant, Feb. 19, 1854, *Journal of Discourses*, 2:11–12.

32. John Taylor, *The Mediation and Atonement* (Salt Lake City: Deseret News Co., 1882), 96–97. My thanks to Blair Hodges for calling this quotation to my attention.

33. Gordon Shepherd and Gary Shepherd. *A Kingdom Transformed: Themes in the Development of Mormonism* (Salt Lake: University of Utah Press, 1984).

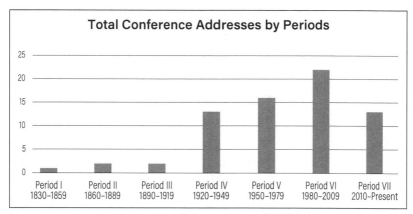

Figure 1

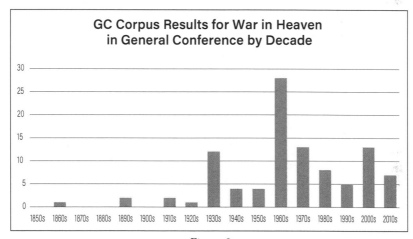

Figure 2

1851 to the present produced by Brigham Young University linguistics professor, Mark Davies. Searching for the specific term "war in heaven" in the *Corpus* reveals a significant increase during the 1930s, 1960s, and the 2000s, decades that have seen challenges to conventional notions of individual moral choice as well as society's political and economic ideals, as we will see below.[34] (See Figures 1 and 2.)

---

34. *Corpus of General Conference Talks,* Brigham Young University, https://www.lds-general-conference.org/. For background on the corpus, see Scott Taylor, "All 24 Million Words of LDS General Conference," April 1, 2011, http://www.deseretnews.com/article/700123380/All-24-million-words-of-lds-general-conference.html. That the BYU corpus does not show the same steady progression in usage as my research can be explained by the fact that, by

From the church's beginnings, the war in heaven narrative has been read as a very literal event in cosmic history. However, that literal event has been given a specific moral function in LDS discourse.

TROPOLOGIC LEVEL

One of the primary functions of the war in heaven narrative has been tropologic—providing a moral message by which church members can orient their lives. This is the most common use of the trope in contemporary LDS conference talks. Representative of this mode is a discourse by First Presidency Counselor James E. Faust in the all-male priesthood session of the October 2001 conference. He warned that the war in heaven "rages today ever more fiercely" and urged his listeners: "As priesthood holders we are marshaled into the great army of righteousness to combat the forces of Lucifer. Each of us needs to train ourselves to be bold, disciplined, and loyal men of the priesthood who are prepared with the proper weapons to fight against evil and to win."[35]

Citing this premortal conflict as an ongoing battle in which all Latter-day Saints are engaged is the most common homiletic use of the narrative in discourses dating from the mid-twentieth century to the present. It is true that Brigham Young cited the war in heaven to caution Latter-day Saints that Satan's followers were sent to earth to "try the sons of men" and admonished the Saints to diligently "improv[e] upon the intelligence given to them, the opportunity for overcoming evil, and for learning the principles which govern eternity, that they may be exalted therein."[36] Likewise John Taylor spoke in a somewhat similar vein, stating that, since the time of the war in heaven, "two grand powers" have opposed each other. "The conflict is between right and wrong, between truth and error, between God and the spirit of

---

searching only one term for the concept, "war in heaven," I am excluding places where a general authority might have spoken of the war in heaven but did not use that terminology, something I am able to take into consideration by going through the talks individually, as I did in my study of the periods. Furthermore, this search breaks down the data by decades rather than the generational periods that the Shepherds employed. Furthermore, it should be noted that in figure 2, the final period, 2010 to the present, only incorporates nine years, whereas the other periods incorporate the twenty-nine years used by the Shepherds. Therefore, it appears that period seven will likely meet if not exceed the previous period.

35. James E. Faust, "The Enemy Within," *Ensign*, Nov. 2000, www.churchofjesuschrist.org/study/ensign/2000/11/the-enemy-within?lang=eng.

36. Brigham Young, Mar. 16, 1856, *Journal of Discourses*, 3:256.

darkness, and the powers of evil that are opposed to Him." Taylor continued, God "has a right to demand obedience from his children," but "that right has been contested from the very first."[37] However, it is more common in early LDS discourse to employ the narrative in the literal, analogical, or anagogical modes.

In 1928, Rulon S. Wells of the First Council of the Seventy warned that "Satan is abroad in the land endeavoring to lead the children of God away here as there, continuing his work of destroying the souls of men." He urged members "to reject the plan of the adversary, with all his sophistry, his false religion, his deception, his evil and all combined," explaining that "to resent and resist that, and to turn away from it, is to overcome sin."[38] In 1935, Rudger Clawson, president of the Quorum of the Twelve Apostles, reminded Latter-day Saints of the war in heaven and warned that now "is a time for the testing of the souls of men."[39] Harold B. Lee, then president of the Quorum of the Twelve Apostles, referred to the war in heaven in April 1972 in the context of lamenting the late-1960s/early-1970s culture of drugs and free love: "Today we are constantly hearing from the unenlightened and misguided, who demand what they call free agency, by which they apparently mean, as evidenced by their conduct, that they have their agency to do as they please or to exercise their own self-will to determine what is law and order, what is right and wrong, or what is honor and virtue." This, Lee saw as "echoing the plan of Satan."[40] In 1989 Elder Russell M. Nelson cited the war in heaven as "the beginning of contention," warning that "Satan's method relies on the infectious canker of contention."[41] Elder Dallin H. Oaks updated the war in heaven in his 1995 warnings about same-gender attraction: "Satan would like us to believe that we are not responsible in this life. That is the result he tried to achieve by his contest in the pre-existence. A person who insists that he is not responsible

---

37. John Taylor, July 29, 1877, *Journal of Discourses*, 19:79.

38. Rulon S. Wells, *Conference Report of the Church of Jesus Christ of Latter-day Saints, April 1928* (Salt Lake City: Church of Jesus Christ of Latter-day Saints, 1928), 70.

39. Rudger Clawson, *Conference Report of the Church of Jesus Christ of Latter-day Saints, April 1935* (Salt Lake City: Church of Jesus Christ of Latter-day Saints, 1935), 66.

40. Harold B. Lee, "A Time of Decision," *Ensign*, July 1972, www.churchofjesuschrist.org/study/ensign/1972/07/a-time-of-decision?lang=eng.

41. Russell M. Nelson, "The Canker of Contention," *Ensign*, May 1989, www.churchofjesuschrist.org/study/ensign/1989/05/the-canker-of-contention?lang=eng.

for the exercise of his free agency because he was 'born that way' is trying to ignore the outcome of the War in Heaven. We *are* responsible, and if we argue otherwise, our efforts become part of the propaganda effort of the Adversary."[42] Elder D. Todd Christofferson sees Satan's attack on traditional families as a continuation of the war in heaven: "the premortal world, Lucifer rebelled against God and His plan, and his opposition only grows in intensity. He fights to discourage marriage and the formation of families, and where marriages and families are formed, he does what he can to disrupt them."[43]

In October 2009, Boyd K. Packer, president of the Quorum of the Twelve Apostles, said that, as a result of the war in heaven, "we were given our agency," adding, "We must use it wisely and remain close to the Spirit; otherwise, we foolishly find ourselves yielding to the enticements of the adversary."[44] During that same conference, Elder Quentin L. Cook stated that "the War in Heaven was fought after Satan said that he would force everyone to obey his ideas. That was rejected." Cook advised members that, "as a result, we have our moral agency and the freedom to choose our course in this life. But we also are accountable for that agency."[45]

Perhaps setting a record for the most references to the war in heaven in one conference, during the October 2010 conference, six speakers cited the war in heaven to emphasize moral principles—including all three members of the First Presidency. President Henry B. Eyring linked Lucifer's fall to a lack of "sufficient trust in God to avoid eternal misery."[46] Elder M. Russell Ballard said that the war in heaven continues today with Satan tempting us with addiction to "artificial substances and behaviors of temporary pleasure."[47] Elder Robert D. Hales described those who followed Satan in the premortal life as

42. Dallin H. Oaks, "Same-Gender Attraction," *Ensign*, Oct. 1995, www.churchofjesuschrist.org/study/ensign/1995/10/same-gender-attraction?lang=eng.

43. D. Todd Christofferson, "Why Marriage, Why Family," General Conference, Apr. 2015, www.churchofjesuschrist.org/study/general-conference/2015/04/why-marriage-why-family?lang=eng

44. Boyd K. Packer, "Prayer and Promptings," *Ensign*, Nov. 2009, www.churchofjesuschrist.org/study/ensign/2009/11/prayer-and-promptings?lang=eng.

45. Quentin L. Cook, "Stewardship—A Sacred Trust," *Ensign*, Nov. 2009, 91–94.

46. Henry B. Eyring, "Trust in God, Then Go and Do," *Ensign,* Nov. 2010, 70–73.

47. M. Russell Ballard, "O That Cunning Plan of the Evil One," *Ensign*, Nov. 2010, 108–10.

lacking "faith to follow the Savior." He cautioned members that Satan and his followers' "only joy is to make us 'miserable like unto [themselves].'"[48] President Dieter F. Uchtdorf told the priesthood session that "pride was the original sin" that "felled Lucifer, a son of the morning," warning that if pride could corrupt "one as capable and promising as this, should we not examine our own souls as well?"[49] And Church President Thomas S. Monson talked of Satan's plan in the premortal sphere to take away agency: "He insisted that with his plan none would be lost, but he seemed not to recognize—or perhaps not to care—that in addition, none would be any wiser, any stronger, any more compassionate, or any more grateful if his plan were followed."[50] Thus, in a single conference, general authorities taught lessons on trust, faith, pride, addiction, and spiritual growth by referring to the war in heaven.

Despite the importance of the war in heaven in LDS theology, it does not seem to occupy a central place in LDS fiction, drama, or poetry. I am aware of only a few examples, and most of them function primarily at the tropologic level, depicting a moral message for the audience to emulate in the here and now. Nephi Anderson's *Added Upon*, a popular didactic novel first published in 1898 (and in continuous print until 2005), depicts the war in heaven through a conversation between pre-mortal spirits Homan and Delsa:

> "What do you think of Lucifer and his plan?" asked she.
> "The talented Son of the Morning is in danger of being cast out if he persists in his course. As to his plan, it is this: 'If I cannot rule, I will ruin.'"
> "And if he rule, it will still be ruin, it seems to me."[51]

"Lucifer's pernicious doctrine," as the novel describes it, casts the war in heaven in terms of universal salvation as was typical in early Mormonism: "To be assured eternal glory and power without an effort on their part, appealed to them as something to be desired. To be untrammeled with laws, to be free to act at pleasure, without jeopardizing their future welfare, certainly was an attractive proposition. The pleasures in the body would be of a nature hitherto unknown. Why not be

---

48. Robert D. Hales "Agency: Essential to the Plan of Life" *Ensign*, Nov. 2010, 24–27.
49. Dieter F. Uchtdorf, "Pride and the Priesthood," *Ensign*, Nov. 2010, 55–58.
50. Thomas S. Monson "The Three Rs of Choice" *Ensign*, Nov. 2010, 67–70.
51. Nephi Anderson, *Added Upon: A Story* (Salt Lake: Deseret News Press, 1898), 16–17.

free to enjoy them? Why this curb on the passions and desires? 'Hail to Lucifer and his plan! We will follow him. He is in the right.'"[52]

Satan's position was not to force humans to be righteous, but to save everyone regardless of their choices. "Lucifer was fast gaining influence among the spirits," the novel relates, "and they had their agency to follow whom they would. The revolting spirit had skill in argument; and the light-minded, the discontented, and the rebellious were won over."[53]

Likewise, Orson F. Whitney's 1904 *Elias: An Epic of the Ages*, one of two epic poems that depict the war in heaven (I discuss the other, by Edward Tullidge, below) depicts the competing arguments put forward by Jesus and Satan, then cuts quickly to the outcome:

> 'T was done. From congregation vast
> Tumultuous murmurs rose;
> Waves of conflicting sound, as when
> Two meeting seas oppose.
> 'T was finished. But the heavens wept;
> And still their annals tell
> How one was choice of Elohim,
> O'er one who fighting fell.[54]

Whitney also described the war in heaven in his poem "Immanuel—A Christmas Idyl," where Lucifer describes his plan as follows: "My saving plan exception scorns— / Man's agency unknown. / As recompense, I claim the right / To sit on yonder Throne!"[55]

The popular 1977 production *My Turn on Earth*, written by Carol Lynn Pearson with music by Lex de Azevedo, has two musical numbers that depict the war in heaven. "I have a plan," sings Satan. "It will save every man. / I will force them to live righteously. / They won't have to choose. / Not one we'll lose. / And give all the glory to me." Jesus responds, "I have a plan. / It is better for man. / Each will have to decide what to be. / And choosing, I know, you'll learn and you'll grow, / And, Father, the glory to thee." In another song, "Shout for Joy," the

---

52. Ibid., 17–18.
53. Ibid., 18.
54. Orson F. Whitney, *Elias: An Epic of the Ages* (New York: Knickerbocker Press, 1904), 34.
55. Orson F. Whitney, "Immanuel—A Christmas Idyl," *The Poetical Writings of Orson F. Whitney* (Salt Lake City: Juvenile Instructor Office, 1889), 136–42.

premortal souls celebrate: "Satan's plan we did destroy! / We'll shout, we'll shout for joy!"[56]

Taking a strikingly different approach is the novel by D. Jeff Burton, entitled *Eternal Borderlands: Detours along the Road to Celestial Glory.*[57] Satirical, though not mocking, the novel explores LDS folk beliefs about premortal life, the unseen spirits tempting humanity, and the postmortal spirit world. In a chapter titled "The Unpleasantness," Candle, an inquisitive premortal spirit, highlights some of the theological implications of the war in heaven, asking "Why would the Council put the most important decision in Creation up for a vote? What would have happened if two-thirds of the Host of Heaven had voted for Lucifer's Plan?" She further comments, "It looks like one single event, one single decision has cost one-third of all our brothers and sisters their eternal lives. Millions of years of progression and a potential eternity of heavenly bliss—poof, gone in one single incidence of poor judgment. Does that make sense to you?"

Finally, evolutionary biologist, poet, and novelist, Steven Peck imagines the two proposals put forward in the war in heaven as a choice between a mechanistic/deterministic universe and evolution, with evolution taking the unique role as God's divine plan. When in the premortal world, God's children ask him how long they would have to wait for human bodies to inhabit, God's response is "No one knows ... what the future holds, / But we must watch and wait until it all unfolds." But what does unfold horrifies God's spirit children as they witness the universe full of pain and suffering competing with pleasure and joy, and they cry out, reminiscent of Christ's words in Gethsemane, "Is there no other way?" At this point, Lucifer arises and proposes an alternate plan:

> Stand still sweet parents swift and bright
> Holding back darkness, wielding light
>
> For I have found the Apollonian way,
> No need for messes, wet with clay

56. Carol Lynn Pearson, *My Turn on Earth*, Excell Entertainment B000FZEQNM, 2006, compact disc.

57. D. Jeff Burton, *Eternal Borderlands: Detours along the Road to Celestial Glory* (Bountiful, Utah: I'VE Press), 12.

No blood, no semen, or menstrual mess
No offal, sickness, age, distress
Make it craftily designed and certain,
Forget this grassy, slimish, verdan'

Here's how …

(And the children listened as he spoke)

Tick tock tick tock
Turn the steel precision gear
Now wind up the iron clock

Metal to metal, key to lock
Torsion, tension, forces shear
Tick tock tick tock

I will teach you how to walk
Set courses given, never veer
Now wind up the iron clock

All is determined, never ad-hoc
All to metronome adhere
Tick tock tick tock

Set with pulley, tackle, block
Let all in lockstep-click appear
Now wind up the iron clock

Toward exact prediction flock!
And every outcome engineer!
Tick tock tick tock!
Now wind up the iron clock!

…

The contriver can be seen
waving his hands and building a scale model
of a universe engineered to be set, certain,
no slop, all is measured and precise,
fixed, so that no surprises enter in.
The machinist shouts, "Where all is arranged from the beginning.

And once in motion it starts to spin—
all ends are determined and from
the beginning laid.

Peck's version of the war in heaven is a contest between a deterministic world and an evolving world of "heaven's ecologies" with "life manifold, diverse within its spheres, / Turning, emerging, knots in knots folding, / Living things striving upward, creative, / Evolving, ascending, to new rife forms."[58]

With only a few exceptions, most references to the war in heaven trope have a common purpose in LDS thought: to inspire individual moral behavior, to remind Latter-day Saints that they are engaged in spiritual warfare, and to reflect on their actions as part of a larger, cosmic drama. The war in heaven provides a moral lesson on the importance of using agency wisely. But it has also served a broader allegorical purpose, defending against threats to church dominion, explaining inequality, and supporting particular economic and political agendas.

ALLEGORICAL LEVEL

The first allegorical use of the war in heaven dates from the succession crisis of 1844. Wilford Woodruff used the narrative to urge members to follow Brigham Young and the Quorum of the Twelve rather than Sidney Rigdon, the sole surviving member of the First Presidency. In an impassioned letter published in the LDS *Times and Seasons* on November 1, 1844, Woodruff compared Rigdon to Lucifer "who made war in heaven." By threatening to "turn traitor, publish against the church in public journals, intimating that he would bring a mob upon the church, stir up the world against the saints and bring distress upon them," Rigdon had, according to Woodruff, proven his treachery and could not be trusted.[59] In a similar vein, Apostle Orson Hyde compared Rigdon's claim to authority to Satan's attempt to seize power during the war in heaven. Hyde stated that "none can bear rule" in God's appointed station, "except such as are appointed and ordained of God. Lucifer once undertook it, but he with all his adherents, was

---

58. Steven Peck, *Gilda Trillim: Shepherdess of Rats* (Abingdon, United Kingdom: Roundfire Books, 2017).

59. Wilford Woodruff, "To the Church of Jesus Christ of Latter day Saints," *Times and Seasons* 5, 20 (Nov. 1, 1844): 698–99.

cast out and thrust down to hell, because of an unlawful ambition in aspiring after a station that Heaven was not pleased to give."[60]

In another defense of the church against a perceived threat, the *Deseret News* published an anonymously written editorial in 1852 that warned against the Spiritualist movement that was then gaining adherents. The editorial cautioned that Lucifer's proposed plan in the premortal council appeared "more liberal, noble, benevolent and kind-hearted" than that proposed by Jesus, and that he drew away one-third of heaven with his "sophistry and false philanthropy." It suggested that spiritualism had real power but that mediums were contacting the wrong kind of spirits.[61] Reference to the war in heaven allowed church leaders to lay out a kind of middle path to successfully navigate any potentially authoritative claims of spiritualists, without rejecting outright the possibility of spiritual continuity and communication after death.

One of the principal uses of the war in heaven trope has been to explain the origins of earthly inequality, especially as it related to the restriction on ordaining Black males to the priesthood prior to 1978.[62] While the curse of Cain or Ham proved a common justification for prejudice and slavery in nineteenth-century America, just as it did in the LDS Church, in 1845 Orson Hyde introduced a new theory that had strong explanatory power for more than a century. He posited that, during the war in heaven, some

---

60. Orson Hyde, *Delivered before the High Priests' Quorum, in Nauvoo, April 27th 1845, upon the Course and Conduct of Mr. Sidney Rigdon, and upon the Merits of His Claim to the Presidency of the Church of Jesus Christ of Latter-Day Saints* (Nauvoo, Illinois: Times and Seasons Press, 1845), 4, www.sidneyrigdon.com/Hyd1845A.htm#pg27a.

61. "To the Saints," *Deseret News*, Feb. 21, 1852. The editor of the paper at this time was Brigham Young's second counselor in the First Presidency, Willard Richards. The editorial was later published as "False and Delusive Spirits" in the *Millennial Star* 14, 18 (June 26, 1852): 277–80. See Davis Bitton, "Mormonism's Encounter with Spiritualism," in his *The Ritualization of Mormon History and Other Essays* (Urbana: University of Illinois Press, 1994), 83–97. As Bitton argued and as this editorial implies, spiritualism posed a difficult dilemma for the LDS Church. To accept spiritualism's claims would be to accept every spiritual manifestation and lose control of the leadership's authority; but to denounce communication with the spirit world would be to deny the very foundation of the LDS message. The approach then was to acknowledge spiritual communication but to maintain that deciphering the intentions of the spirits thus encountered would require spiritual discernment available to LDS priesthood holders.

62. Lester E. Bush and Armand L. Mauss, eds., *Neither White nor Black: Mormon Scholars Confront the Race Issue in a Universal Church* (Salt Lake City: Signature Books, 1984), have abundantly outlined this history, so only a brief summary is necessary here. See also Armand L. Mauss, *All Abraham's Children: Changing Conceptions of Race and Lineage* (Urbana: University of Illinois Press, 2003).

spirits "did not take a very active part on either side, but rather thought the devil had been abused, and considered he had rather the best claim to government." Thus, according to Hyde, these spirits were born into the "African race," the "accursed lineage of Canaan" as a sort of punishment. Brigham Young publicly repudiated Hyde's hypothesis, likely for theological reasons, despite his own characterization of blacks as "uncouth, uncomely, disagreeable in their habits, wild and seemingly deprived of nearly all blessings of the intelligence that is bestowed upon mankind." Nevertheless, Young assured members of the church that "all spirits are pure that came from the presence of God. The posterity of Cain are black because he committed murder."[63]

Young's repudiation of the idea of premortal neutrality did not stick after his death, however. In 1885, B. H. Roberts of the First Council of the Seventy suggested that Blacks may not have "rebelled against God and yet were so indifferent in their support of the righteous cause of our Redeemer that they forfeited certain privileges and powers granted to those who were more valiant."[64] In 1889, Wilford Woodruff hinted that there might have been souls "astride the fence" in the war in heaven.[65] A letter from the First Presidency to Milton H. Knudson, dated January 13, 1912, seemed to contradict this line of reasoning, however: "So far as we know, there is no revelation, ancient or modern, neither is there any authoritative statement by any of the authorities of The Church of Jesus Christ of Latter-day Saints in support of that which many of our elders have advanced as doctrine, in effect that the negroes are those who were neutral in heaven at the time of the great conflict or war, which resulted in the casting out of Lucifer and those who were led by him, said to number about one-third of the hosts of heaven."[66]

The 1931 publication of Apostle Joseph Fielding Smith's *The Way to Perfection* trod a middle ground, stressing that Black people had not

63. Brigham Young, qtd. in Bush and Mauss, *Neither White nor Black*, 72–73; Hyde, *Delivered before the High Priests' Quorum*, 30.
64. B. H. Roberts, "To the Youth of Israel," *The Contributor* 6, 8 (May 1885): 296–97.
65. Wilford Woodruff, "Eternal Variety of God's Creations," July 14, 1889, in Brian H. Stuy, comp. and ed., *Collected Discourses Delivered by Wilford Woodruff, His Two Counselors, the Twelve Apostles, and Others, 1886–1898*, 5 vols. (Burbank, California: BHS Publishing, 1987–92; Vol. 3 published in Sandy, Utah), 1:311.
66. Gary James Bergera, comp., *Statements of the LDS First Presidency: A Topical Compendium* (Salt Lake City: Signature Books, 2007), 369. The First Presidency then consisted of Joseph F. Smith, Anthon H. Lund, and Charles W. Penrose

necessarily been neutral but rather that they "did not stand valiant-ly."[67] In April 1939 general conference, Apostle George F. Richards repeated Smith's concept of non-valor.[68] Echoing Smith's position, the First Presidency wrote to sociology professor Lowry Nelson on July 17, 1947: "From the days of the Prophet Joseph [Smith] even until now it has been the doctrine of the Church, never questioned by any of the Church Leaders, that the Negroes are not entitled to the full blessings of the Gospel." Evidently church leaders were unaware of the priesthood ordinations of Elijah Abel in 1836, Walker Lewis in 1844, William McCary in 1846, and Abel's son Enoch in 1900 and grandson Elijah in 1935.[69] The letter goes on: "Some of God's children were as-signed to superior positions before the world was formed" based on the "preexistence of our spirits, the rebellion in heaven, and the doctrines that our birth into this life and the advantages under which we may be born have a relationship in the life heretofore."[70] Two years later in 1949, the same First Presidency announced this theory as a principal reason for priesthood denial to Black men.[71]

The idea that Blacks were less valiant in the war in heaven appears in the 1956 young adult novel *Choose Ye This Day* written by Emma Marr Petersen, the wife of Elder Mark E. Petersen.[72] In the novel, when Milo Patterson, a Black athlete from Los Angeles, joins the college football team, several southern athletes stage a boycott. Two LDS stu-dents, Kent and Steve, debate the school's position that the team be integrated. Steve is willing to play with Milo, but Kent does not like the idea. "Even the Church holds out against the Negros," Kent states (45).

---

67. Joseph Fielding Smith, *The Way to Perfection* (Salt Lake City: Deseret Book Co., 1931), 43–45.

68. George F. Richards, "Punishment of Those Not Valiant," *Conference Report of the Church of Jesus Christ of Latter-day Saints, April 1939* (Salt Lake City: Church of Jesus Christ of Latter-day Saints, 1939), 58–59.

69. Bush and Mauss, *Neither White nor Black*, 131, 133, 147n75; "Black History Timeline, Blacklds.org," www.blacklds.org/history.

70. Lowry Nelson, *In the Direction of His Dreams: Memoirs* (New York: Philosophical Library, 1985), 339. The First Presidency then consisted of George Albert Smith, J. Reuben Clark Jr., and David O. McKay. My thanks to Gary James Bergera for calling this source to my attention.

71. The full text of the letter, dated August 17, 1949, appears in Bush and Mauss, *Neither White nor Black*, 221. The First Presidency still consisted of George Albert Smith, J. Reuben Clark Jr., and David O. McKay.

72. Emma Marr Petersen, *Choose Ye This Day* (Salt Lake City: Bookcraft, 1956).

Steve suggests they talk about it with Hank Weston, a "crippled" hamburger stand owner "known for his honesty and practical good sense" (7). Hank opines that his "attitude on this subject is pretty well guided by my religious views ... so I hope you won't mind if I mix a little religion with what I say" (47). Hank then teaches the students that Blacks are cursed in mortality because they were not as valiant in the war in heaven. He confesses, though, that he has "heard some of our [church] leaders teach that even the Negro can go to the celestial kingdom if he is faithful. However, he can be only a servant there." He justifies this idea by adding: "That is more than many white people will receive, for many of them will be placed in the lower degrees of glory in the next world, because they did not live righteously. So in some respects, Negroes, if they are faithful, may receive a higher glory in the world to come than those of other races who defile their birthright" (49). Hank concludes: "Each race may develop within itself. So far as the Negroes are concerned, we will give them every right and privilege within their race that we claim for ourselves within our own race, but we will not become intimate with them in any way, and we will not intermarry with them. ... I believe that is a fair position to take, and I believe it squares with the word of God" (49–50). Hank's position is finally summed up by one of the students: "So you would be in favor of allowing a Negro to play on our football team, as long as we did not take him so far into our social life that some white girl might become infatuated with him" (50). "That is just what I believe," responds Hank (51).

After the 1978 revelation extending the priesthood to all worthy male members of the LDS Church, Apostle Bruce R. McConkie, who himself had perpetuated the idea of premortal "neutrality" in his highly influential *Mormon Doctrine*, stated: "Forget everything that I have said, or what President Brigham Young or President George Q. Cannon or whoever has said in days past that is contrary to the present revelation. We spoke with a limited understanding without the light and knowledge that now has come into the world."[73]

---

73. Bruce R. McConkie, *Sermons and Writings of Bruce R. McConkie* (Salt Lake City: Deseret Book Co., 1979), 165. The entry for "Negroes" in editions of *Mormon Doctrine* prior to 1979 stated: "In the preexistent eternity various degrees of valiance and devotion to the truth were exhibited by different groups of our Father's spirit offspring. ... Those who were less valiant in preexistence and who thereby had certain spiritual restrictions imposed upon them during mortality are known to us as the negroes." This material was all deleted

The war in heaven narrative has also been employed to explain more generally the origins of inequality. In 1954, Apostle Mark E. Petersen speculated that the circumstances of our birth, whether we were born in "darkest Africa, or in flood-ridden China, or among the starving hordes of India, while some of the rest of us are born in the United States" is a "reflection of our worthiness or lack of it in the pre-existent life."[74] Likewise, in 1961, Alvin R. Dyer, who was then serving as Assistant to the Quorum of the Twelve and would later join the First Presidency, asked: "Why is it that you are white and not colored? Have you ever asked yourself that question? Who had anything to do with your being born into the Church and not born a Chinese or a Hindu, or a Negro? … There were three divisions of mankind in the pre-existence, and when you are born into this life, you are born into one of these three divisions of people. There is an imposed judgment placed upon everyone who leaves the Spirit World just the same as there will be when they leave this life and go into one of three places."[75]

It is fascinating to note, however, that another strand of this argument takes the exact opposite position. While suggesting that Blacks *were* denied the priesthood because of their "degree of faithfulness, by the degree of development in the pre-existent state," B. H. Roberts denied that wealth and privilege were indications of premortal righteousness. "The favored sons of God are not those furthest removed from trial, from sorrow, from affliction. It is the fate, apparently, of those whom God most loves that they suffer most, that they might gain the experience for which men came into this world."[76] Thus, whom

in post-1979 editions of the book. See also Marvin Perkins. "Blacks and the Priesthood," FAIR, Sept. 8, 2002, www.fairlds.org/Misc/Blacks_and_the_Priesthood.html. Perkins astutely notes that, in the Book of Abraham, where the notion of different levels of valor is stated, "the discussion regarding varying degrees of valiancy or greatness … actually comes before the plan was laid out and presented, and before the rejection of the plan and rebellion by Satan, instead of after, as the tradition would have us believe."

74. Mark E. Petersen, "Race Problems as They Affect the Church: A Speech Delivered at the Convention of Teachers of Religion on the College Level," Brigham Young University, Aug. 27, 1954, 9–10, www.mormonismi.net/mep1954/00.html.

75. Alvin R. Dyer, "For What Purpose," Mar. 18, 1962, at Oslo, Norway Missionary Conference, qtd. in Jerald and Sandra Tanner, *The Negro in Mormon Theology* (Salt Lake City: Modern Microfilm, 1963), 48–58. Also available at www.scribd.com/doc/13500724/For-What-Purpose.

76. B. H. Roberts, Jan. 27, 1895, Stuy, *Collected Discourses*, 4:235–38. Roberts also stated, "If all … affliction was for the 'good' of one of the most favored of God's sons, is

God loves, he sends not riches but trials, suggested Roberts. Reflecting perhaps more concern for diversity as the LDS Church becomes a world religion, BYU religion professor Terry Ball posed exactly the same question in a 2008 BYU Devotional as Dyer had in 1961 but drew the opposite conclusion: "Have you ever wondered why you were born where and when you were born?" Ball continued, "We believe that when it came time for us to experience mortality, a loving Heavenly Father who knows each of us well sent us to earth at the time and place and circumstances that would best help us reach our divine potential and help Him maximize his harvest of redeemed souls."[77]

In short, for Mark E. Petersen and Alvin R. Dyer, inequality is an outward sign of premortal apathy—the worse your condition in this life, the more likely your indifference in the preexistence. Others have taken a much more charitable view of humanity. For B. H. Roberts, inequality may be a sign of premortal righteousness, while Terry Ball sees it as a result of divine understanding.

Perhaps the most common allegorical function the war in heaven has served in LDS thought is to justify and defend certain political and economic structures. Brigham Young saw it as a warning against the type of political factions that had created the Civil War. Citing the division that existed in the war in heaven, Young concluded, "Where such disunion exists in any government, it ultimately becomes the means of the utter overthrow of that government or people, unless a timely remedy is applied. Party spirit once made its appearance in heaven, but was promptly checked." Young continued, "if our Government had cast out the Seceders, the war would soon have been ended." Young's position was that the Mormons were witnessing the judgments of God against the United States for America's treatment of the church members. "The people in the States have violated the Constitution in closing their ears against the cries of the oppressed, and in consenting to shedding innocent blood, and now war, death and gloom are spread like a pall over the land."[78]

---

it not a fair conclusion that the trials and adversities of the other sons of God are for their 'good?'" *The Gospel and Man's Relationship to Deity* (Salt Lake City: George Q. Cannon & Sons, 1893), 345–50.

77. Terry Ball, "To Confirm and Inform: A Blessing of Higher Education," BYU Devotional Address, Mar. 11, 2008, 6, www.speeches.byu.edu/?act=viewitem&id=1764.

78. Brigham Young, Aug. 3, 1862, *Journal of Discourses*, 9:333.

Fifty years later B. H. Roberts took a different position and defended U.S. entry into World War I by suggesting that the war in heaven proves that God does take sides in war, and surely he is on the side of the allies. To those who would say wars are "merely the machinations of men," Roberts stated, "I would ask what of the war in heaven when Michael [sic, Lucifer] and his angels revolted and became the devils of this world?" He continued, "I have absolute faith and confidence that so far as the United States is concerned, God is with us."[79] On another occasion, Roberts linked the patriots of the American Revolution with an ongoing fight for freedom that began when Satan was cast out of heaven. "We read that there was war in heaven," Roberts stated. "I think God was in that war, for Satan was overthrown and forced from heaven. I cannot help but think that when the patriot fathers who founded our nation drew the sword against the great empire of England, in the maintenance of their avowed rights, and for the establishment of free government in this world, God sustained their feeble arms and crowned them with glory."[80] Likewise, in 1917 Presiding Bishop Charles W. Nibley saw World War I as a continuation of the struggle for freedom begun in the war in heaven and encompassing Henry VIII's break with the Pope, Cromwell's rupture with the Stuarts, George Washington's clash with George III, and Abraham Lincoln's opposition to the South. "The spirit of that contention did not cease to exist. It has existed and has come down to us through the ages; one side contending for individual liberty and the rights of man, and the other side contending for rule by force and by compulsion. That was essentially the issue in that great conflict before the world was. Christ stood for government by persuasion, by long suffering, by kindness and gentleness and love unfeigned. The other power was for government and salvation for all, to be secured by the spirit of force and compulsion, wherein all would be saved without agency, or what we call common consent."[81] In a similar vein, Apostle Melvin J. Ballard

---

79. B. H. Roberts, qtd. in "Says God Takes Part in Certain Great Conflicts," *Deseret News*, Aug. 27, 1917, 5. Since this is a report of Roberts's speech, it is not clear whether he misspoke, saying that Michael rather than Lucifer revolted, or if it is the error of the reporter.

80. B. H. Roberts, *Conference Report of the Church of Jesus Christ of Latter-day Saints, October 1914* (Salt Lake City: Church of Jesus Christ of Latter-day Saints, 1914), 109.

81. Charles W. Nibley, *Conference Report of the Church of Jesus Christ of Latter-day Saints, April 1917* (Salt Lake City: Church of Jesus Christ of Latter-day Saints, 1917), 144.

denounced the German Kaiser Wilhelm II as leading the forces of evil in a continuation of the war in heaven. "The forces of evil were cast down to the earth, and here they have been and here the war wages and never have these combats ceased," said Ballard. "When shall the conflict end? There is no doubt in our minds what the result will be when that end shall come."[82]

The trope took a new direction after Franklin Delano Roosevelt was elected US president in 1932. As historians have documented, LDS President Heber J. Grant became increasingly wary of FDR's New Deal policies. When Roosevelt sought an unprecedented third term in office, Grant authorized the publication of an anti-Roosevelt editorial in the *Deseret News* on October 31, 1940. Days later, the November *Improvement Era* featured an editorial, penned by Richard L. Evans, stating that "the ability to influence public opinion is not always accompanied by a like degree of integrity or honesty or honorable motive. A man may be a spellbinder and a scalawag at the same time." The editorial pointedly drew a comparison with "Lucifer, a brilliant personality" who "waged war in heaven and misled a third of the hosts thereof to their own downfall and to his," reminding readers to keep this duplicity in mind "before we set aside any hard-won and quickly-lost right of liberty or tradition of freedom."[83]

The United States' entrance into World War II brought out the war in heaven narrative once again. On April 5, 1942, general conference was ripe with significance: The world was celebrating Easter and entering a war. American soldiers had been arriving in Great Britain since January. David O. McKay, second counselor in the First Presidency, addressed the audience gathered in the upper room of the Salt Lake temple, stating, "On this Easter Day, the Risen Christ beholds in the world not peace, but war." McKay continued: "War impels you to hate your enemies. The Prince of Peace says, Love your enemies. War says, Curse them that curse you. The Prince of Peace says, Pray for them that curse you. War says, Injure and kill them that hate you. The Risen Lord says, Do good to them that hate you. Thus we see that war is incompatible with Christ's teachings. The gospel of Jesus Christ is the gospel of peace.

---

82. Melvin J. Ballard, *Conference Report of the Church of Jesus Christ of Latter-day Saints, October 1918* (Salt Lake City: Church of Jesus Christ of Latter-day Saints, 1918), 149.

83. "Editorial," *Improvement Era*, Nov. 1940, 672.

War is its antithesis, and produces hate. It is vain to attempt to reconcile war with true Christianity." McKay then used the war in heaven as an example of a war that is justifiable: "In that rebellion Lucifer said in substance: 'By the law of force I will compel the human family to subscribe to the eternal plan, but give me thine honor and power.'" Depriving another of agency, McKay stated, "may justify a truly Christian man to enter—mind you, I say enter, not begin—a war."[84]

One of the most esoteric works on the war in heaven was Nels L. Nelson's 1941 *The Second War in Heaven as Now Being Waged by Lucifer through Hitler as a Dummy*. Nelson had taught English, philosophy, public speaking, and religion at BYU between 1883 and 1920, except for a short hiatus between 1885 and 1887 while serving in the Southern States Mission, and had published many articles and three books: *Preaching and Public Speaking*, *The Mormon Point of View*, and *Scientific Aspects of Mormonism*. When *The Second War in Heaven* was published, Nelson was seventy-nine, respected by church leaders, and, as Davis Bitton states, "we can safely say that Nelson's name was well-known in the Mormon community."[85] The book combines a sort of New Age philosophy with political commentary to stress that the totalitarian regimes of Stalin, Mussolini, and, in particular, Hitler are "trying to destroy" what Nelson calls the "I am principle in man" and that these dictators oppose the "psychic evolution" of "pre-existence, earth-life, and after-earth life."[86]

Church President Joseph F. Smith had a deep respect for Nelson and his writing, going so far as authorize the church to loan Nelson $800 to publish his book *Scientific Aspects of Mormonism*. As Richard Sherlock has written, Smith "sent [Nelson] manuscripts to review before

<hr/>

84. David O. McKay, *Conference Report of the Church of Jesus Christ of Latter-day Saints, April 1942* (Salt Lake City: Church of Jesus Christ of Latter-day Saints, 1942), 70–71.

85. Davis Bitton, "N. L. Nelson and the Mormon Point of View," *BYU Studies* 13, 2 (Winter 1973): 157.

86. N[els]. L. Nelson, *The Second War in Heaven as Now Being Waged by Lucifer through Hitler as a Dummy* (Independence, Missouri: Zion's Printing, 1941), 5. Biographical information about Nelson is scarce, but a brief notice is found in T. Earl Pardoe, *The Sons of Brigham* (Provo, Utah: Brigham Young University Alumni Association, 1969), 156–60. Concerning Nelson's attempt to synthesize science and religion, see Richard Sherlock, "A Turbulent Spectrum: Mormon Reactions to Darwinist Legacy," in *The Search for Harmony: Essays on Science and Mormonism*, ed. Gene A. Sessions and Craig J. Oberg (Salt Lake City: Signature Books, 1993), 67–91. Bitton, "N. L. Nelson and The Mormon Point of View," 1–12, discusses a short-lived periodical Nelson published.

deciding whether they should be published by the church. From the mass of letters between Nelson and church leaders, it is clear that he was on close terms with Smith and others."[87] However, *The Second War in Heaven* struck a nerve with President J. Reuben Clark, First Counselor to President Heber J. Grant. Clark took Nelson to task in a six-page personal letter critiquing Nelson's manuscript, calling it "too philosophic to be good propaganda, and too 'propagandish' to be good philosophy." Despite Nelson's appeal to the war in heaven, Clark's position as a laissez-fair conservative caused him to regard foreign entanglements with suspicion. For Clark, Hitler should not be singled out in the world's history of evil. "It seems to me that the 'second war in heaven' began with Satan's temptation of Eve, and swung into full march with Cain's murder of Abel. From that date until the present ... it has been the conflict between the two great forces, Good and Evil." As he put it, "I think you have largely spoiled [the book] by over-emphasizing and over magnifying Hitler and his particular regime." Clark was not siding with Hitler, stating "I am willing to convict him" but also adjudging that "the situation has created the man." Recognizing the economic difficulties in Germany caused by reparations after World War I, Clark believed that Hitler "was to the Germans as a voice crying in the wilderness and offering to lead them out of the economic and political bondage in which the Treaty of Versailles left them." And of the situation in Germany, Clark cautioned, "I should like you to excuse my warning you against your assuming as truth most of the criticism you see leveled against Hitler and his regime in Germany. ... Hitler is undoubtedly bad from our American point of view, but I think that Germans like him." Clark further warned Nelson about taking the side of Jews. "There is nothing in their history which indicates that the Jewish race loves either free-agency or liberty. 'Law and order' are not facts for the Jews."[88]

The war in heaven narrative gained even greater traction as an allegory for the proper role of government in light of Communism. One of the earliest references came from Rulon S. Wells of the First Council

---

87. Sherlock, "A Turbulent Spectrum," 80.

88. J. Reuben Clark, Letter to N. L. Nelson, June 24, 1941, 6, J. Reuben Clark Papers, MSS 303, Box 363, fd. 2, L. Tom Perry Special Collections, Harold B. Lee Library, Brigham Young University, Provo, Utah. D. Michael Quinn cites this revealing letter in *Elder Statesman: A Biography of J. Reuben Clark* (Salt Lake City: Signature Books, 2002), 291–92, 335.

of the Seventy in the April 1930 general conference. Wells stated that "the war begun in heaven is continued here on earth. To follow the enemies of God means to follow them into slavery, but to serve God means freedom." Wells continued, "Think of poor afflicted Russia now under Soviet rule." Russia had suffered under the czars and had "good reason to rise up against such conditions," but had "no sooner liberated themselves" than the "Soviet seeks to plunge them into the still more deadly slavery of atheism."[89]

During the post-World War II developments of heightened diplomatic and military tensions known as the Cold War, the war in heaven became the primary metaphor for LDS thinking about the Soviet Union and concerns about the spread of Communism throughout the world. Apostle Ezra Taft Benson frequently spoke of the fight against Communism as a continuation of the war in heaven. "It is time, therefore, that every American, and especially every member of the priesthood, became informed about the aims, tactics, and schemes of socialistic-communism," Benson stated in the October 1961 general conference. "This becomes particularly important when it is realized that communism is turning out to be the earthly image of the plan which Satan presented in the pre-existence. The whole program of socialistic-communism is essentially a war against God and the plan of salvation—the very plan which we fought to uphold during 'the war in heaven.'"[90] But he also began to link his anti-Communism discourse with any form of "welfare government" that would "force us into a greater socialistic society." When some church members took umbrage at his increasingly far-right agenda, Benson responded in a 1966 BYU devotional address: "We cannot compromise good and evil in an attempt to have peace and unity in the Church any more than the Lord could have comprised with Satan in order to avoid the War in Heaven."[91] Strikingly, Benson characterized differences of opinion within the church

89. Rulon S. Wells, *Conference Report of the Church of Jesus Christ of Latter-day Saints, April 1930* (Salt Lake City: Church of Jesus Christ of Latter-day Saints, 1930), 70–72.

90. Ezra Taft Benson, *Conference Report of the Church of Jesus Christ of Latter-day Saints, October 1961* (Salt Lake City: Church of Jesus Christ of Latter-day Saints, 1961), 70. In that same talk, Benson urged members to read W. Cleon Skousen's *Naked Communist* (Salt Lake City: Ensign Publishers, 1962). See also Ezra Taft Benson, *The Red Carpet* (Salt Lake City: Bookcraft, 1962), 111; *An Enemy Hath Done This* (Salt Lake City: Bookcraft, 1969), 281–82; *God, Family, and Country* (Salt Lake City: Deseret Book Co., 1974), 389.

91. Ezra Taft Benson, "Our Immediate Responsibility," BYU Devotional Address, Oct. 25, 1966, qtd. in D. Michael Quinn, "Ezra Taft Benson and Mormon Political Conflicts,"

as a continuation of the war in heaven, with his own right-leaning rhetoric defending the side of the angels.

The war in heaven continued to be employed against the spread of Communism, but also against liberalism in general. In his self-published 1964 book *Prophets, Principles, and National Survival*, Jerreld Newquist, an Air Force major during World War II and convert to the LDS Church, claimed that any "collectivist philosophy" is related to the plan proposed by Lucifer prior to the war in heaven. Likewise, Hyrum Andrus's 1965 *Liberalism, Conservatism, Mormonism* branded "liberalism, like the plan proposed by Lucifer and his hosts in the war in heaven," as "deficient and perverse."[92] The war in heaven was also used to justify greater political moderation and support for pluralism. For example, one letter to the editor of *Dialogue: A Journal of Mormon Thought* suggested that, by ignoring the rights of other nations to self-determination—to impose our ways on them despite the fact that their people have duly elected a Communist government—the United States was "getting close to" supporting Lucifer's plan. Hugh Nibley took the position that "Satan wasn't cast out of heaven for voting the wrong way ... [but] for refus[ing] to accept the verdict. ... Satan was cast out for refusing to accept the popular vote."[93] Voices on both sides of the debate could make their case by appealing to the war in heaven.

Dialogue: A Journal of Mormon Thought 26, 2 (Summer 1993): 56–57, MP3 format, www. speeches.byu.edu/?act=viewitem&id=1611.

92. Jerreld L. Newquist, *Prophets, Principles, and National Survival* (Salt Lake City: Publishers Press, 1964), viii; Hyrum L. Andrus, *Liberalism, Conservatism, Mormonism* (Salt Lake City: Deseret Book Co., 1965), 69–70. Receiving substantially less attention were reviews to these books published in *Dialogue: A Journal of Mormon Thought*. Thomas G. Alexander responded to Newquist's claim about collectivism by stating: "Had opposition to collectivism been an eternal principle related to the War in Heaven and to man's free agency, the Lord would never have had his Church practice it" as the Saints had in the nineteenth century. Martin Hickman suggested that Andrus was implying that only right-wing conservatives could be good members of the church and that, "if the arguments of this book ever become widely accepted in the Church, criteria other than devotion to the gospel will be used to measure acceptable Church behavior, Church members will become confused about the nature and mission of the Church, divisions[,] and bitterness arising from political differences will be infused into Church relationships, and members will be distracted from the principal task of giving effect to the teachings of Christ in their lives." Alexander, "An Ambiguous Heritage," *Dialogue: A Journal of Mormon Thought* 2, 3 (Autumn 1967): 127–34; Hickman, Review of *Liberalism, Conservatism, Mormonism*, *Dialogue: A Journal of Mormon Thought* 2, 2 (Summer 1967): 115–22.

93. Alvin Guy Van Alstyne, Letter to the editor, *Dialogue: A Journal of Mormon Thought* 3, 1 (Spring 1968): 7. Hugh Nibley, "Alma 1–2: Alma Escapes Wealth," *Teachings of the Book of Mormon*, 4 vols. (Provo, Utah: FARMS, n.d.), 2:237.

Returning to the tendency to use the war in heaven to justify the United States in times of war, Sterling W. Sill of the First Council of the Seventy invoked the narrative in 1970, the year US and South Vietnamese forces invaded Cambodia and National Guardsmen fired on protesters at Kent State. Sill lauded the examples of war heroes like Generals Black Jack Pershing, Douglas MacArthur, and Dwight D. Eisenhower, as well as "our present great commander-in-chief, Richard M. Nixon," and admonished church members to remember that "the greatest of all military men was the Son of God himself. In the war in heaven, he led the forces of righteousness against the rebellion of Lucifer." Sill apparently saw Christ as displacing Michael's role in the premortal conflict. He continued, "We can also draw great significance from the fact that before the Savior of the world was the Prince of Peace, he was Jehovah the warrior."[94]

Despite the fall of the Soviet Union in 1991, conservative writers and commentators like Glenn Beck have continued to use the war in heaven narrative to warn against what they regard as "socialism" and to denounce the progressive goals of universal health care and governmental efforts to alleviate poverty. A perusal of blog posts and web pages reveals conservative Latter-day Saints using the war in heaven to argue against paying taxes, voting for Harry Reid, and the creeping "socialism" into which they saw the nation sliding.[95] In his 2001 self-published book *The Hidden Things of Darkness*, Christopher S. Bentley, a Latter-day Saint who has served as the director of operations for the John Birch Society, argued that the war in heaven "did not cease after Satan was cast out" but has rather intensified. It continues here

---

94. Sterling W. Sill, "God and Country," *Improvement Era* Dec. 1970, 79. Sill repeats much of this material in "The Unknown Soldier," in his *That Ye Might Have Life* (Salt Lake City: Deseret Book Co., 1974), 51.

95. For example, see Christopher Hansen, "Tea–2010 AD Handbook," *The Tea Party*, Nov. 19, 2010, www.ateapartyblog.blogspot.com/2010/11/tea-2010-ad-handbook.html; Kelly Smith, "7 Reasons Why This Mormon Is Not Voting for Harry Reid," *Inspiration Is Light*, Sept. 3, 2010, www.kellywsmith.com/mormon_not_voting_for_harry_reid.html; LDS Patriot, "Will the Mormons Please Excommunicate Harry Reid Already?" *LDS Patriot*, June 7, 2006, www.ldspatriot.wordpress.com/2006/06/07/will-the-mormons-please-excommunicate-harry-reid-already/; Chauncy Childs, "Awake to Our Awful Situation," *LDS Liberty*, www.ldsliberty.org/awake-to-our-awful-situation/; Brian Mecham, "The Book of Mormon Warns America, Are You Listening?" *Latter-day Conservative*, Dec. 4, 2009, www.latterdayconservative.com/blog/the-book-of-mormon-warns-america-are-you-listening.

on earth in the form of "Satanocracy," "the ongoing effort to enslave mankind" by "convert[ing] government into a destroyer of rights."[96]

In 2003, church president Gordon B. Hinckley compared the fight against terrorism to the war in heaven.[97] And during the 2008 debate over California's Proposition 8 to repeal gay marriage, LDS pollster and author Gary Lawrence published an article in the online *Meridian Magazine* claiming that "the new battlefield" of the war in heaven was now California and arguing that Lucifer employed arguments of equality and sympathy to win over converts. Lawrence wrote, "If the arguments used in the war in heaven were persuasive enough to draw billions of God's spirit children away from him, why should we not expect them to be used on the present battlefield? The same minions cast out from the Father's presence still remember what worked up there."[98] In the October 2010 General Conference, Elder Quentin L. Cook argued in that the war in heaven continues today as an attack on religious liberty, often a code word used by church leaders in fighting gay rights proposals. "Since the War in Heaven, the forces of evil have used every means possible to destroy agency and extinguish light. The assault on moral principles and religious freedom has never been stronger."[99]

On his January 12, 2010 radio show, LDS convert Glenn Beck, went "all Jesus Freak" by linking the progressive agenda with Satan's plan in the premortal world: "If you believe in the war in heaven where a third of the angels were cast out and all of that stuff, it was about man's choice … and Satan's plan was 'hey, I'll save everybody; give me the credit … I'll make sure everybody returns home. It's going to be fantastic. You just take away their choice and give me the credit.' Well, gee, I think that plan was rejected because God knew that failure was important for growth."[100] Similarly, in June 2011 when *Newsweek*

---

96. Christopher S. Bentley, *Hidden Things in Darkness: An Exposé of the Enemies of Christ* (Orem, Utah: Sunrise Publishing, 2006), 27, 97.

97. Gordon B. Hinckley, "War and Peace," *Ensign*, May 2003, 78.

98. Gary Lawrence, "Wonder What the War in Heaven Was Like? Watch California This Fall," *Meridian Magazine*, www.meridianmagazine.com. The link to this article appears to have been disabled but it can still be accessed at www.web.archive.org/web/*/http://www.meridianmagazine.com/ideas/080711war.html.

99. Quentin L. Cook "Let There Be Light!" *Ensign*, Nov. 2010, 27–30.

100. Glenn Beck, Jan. 12, 2010. The audio is available in hour two, *The Glenn Beck Program,* www.glennbeck.com/content/show/2010-01-12/. The specific audio clip may most easily be found at "Beck: Progressives, like Satan, Are Supplanting God and Taking Away

celebrated "The Mormon Moment" in an article authored by Walter Kirn, Congressman Jeff Flake (R–Ariz.) was quoted as seeing "an even deeper connection between his faith and his economic and political views. According to Mormon tradition, God and Satan fought a 'war in heaven' over the question of moral agency, with God on the side of personal liberty and Satan seeking to enslave mankind. Flake acknowledged that the theme of freedom—and the threat of losing it—runs through much of Mormonism, and 'that kind of fits my philosophy.'"[101] Arriving at a similar conclusion, a non-member freelance writer opined following Mitt Romney's defeat in 2012 that Latter-day Saints are "the most politically wise human beings on the planet" and touted the connection between the religion's unique war in heaven narrative and the narrative's relevance to modern politics. "For a Mormon, the battle for liberty is not unique to this life; it is the core battle of the ages. Lucifer lost the war in heaven (he really thought he could beat God?), but the war continues on earth. So seeing the government become more and more tyrannical is not just a political concern; it's a fundamental, eternal concern."[102]

More recently, the narrative has been cited in social media posts and blogs to oppose government-imposed shuttering of businesses and shelter-in-place orders in response to the COVID-19 pandemic. One person posted to a Facebook discussion group that "I always wondered how Satan could get 'even the elect' to fall for his plan and then it happened. I see members of The Church of Jesus Christ of Latter-day Saints willing to give up their agency instead of fighting for it. This virus is not what people think it is. It is part of a plan to take away the agency we fought for long ago."[103] A blog post by a man known as

---

Choice," *Media Matters*, www.mediamatters.org/mmtv/201001120016. Beck returned to the theme again when discussing comments made by Al Gore and alleged comments made by Obama about "collective salvation." "Glenn Beck—Gore to 12 Year Olds: 'You Know Things Older People Don't Know,'" *The Glenn Beck Program*, Feb. 4, 2010, www.glenn-beck.com/content/articles/article/198/21049/, "Obama: Individual Salvation Depends on Collective Salvation," *The Glenn Beck Program*, July 9, 2010, www.glennbeck.com/content/articles/article/198/42764/.

101. Walter Kirn, "The Mormon Moment," *Newsweek*, June 5, 2011, www.newsweek.com.

102. Mike Jensen, "Smart Mormons" *Canada Free Press*, Jan. 22, 2013, www.canada-freepress.com/article/smart-mormons.

103. Posted on "Latter-day Saints of Jesus Christ Discussing Last Days Prophecies," a private Facebook group, May 14, 2020.

Jeremy compared the war in heaven to government responses to the pandemic, stating that "today we have real-life examples" of God's plan of agency versus Satan's plan of force. "We have leaders of the world trying to force their citizens to do what they deem is best. They have suspended God-given rights, they have shut down small businesses, destroyed entire economies and the livelihood of millions of people, all because they do not believe we will choose the right, but that we must be coerced to do so." He compared these plans to the church's response to the crisis "encouraging people to voluntarily do everything in their power to stop the spread without government mandates and threats."[104] Incidentally, the church's First Presidency issued a formal letter encouraging members to be "good citizens" and "follow the directions carefully from national, state, and local leaders in many countries in response to the COVID-19 pandemic."[105]

Interestingly, when issuing cautions about economic issues or political tyranny, LDS authors and speakers have tended to stress that the war in heaven was about taking away agency; however, when the debate is about sexuality, the emphasis gets switched to Satan's rhetorical power. The war in heaven is used to defend libertarian policies concerning governmental regulation and free-market economics. However, it is also used, with different emphasis, to argue against gay marriage, despite the fact that the opposing side could use the same narrative to justify a libertarian argument.

Perhaps, however, LDS discourse has conflated the issues of freedom and agency. Garth Mangum made this point in a short but insightful essay in *Dialogue*. Citing 2 Nephi 2:16–27, Mangum emphasized: "Free agency was 'given unto man' and he is 'free forever' to act for himself and take the consequences. In that sense, the War in Heaven was definitive." The point, Mangum stressed, is that "regardless of what happens to freedom, free agency is not in danger."[106] As Victor Frankl

---

104. Jeremy, "What Corona Virus and the War in Heaven Have in Common," *GoGo Goff,* Apr.9, 2020, www.mylifebygogogoff.com/2020/04/what-coronavirus-and-the-war-in-heaven-have-in-common.html

105. First Presidency, Letter on Administrative Principles in Challenging Times, Apr. 16, 2020, www.newsroom.churchofjesuschrist.org/article/first-presidency-letter-administrative-principles-in-challenging-times

106. Garth L. Mangum, "Free Agency and Freedom—Some Misconceptions." *Dialogue: A Journal of Mormon Thought* 1, 4 (Winter 1966): 43–49.

put it in his powerful memoir of surviving the German concentration camps, "Everything can be taken from a man but one thing: the last of human freedoms—to choose one's attitude in any given set of circumstances, to choose one's own way."[107] Dallin Oaks has come to a similar conclusion in a speech to a BYU Symposium on the Book of Mormon in 1987. He stated, "[B]ecause *free agency* is a God-given precondition to the purpose of mortal life, no person or organization can take away our free agency in mortality."[108]

ANAGOGICAL LEVEL

Finally, the war in heaven narrative serves an anagogical function within LDS thought, highlighting the prophetic events of church history and its eventual triumph over adversity. Persecution of the church was early on seen as a continuation of the war in heaven and as evidence that members were on the right side of that battle. As Apostle George Q. Cannon told church members in 1866:

> The war which was waged in heaven has been transferred to the earth, and it is now being waged by the hosts of error and darkness against God and truth; and the conflict will not cease until sin is extinguished and this earth is fully redeemed from the power of the adversary, and from the misrule and oppression which have so long exercised power over the earth. Do you wonder, then, that there is hatred and bitterness manifested; that the servants of God have had to watch continually to guard against the attacks of the enemy; that the blood of Joseph and Hyrum [Smith], David Patten, and others has been shed, and that the Saints, whose only crime was desiring to serve God in truth, virtue, uprightness, and sincerity, have been persecuted and afflicted all the day long? I do not wonder at it; there is no room for wonder in the minds of those who understand the work in which we are engaged.[109]

Likewise Wilford Woodruff stated that those who were cast out of heaven—the "thousands and millions of fallen spirits"—dwell on the earth and strive to "make war upon the Saints of God, wherever or whenever they are found upon the earth."[110] In his introduction to the third volume of the *History of the Church*, editor B. H. Roberts opined

---

107. Viktor Frankl, *Man's Search for Meaning* (Boston: Beacon, 1959), 66.
108. Dallin H. Oaks, "Free Agency and Freedom," Oct. 11, 1987, BYU Speeches, www.speeches.byu.edu/talks/dallin-h-oaks/free-agency-freedom/.
109. George Q. Cannon, May 6, 1866, *Journal of Discourses,* 11:229–30.
110. Wilford Woodruff, May 14, 1882, *Journal of Discourses*, 23:126–27.

that since "in heaven [Satan] opposed the gospel of Jesus Christ; cast out into the earth will he not oppose it there?" Roberts thus saw the persecution of the Latter-day Saints as a manifestation of Lucifer's hatred for the "institution wrought out in the wisdom of God to bring to pass the salvation of man."[111] Edward Tullidge launched an ambitious effort in "A Chapter from the Prophet of the Nineteenth Century," an unfinished Miltonian epic poem written in rhymed couplets of iambic pentameter. He linked opposition to the Restoration with a continuation of the war in heaven. Only a fragment of the epic poem was ever published. It depicts Satan calling the forces of fallen angels together to glory in their past rebellion. "We were not crushed. Our strength and hate remained; / And even now the loss might be regained." Satan announces to the host that the "councils of the skies" had created a plan to "break our spells and rescue fallen man":

> I need not tell you how the Seers of old,
> By vain illusions and conceits made bold,
> Foretold that in the latter times should rise
> A mighty kingdom towering to the skies,—
> That Saintly dreamers held a foolish boast
> That it should break and scatter all our host.
> Know, then, my lords, those vaunted times now loom,
> And we must conquer or receive our doom.

This kingdom would be ushered in by an "Anointed and pre-ordinated Seer" who must be opposed, concludes Satan. He urges his forces: "Away, my lords! Crush all who brave our sway! / Flood them—drown them with hate! Away, away!"[112] Tullidge, Roberts, Cannon, and Woodruff saw LDS Church history as a continuation of the war in heaven with persecution as a sign that the church was fully engaged in the battle against Satan. The narrative ties the history of the LDS Church to a larger, cosmic history.

But even though the Saints will suffer persecutions in this continuing battle, they are assured of eventual success. President Gordon B.

---

111. B. H. Roberts, "Introduction," *History of the Church*, 3:lix–lxl.

112. E. W. Tullidge, "A Chapter from the Prophet of the Nineteenth Century," *Millennial Star* 20, 1 (Jan. 2, 1858), 14–16; Blair Hodges "Edward Tullidge's Miltonian 'Gathering of the Grand Council of Hell,'" *Faith-Promoting Rumor: Exploring Mormon Thought, Culture, and Texts*, Feb. 4, 2011, www.faithpromotingrumor.com/2011/02/edward-tullidges-miltonian-gathering-of-the-grand-council-of-hell/.

Hinckley spoke of it as "the war we are winning" and "a victory assured."[113] And as Elder James Hamula reminded young men at the October 2008 general conference, "We are entering the final stages of a great war." He urged these young men to live righteous lives, assuring them: "His salvation will come, delivering you and yours from every evil."[114] In a very real way, members of the LDS Church sense they are engaged in a great battle against evil, but one they will eventually win, just as the forces of God triumphed over Satan in the war in heaven.

CONCLUSION

The war in heaven narrative has provided moral meaning for individual LDS lives; served an allegorical function, challenging threats to the church, explaining earthly inequalities, and promoting individual economic and political agendas; and linked the mission of the church to a sacred history, beginning with the premortal councils of heaven and culminating with the final judgment and millennial reign of Christ. At the personal level, the narrative provides a sublime sense of meaning for Latter-day Saints. At the community level, it provides a sense of shared purpose and values. In both the individual and community, it can help make sense of an increasingly complex world. By examining the ways the narrative is used, we see how it shapes and defines both the individual and the community.

With the current political discussion focusing on issues like "big government" and same-sex marriage, the war in heaven will continue to occupy the collective imagination of Latter-day Saints for some time to come. However, a cautionary note is in order: When this narrative is employed as a tool for earthly, political debate, the results can be quite ugly, at least from the vantage point of history. For believing Saints, it is challenging, to say the least, to encounter statements by church authorities that by twenty-first-century standards seem discomfiting at best, disgusting at worst. But only by confronting the past can a people learn from it. If we bury this past, as psychologists warn, it will only come back to haunt us.

113. Gordon B. Hinckley, "The War We Are Winning," *Ensign*, Nov. 1986, www.churchofjesuschrist.org/study/ensign/1986/11/the-war-we-are-winning?lang=eng; and his "An Unending Conflict, A Victory Assured," *Ensign*, June 2007, www.churchofjesuschrist.org/study/ensign/2007/06/an-unending-conflict-a-victory-assured?lang=eng.

114. James J. Hamula, "Winning the War against Evil," *Ensign*, Nov. 2008, 50–53.

Furthermore, we should be more conscious of how we use scripture. We often use scripture as if it is the final, ultimate proof in a debate. In this case, if one can compare an opponent's position to Satan's in the war in heaven, the argument appears settled. But these scriptural narratives are really the beginning of conversation, not the end of it. Language is slippery, and stories are always elusive, hinting at meaning while evading our grasp. At the same moment, one reader will use the war in heaven narrative to describe the evil of limiting agency, while another reader will apply that narrative to describe the dangers of listening to a charismatic secular leader. Even more troubling is attempting to read the narrative consistently across different debates. For surely the war on heaven can be seen as a morality tale on the importance of preserving agency, but consistently placing agency over *all* other principles results in the need to defend things one may not want to defend. The libertarian interpretation of the war in heaven narrative can be used to support limited government and free market economics, but it may also be used to support the right to abortion, the legalization of drugs, same-sex marriage, or guns in schools. We soon discover that allegories applied consistently only prove the open-endedness of the allegory.

Finally, this narrative, as sublime to the individual soul and community ethos as it is, does not, in the final analysis, productively grapple with the complicated issue of earthly inequality. The motive behind such misguided thinking is, like Milton's, a noble desire "to justify God's ways to man." It attempts to account for the unjust conditions in a world created by a just God. While this reasoning may let God off the hook, it does not let humanity off the hook with God. Furthermore, as we have seen, it is just as easy to argue that those who were valiant in the war in heaven are given greater trials in mortality as it is to argue that they are given greater blessings. Since LDS theology holds that all who came to earth with physical bodies passed the premortal world's testing, it is safest, and indeed most doctrinally sound, to assume that all fought, and fought valiantly, on the side of the angels.

FIVE

THREE SUB-DEGREES IN THE CELESTIAL KINGDOM?

SHANNON P. FLYNN

Almost forty years ago, I attended a B. H. Roberts Society lecture in the University of Utah physics department's lecture hall in Salt Lake City at which the speaker was Van Hale.[1] Though the LDS concept of a post-mortal celestial kingdom was not the main subject of Hale's talk, he mentioned his belief that there were not three sub-degrees in the celestial kingdom and that the teaching of three sub-degrees was an invention of some church member or members sometime after 1900. He said he had read extensively, maybe even exhaustively, in the relevant pre-1900 literature, and he could find no reference to a concept of three sub-degrees in the celestial kingdom as described in LDS Doctrine and Covenants 76. Hale's comment came as a surprise to me since I had grown up in the milieu of Wasatch Front Mormonism, and celestial sub-degrees was a commonly held belief, including speculations regarding what was included in each sub-degree and which post-mortal beings went where.

As time went on, I found that Hale's assertion became more convincing and that adding sub-degrees seriously complicated and confused the scheme laid out in Sections 76, 88, and 132 of the Doctrine and Covenants. I talked about this to friends and others throughout the ensuing years and found a few who agreed that there probably were not three sub-degrees, but most of the others had very strong negative reactions to the possible absence of three sub-degrees. Ten years ago, I made an appointment with Hale to make sure I had understood him correctly and that I was transmitting the information correctly. He confirmed

---

1. The B. H. Roberts Society was an independent affiliate of the Sunstone Foundation and periodically hosted evening presentations on topics of special relevance to LDS Church members. Van Hale has hosted a radio talk show since 1980 on Mormon subjects, *Mormon Miscellaneous*, that airs Sunday evenings on K-TALK in Utah.

that he had given a lecture at the Roberts Society and that a discussion of three sub-degrees of the celestial kingdom was part of his remarks. He went on to say that he had found nothing in the intervening years to change his mind. I asked if he knew where and when the change in "doctrine" had occurred, and he said he had no idea. He then issued a challenge to find out where and when the change had taken place. I took up the challenge and have been researching the topic, on and off, ever since. Many years later, I have found that Hale was not entirely correct. In my research, I have discovered five instances in talks, articles, or books that contain some reference to three degrees or undefined degrees in the celestial kingdom prior to 1900. After discussing the background to this concept, I treat each of these nineteenth-century statements and the implications I believe they have in relation to my thesis.

WHENCE THE IDEA OF THREE CELESTIAL SUB-DEGREES?

I would imagine that most LDS Church members, if asked about there not being three sub-degrees in the celestial kingdom, would point immediately to Doctrine and Covenants 131:1 and, with no small amount of satisfaction, read out loud: "In the celestial glory there are three heavens or degrees." But does this verse actually mean that in the celestial kingdom, as defined in Doctrine and Covenants 76, there are three sub-degrees? In my opinion, upon close examination, it does not.

I contend that the original intent of the verses in Section 131 was never to describe an expanded vision of the internal workings of the celestial kingdom. Verses 1–4 of Section 131 were originally extracted from the private journal of William Clayton (1814–79), who was a secretary, amanuensis, and confidant of LDS prophet Joseph Smith (1805–44). Clayton was an early English convert who was baptized late at night in the River Ribble by church apostle Heber C. Kimball on October 21, 1837. Clayton later immigrated to the United States with the voyage starting from Liverpool on September 8, 1840, and arrived in Nauvoo two months later.[2] Clayton had considerable skills at writing and copying and was soon employed in his area of expertise. Smith made him an official secretary, and, as such, Clayton spent considerable time as one of Smith's closest confidants. It was in this

---

2. For a treatment of Clayton's life, see James B. Allen, *No Toil Nor Labor Fear: The Story of William Clayton* (Provo, Utah: BYU Studies, 2002).

capacity that Clayton was with Smith on the evening of May 16, 1843, the day in Clayton's journal entry from which the first four verses of Section 131 were later taken.

A small group of people left Nauvoo in the morning of May 16, 1843, including Smith and Clayton. They headed first to Carthage and, after meeting with people there, continued their journey to Ramus, Illinois. They arrived at 3:30 p.m. at the house of Benjamin F. Johnson. Smith and Clayton stayed the night there, the others finding lodging elsewhere. It was Smith's purpose in staying with the Johnsons to teach his friends the new principle of plural marriage.[3] The only contemporary account we have of the evening's discussion comes from Clayton's journal. From the structure of the entry, it seems likely that Clayton composed the entry at the end of the day:

> pres[t] J. & I went to B[enjamin] F. Johnsons to sleep.[4] Before we retired the pres[t] gave bro Johnson & wife some instructions on the priesthood. He put his hand on my knee and says "your life is hid with Christ in God." and so is many others." Addressing Benjamin says he "nothing but the unpardonable sin can prevent him (me) from inheriting eternal glory for he is sealed up by the power of the priesthood unto eternal life having taken the step which is necessary[5] for that purpose." He said that except a man and his wife enter into an everlasting covenant and be married for eternity while in this probation by the power and authority of the Holy priesthood they will cease to increase when they die (I e. they will not have any children in the resurrection, but those who are married by the power & authority of the priesthood in this life & continue without committing

---

3. In the years before polygamy became an open doctrine, Smith would use private moments such as these to quietly present the controversial idea to trusted associates.

4. On this visit, according to Johnson's later reminiscences, Smith stayed with Johnson's sister Almera "as man and wife" and "occupied the same room and bed with my sister, that the previous month he had occupied with the daughter of the late Bishop Partridge as his wife." "Benjamin F. Johnson's Testimony," *Historical Record*, 6:222; Benjamin F. Johnson, Letter to George F. Gibbs, 1903, M273.2 J66i 1911, Church History Library, Church of Jesus Christ of Latter-day Saints, Salt Lake City (hereafter CHL). Almera confirmed her marriage to Smith in an 1883 affidavit: "On a certain occasion in the spring of the year 1843, the exact date ^of^ which I do not now recollect, I went from Macedonia to Nauvoo to visit another of my sisters, the one who was the widow of Lyman R. Sherman, deceased, at which time I was sealed to the Prophet Joseph Smith" (MS 3423, CHL). Johnson's eldest sister, Delcena (widow of Lyman Sherman), had also become a plural wife of Smith.

5. This refers to the fact that Clayton had been married to his first plural wife on April 27, 1843, just three weeks earlier. Clayton had married Ruth Moon on October 9, 1836, in England and then married Ruth's sister Margaret as his first plural wife.

the sin against the Holy Ghost will continue to increase & have children in the celestial glory. The unpardonable sin is to shed innocent blood or be accessary thereto. All other sins will be visited with judgement in the flesh and the spirit being delivered to the buffetings of Satan untill the day of the Lord Jesus." I feel desirous to be united in an everlasting covenant to my wife and pray that it may soon be.

pres^t. J. said that the way he knew in whom to confide. <u>God told him</u> in whom he might place confidence. He also said that in the celestial glory there was three heavens or degrees, and in order to obtain the highest a man must enter into this order of the priesthood and if he don't he cant obtain it. He may enter into the other but that is the end of his kingdom he cannot have an increase.[6]

It is the last two sentences—the fifty-four words beginning with "in the celestial glory"—that were excerpted by church apostle Orson Pratt as verses 1–4 of Section 131 of the 1876 edition of the Doctrine and Covenants. It is important to understand the context of Clayton's journal entry. Smith had a very specific purpose in mind as he stayed the night with the Johnsons: to instruct them in his new doctrine of plural marriage.[7] As he had done previously, Smith was introducing or further clarifying the concept privately to people he thought he could trust with such a controversial subject. Smith's point that evening was not to modify or amplify concepts about the celestial kingdom as first revealed in 1832 (in what is now Doctrine and Covenants 76), but to teach and discuss plural marriage. Clayton's report of the meeting tied together various threads of Smith's teachings—namely, that "in the celestial glory there was three heavens or degrees." Following Section 76, those three heavens or degrees are the celestial, terrestrial, and telestial kingdoms. (A fourth post-mortal realm is Outer Darkness, intended only for the most truly damned, for those who experienced God's presence and rejected it.)

The term "celestial glory" is what causes confusion. It is important to understand what would have been the common definition of "celestial glory" in 1843 and what Clayton, an Englishman living in the United States, would have understood by it.

---

6. Instruction, May 16, 1843, as reported by William Clayton, Joseph Smith Papers, at www.josephsmithpapers.org.

7. I use the terms plural marriage or polygamy interchangeably and without nuanced definitions. It is not my point here to enter into a discussion of exact meanings at the time or now.

There were two prominent, influential dictionaries in use at the time Clayton wrote the entry in his diary. The first was Samuel Johnson's *Dictionary of the English Language*. Produced in Great Britain and printed for the first time in 1755, Johnson's dictionary was the authoritative resource for word definition for someone who had grown up in England at the time Clayton did and, more importantly, reflected the common usage at the time. The definition found in Johnson's dictionary reads:

Celestial adj.
    1. Heavenly; relating to the superiour regions. ...
    2. Heavenly; relating to the blessed state.[8]

The other key dictionary, reflecting American usage, was produced by noted lexicographer Noah Webster, entitled *An American Dictionary of the English Language*. The pertinent entry in this reference work is:

Celestial, a.
    1. Heavenly; belonging or relating to heaven; dwelling in heaven; as *celestial* spirits; *celestial* joys. Hence the word conveys the idea of superior excellence, delight, purity, &c.[9]

It is clear from both Johnson's and Webster's dictionary definitions and from the context and common usage at the time that Clayton intended—in his journal entry—to report Joseph Smith's teaching that in the next life, that is, the hereafter, there are three degrees/divisions of glory: celestial, terrestrial, and telestial, as laid out in Doctrine and Covenants 76. In addition, for a person to dwell in the celestial portion, he or she needs to be married. Thus, if Clayton had written the words "in the next life," "in the resurrection," or "in the hereafter," instead of writing "celestial glory," probably none of the controversy surrounding three celestial sub-degrees would be taking place today. Section 131, verses 1–4, is the only place in LDS scripture that supports the idea of subdividing the celestial kingdom into sub-degrees. That said, it is also clear that Section 131:1, in fact, does not teach that there are three sub-degrees in the celestial kingdom.

Context and original intent form a crucial part of our exegesis of

---

8. *A Dictionary of the English Language*, 8th ed., 2 vols. (London: J. Johnson, et al., 1799), s.v. "celestial."

9. *An American Dictionary of the English Language*, 2 vols. (New York: S. Converse, 1828), s.v. "celestial."

scripture. This discussion says something significant about the way we view scripture, the way that words from the past are transmitted to us, and when and how words that may have only been a phrase or two written in passing may eventually be canonized and/or form the basis of significant beliefs. I believe that it would be surprising to William Clayton to learn that the sentence he wrote in his journal—"In the celestial glory there are three heavens or degrees"—has been interpreted the way it has been and has taken on a life of its own. I do not believe he ever intended the interpretation to come out the way it has.

The statements recorded by Clayton were incorporated into Smith's official history, first in manuscript form and then published in the *Deseret News* in 1856. However, they were likely not widely read before being formally canonized in the Doctrine and Covenants in 1876. During this period, Orson Pratt occasionally referred to the celestial kingdom and the possibility of division therein. In these remarks, he posits that there are many different places in all of the kingdoms and there are places in the celestial for a variety of degrees of worthiness. It is my view that Pratt was putting forth his own ill-defined opinions and that some of these ideas would not be accepted today.[10]

This becomes even more significant in light of the fact that there are two other instances before 1900 where a three-part division in the celestial kingdom is mentioned in written works. The first is in an article published in the *Deseret Weekly* in 1888 regarding the resurrection. Joseph E. Taylor, longtime counselor in the Salt Lake Stake presidency, stated that "Joseph [Smith] has made it known that 'in the celestial kingdom are three heavens or degrees,' and that the highest can only be reached by observing the patriarchal order of marriage."[11] It seems to me that Taylor has misquoted the first sentence of Section 131

---

10. For example, in an intriguing example from 1875, Orson Pratt preached that there are "millions and millions that may reach the celestial Kingdom if they embrace the gospel that will not reach the higher order of glory in that Kingdom for there are different degrees of glory even in that one Kingdom that celestial world." Discourse, May 30, 1875, reported by David Evans in shorthand, transcribed by LaJean Purcell Carruth, Church History Department Pitman Shorthand transcriptions, CR 100 912, CHL. My thanks to LaJean for her assistance. For the other references by Pratt to this topic, see his August 28, 1859, sermon, *Journal of Discourses*, vol. 7 (Liverpool, Eng.: Amasa Lyman, 1860), 89; and sermon, Jan. 19, 1873, *Journal of Discourses*, 15:19.

11. "The Resurrection," *Deseret Weekly*, Dec. 29, 1888. The lengthy lecture—which discussed various topics including the Adam–God doctrine—was first delivered in the Logan temple.

and in so doing has made the jump from "celestial glory" to "celestial kingdom." My contention is that he misunderstood the first verse of Section 131, as he probably had no context or background. Furthermore, publication in a weekly newspaper would not likely lend itself to widespread repetition.

The second—and more notable—occurrence comes from the pen of B. H. Roberts. In his *Outlines of Ecclesiastical History*, designed to be used for study by elders and seventies, he wrote, "The Prophet Joseph taught that in the celestial glory there are three heavens or degrees. ... From this it is evident that there are different degrees of glory within the celestial and telestial glories."[12] I believe this is very similar to the Joseph Taylor statement—a writer who is not familiar with or is not taking into account the context of Section 131. In both cases, especially with Roberts, this is such a minor part of their treatise that it carries almost no weight or prominence in the text in question. Importantly, I am not aware of either of these statements being mentioned again in the footnotes of any published work on the topic of the three degrees.[13] My sense is that, while the two passages may have stuck in the minds of some readers, they do not seem to have resulted in any change in the general thinking of the majority of church members.

Nothing appears in print about three sub-degrees in the celestial kingdom, to my knowledge, until after the turn of the twentieth century. One potential landmark occurred in 1919, when the first book-length commentary on the Doctrine and Covenants was published. The thick tome was ostensibly the work of Apostle Hyrum M. Smith, who was listed as the author, but, as it turns out, he had little to do with the actual writing. The bulk of the work was carried out by Janne M. Sjodahl[14] and a committee consisting of Orson F. Whitney, Joseph Fielding Smith, John E. Cottam, George F. Richards, and Junius F. Wells. Hyrum M. Smith was an apostle and son of Joseph F. Smith, LDS Church president. Work on the commentary had been underway since 1916, at least. Hyrum Smith passed away in January 1918—of a ruptured appendix—and the work was completed and published in

---

12. *Outlines of Ecclesiastical History* (Salt Lake City: George Q. Cannon & Sons, 1893), 426.

13. Roberts included this same paragraph two years later in a similar work: *A New Witness for God* (Salt Lake City: George Q. Cannon & Sons, 1895), 390–91.

14. In recognition of Sjodahl's contribution, he was listed as co-author in subsequent editions.

1919 with Smith listed as author. In 1917, Joseph F. Smith sent an interesting note to Orson Whitney concerning the content of the book: "I should be pleased to have you and Joseph F. [Smith] Jr. act as a committee to hear the reading of a work on the Doctrine and Covenants by Hyrum M. You will please render your best assistance to see that no error in doctrine or inaccuracy in history, should there be any, escape notice. Hyrum will confer with you as to the time that will be convenient for the reading."[15]

When one reads the commentary for Section 131, there is nothing mentioned about three sub-degrees. Nor is there anything relevant in the commentary for Section 76. It is difficult to argue from a negative or from a paucity of information, but the absence of any reference to sub-degrees in the celestial kingdom at this point—and in a book of quasi-official production and status—seems convincing that the concept of three sub-degrees in the celestial kingdom was not normative at this time. The first edition was printed in 1919 and the last, of dozens of editions, was printed in 1978. There was no change in the wording for the relevant verses in Sections 76 or 131.

THE SHIFT

In my view, the beginnings of a major shift in the interpretation of 131:1 came just three years after the publication of the *Doctrine and Covenants Commentary*. On September 22, 1922, LDS apostle Melvin J. Ballard (d. 1939) gave a talk in the Ogden, Utah, tabernacle on the topic of "Three Degrees of Glory." A transcript was first published in pamphlet form in October 1924 under the direction of the Mount Ogden (Utah) Stake Genealogical Committee.[16] The publication was probably a fund-raising effort for the stake's genealogical society as a price of 15 cents is printed on the cover. Ballard talks about a variety of subjects and tries to answer many questions about who goes where in

---

15. Dennis Horne, "Mormon Book Bits #18: Hyrum M. Smith and Janne M. Sjodahl, Doctrine and Covenants Commentary," www.truthwillprevail.xyz.

16. The 48-page pamphlets were printed by the Neuteboom Printing Company in Ogden. The president, Evert Neuteboom, was a member of the Mount Ogden Stake high council. In the LDS Church, a stake is similar to a Catholic diocese; a ward, to a parish. The pamphlet had at least five printings before 1930 and more afterward; subsequent editions number in the dozens, and new copies are still available today.

the next life, how choices and actions in this life affect one's final destination in the next life, and his views on wayward children in this life.

Among other topics, Ballard outlines his understanding of the structure of the celestial kingdom, declaring:

> Now, I wish to say to you that the only possible candidates to become what God is are those who attain Celestial Glory, and those who fail in that will never, worlds without end, be possible candidates to become what God is. Then I wish to say to you that there are three degrees of glory in the Celestial Kingdom and only those who attain the highest degree of Celestial Glory will be candidates to become what God is, and graduate.[17]

Ballard says nothing more about this subject anywhere else in the talk. He makes no clarification of who is destined for the three subdivisions or what differences there may be among the three sub-realms. What is noteworthy is Ballard's interchangeable use of "Celestial Kingdom" and "Celestial Glory" in one sentence which, I suggest, gets at the heart of the problem. When William Clayton recorded the journal entry in 1843, the common understanding of the word "celestial" was "heavenly." At the time Clayton's entry was written, "celestial glory" was synonymous with "heaven": thus, in "heaven" or "the next life" there are three heavens or degrees. This is what is taught in Doctrine and Covenants 76 and in every other scriptural instance.

While this is the first time Ballard's thoughts on the topic appeared in print, he had taught the same thing previously. He is listed in the program for a genealogical conference in Salt Lake City's Ensign Stake, six months earlier, on March 4, 1922. Billed as the main Thursday night speaker, he took as his topic "The Three Degrees of Glory." While the text for the talk is not extant, it seems likely that it would be the same as the talk in Ogden six months later. This indicates that Ballard had been thinking about the three-degree concept for some time before the pamphlet was published. Furthermore, one assumes that, in addition to published statements, Ballard was discussing his ideas privately with others.

It is possible to make an attempt at bracketing Ballard's thinking on the subject. In October 1917, while president of the Northwestern

---

17. *Discourse: Three Degrees of Glory* (Published under the direction of Mount Ogden Stake Genealogical Committee, n.d.), 10.

States Mission, he delivered a discourse in general conference that centered around the qualifications for the celestial kingdom. What happens in the next life seems to have been a lifelong concern for him. Early in his sermon, he remarked, "The Latter-day Saints will recall that there is one glorious place, the highest of all, to which all souls may possibly attain, the celestial kingdom, where God and Christ live, whose glory Paul has said was like unto the glory of the sun."[18] Without trying to read too much into it, Ballard here seems to speak of the celestial kingdom as one undivided sphere. Five years later, he declared that there are three divisions within the celestial kingdom. It is impossible to know exactly when (or precisely if) he changed his mind on the subject, but it appears that, as late as 1917, he still envisioned the celestial kingdom as a single realm.

An important point to remember is that Ballard was born in 1873, making him forty-nine years old when he gave this 1922 talk. He had no distinct memory of early church apostle and president Brigham Young (d. 1877) or Young's contemporaries or their teachings. Also, Section 131 was published for the first time as official scripture in 1876, meaning that the section was part of the LDS canon from the time Ballard could read.

I do not believe that Ballard had any idea he was introducing a radically new concept. It is impossible to know how long he harbored the idea of three sub-degrees previous to this talk, but it seems likely that the teaching was not yet widely held within the LDS community. In my view, announcing three sub-degrees as official church doctrine was a simple mistake on the part of the popular apostle and speaker. However, the concept gradually took hold in the LDS community. It is my belief that all religions make attempts to amplify or clarify sacred texts that are ambiguous. This is especially so when the text does not give clear understanding or makes room to introduce concepts that will provide comfort or encouragement in times of stress. The question of what happens in the next life must rank as one of the chief concerns of humanity. The LDS tradition has added significantly to Christian doctrine, so there is a tendency to add even more, especially as it relates to the highest glory, the celestial kingdom. There seems to be a

---

18. *Eighty-Eighth Semi-annual Conference of the Church of Jesus Christ of Latter-day Saints* ([Salt Lake City]: Deseret News, 1917), 108.

powerful need in the LDS Church to make the circumference of the celestial kingdom larger and larger. This new doctrine goes a long way to accomplishing that.

It is my argument that the Ballard pamphlet becomes the major catalyst for changing LDS doctrine. While there were several instances where either a nebulous description of multiple sub-degrees or three specific sub-degrees in the celestial kingdom were mentioned in a discourse or appeared in a printed source, I believe none of them had a lasting influence. The Ballard pamphlet, on the other hand, was reprinted dozens of times, with potentially hundreds or thousands of copies in each printing. After the copyright expired, several publishers issued competing editions. In my own personal collection, I have copies from Joseph Lyon and Associates, Magazine Printing, and Deseret Book, along with several from Neuteboom Printing. Though Lyon and Associates are out of business, copies are still available from them as well as from various printers specializing in titles now in the public domain. This talk became the subtle missionary for this doctrine and spread the message far and wide.

Despite there being no official acknowledgment or promotion of the concept, some portions of the LDS community started to promote the idea. In 1939, prolific compiler N. B. Lundwall included portions of Ballard's discourse in his popular LDS collection *The Vision*.[19] A decade later, Leonidas DeVon Mecham, described in his obituary as a "noted lecturer on Genealogy, Books of Remembrance, Priesthood Lineage and Family Histories,"[20] produced a chart entitled *Free Agency* depicting the LDS concept of the plan of salvation. In the top right corner is the "Celestial Kingdom" with three concentric circles or degrees—"celestial marriage" is the restricting requirement of the innermost circle/degree, presumably the most exalted realm in the celestial kingdom. Mecham's illustration is just one of what must be now be hundreds of similar illustrations.

Over the next few decades, the concept continued to gain traction in several widely read LDS publications. In 1958, Bruce R. McConkie,

---

19. In the preface, Lundwall notes that he submitted the manuscript to Ballard for review before his death that year. "Authenticity of This Book," *The Vision or The Degrees of Glory* (N.p.: n.p., 1939).

20. Obituary, FamilySearch, person ID KWCQ-47J, www.familysearch.org.

then a member of the LDS Church's Council of Seventy and later an LDS apostle, discussed the idea in the enormously influential *Mormon Doctrine*. McConkie noted that "in the same sense that baptism starts a person out toward an entrance into the celestial world, so celestial marriage puts a couple on the path leading to an exaltation in the highest heaven of that world."[21] Two years later, popular author and BYU religion professor Sidney B. Sperry stated unequivocally, "[B]efore a man can be exalted in the Celestial Kingdom, he must have had a wife sealed to him by proper authority. If he does not, he cannot obtain exaltation, the highest glory of all. He may enter into one of the two lower degrees of the celestial kingdom, but that is the end of his kingdom." Sperry also outlined the murkiness of the other two levels: "Nevertheless, we must bear in mind that the Lord has not revealed to us or made it possible to deduce many of the situations that may relegate a man into the second heaven or degree in the Celestial World, much less those which may relegate him to the last or third heaven."[22]

By the second half of the twentieth century, the subdivision of the celestial kingdom had acquired seemingly official status. A 1981 a manual for the college-age institute program of the LDS Church Education System (which had undergone review for doctrinal purity by the church's correlation department) included the following as part of the commentary on Doctrine and Covenants 131:

> The Lord has not revealed to the Church who will live in two of the three degrees in the celestial kingdom. Any discussion on this topic is speculation. More has been revealed about the highest degree of the celestial kingdom, or exaltation. That is where the Father would have all of His children live if they keep His commandments. In Doctrine and Covenants 76:50–70 the Lord outlines the requirements to obtain the highest degree in the celestial kingdom.[23]

By this point, the portion of Section 76 dealing with the celestial kingdom is now seen as describing only the highest of the three degrees in the celestial kingdom, rather than the kingdom as a whole. A

---

21. Bruce R. McConkie, *Mormon Doctrine* (Salt Lake City: Bookcraft, 1958), s.v. "Celestial Kingdom."

22. *Doctrine and Covenants Compendium* (Salt Lake City: Bookcraft, 1960), 701.

23. *The Doctrine and Covenants Student Manual*, Religion 324–25 (Salt Lake City: Church of Jesus Christ of Latter-day Saints, 1981), 325.

popular commentary from that period reinforced this idea: "The celestial glory ... has within it three heavens or degrees. (D&C 131.) Those persons who receive exaltation are in the highest degree of the celestial glory."[24] An essay on the "Kingdoms of Glory" posted on the LDS Church's official website today teaches:

> From another revelation to the Prophet Joseph [Smith], we learn that there are three degrees within the celestial kingdom. To be exalted in the highest degree and continue eternally in family relationships, we must enter into "the new and everlasting covenant of marriage" and be true to that covenant. In other words, temple marriage is a requirement for obtaining the highest degree of celestial glory.[25]

I have reviewed all of the LDS Church's general conference talks from 1859 to present[26] for any mention of three degrees in the celestial kingdom. I have found only three instances—two from Milton R. Hunter and one from Royden G. Derrick.[27] Talks given by Hunter in 1949 and 1969 mention three sub-degrees but give no clarification or additional information regarding what may be contained in each. Hunter's two comments were made in passing and represent a misreading of Doctrine and Covenants 131:1 or exposure to Ballard's pamphlet. Derrick's mention follows the same lines. His talk, given in 1989, makes clear that he has heard or read about the sub-degrees, which he assumes is the common, accepted understanding. In both cases, there is no explaining or expanding on the doctrine, just a repetition of folklore. All three talks come years after the Ballard pamphlet. I can find no such mentions before 1922 and nothing before 1949 in official general conference settings.

There are other places where the concept of three sub-degrees may be found in LDS literature, but suffice it to say that the idea started off slowly and gained steam until it is generally believed, I suspect, by the majority of church members today. In my opinion, more details regarding the three sub-degrees have not been forthcoming because

---

24. Daniel H. Ludlow, *A Companion to Your Study of the Doctrine and Covenants* (Salt Lake City: Deseret Book Co., 1978), 2:38

25. "Kingdoms of Glory," *Gospel Topics*, online at www.churchofjesuschrist.org.

26. These were published in various venues such as the *Journal of Discourses, Conference Reports,* and the *Ensign.*

27. All of the Orson Pratt sermons discussed above were delivered in other venues than general conference.

there were none to begin with. The concept of subdividing the highest kingdom of glory does nothing but add confusion because of the speculation that it generates based on what can only be called a mistaken interpretation. A large part of the problem is that Ballard did not take into account the historical context—William Clayton's diary—for the verses in Section 131 which led in an erroneous direction. At least a part of this was not Ballard's fault. There was simply not much, if anything, in the way of reliable historical studies or interpretive work at the time, certainly nothing compared to what is available today. He could have had access, at least, to a small amount of background to that section by looking at the relevant portion of Joseph Smith's *History of the Church*,[28] but that would have required a close reading of the historical record, which does not seem to have been in Ballard's nature. It is unlikely that the concept arose from deliberate error on his part but rather is a mistake based on his misreading and misunderstanding of Doctrine and Covenants 131:1.

Such errors happen regularly in every religion, including the Mormon Church.[29] A leader or authority makes a statement based on his/her limited understanding without the benefit of research or an awareness of background contexts. The statement is soon repeated until it essentially takes on a life of its own, after which it becomes widely disseminated as established fact. Eventually, the statement forms the basis for all kinds of additional, expanded, increasingly fanciful speculation. But no amount of certainty, dogmatism, and conviction-bearing can change the fact that it is wrong.

28. The pertinent volume had been published more than a decade before. B. H. Roberts, ed., *History of the Church*, vol. 5 (Salt Lake City: Deseret News, 1909), 391–92.

29. Two other prominent examples from the twentieth century (both also seemingly originating from apostles) are: (1) the idea first presented by Elder Orson F. Whitney in 1929 that children sealed to faithful parents are guaranteed exaltation by virtue of the sealing covenant; and (2) the concept that *all* covenants are renewed during the weekly partaking of the sacrament, first promulgated by Elder Delbert L. Stapley in 1965. Whitney, *Ninety-Ninth Annual Conference of the Church of Jesus Christ of Latter-day Saints* (Salt Lake City: Church of Jesus Christ of Latter-day Saints), 110. Stapley, *Official Report of the One Hundred and Thirty-Fifth Semi-annual General Conference of the Church of Jesus Christ of Latter-day Saints* ([Salt Lake City]: Church of Jesus Christ of Latter-day Saints), 14.

HEAVENLY MOTHER
THE MOTHER OF ALL WOMEN

BLAIRE OSTLER

Heavenly Mother is a cherished doctrine among many Latter-day Saints. Her unique esthetic of feminine deity offers Latter-day Saint women a trajectory for godhood—the ultimate goal of LDS theology. Though Heavenly Mother offers a uniquely feminine perspective of God, there are some problematic aspects. First, Heavenly Mother can be discouraging for some Latter-day Saint women who desire more equitable representation among gendered deities. Since Latter-day Saint women are discouraged from directly worshiping, communing, and praying to Her, She is disconnected from Her spirit children in ways that Heavenly Father is not.[1] Second, the standard Heavenly Mother esthetic does not offer a trajectory for women who desire godhood without motherhood. The inherent nature of Heavenly Mother implies all women would desire eternal motherhood. In this sense, motherhood becomes the gatekeeper of a woman's godly potential. Third, the Heavenly Mother concept of godhood combined with Latter-day Saint culture can be harmful to some Latter-day Saint women who struggle with fertility—especially when godliness is connected to the ability to produce children. Last, the cisgender,[2] heterosexual[3] Heavenly Mother esthetic fails to give queer[4] women a feminine trajectory that

---

1. Though many editorial manuals of style do not uppercase deity-related pronouns, I intentionally use upper case letters.
2. Cisgender is a label used to describe people whose gender identity matches their assigned gender at birth.
3. Heterosexual is a label used to describe those who are attracted to members of the opposite sex.
4. Queer is used as an umbrella term to describe people in the LGBTQIA+ community. For example, "queer women" includes lesbians, bisexual women, intersex women, and trans women—just to name a few.

exemplifies their earthly experience and desires. Though Her example may appeal to conventional, heterosexual, cisgender women, there is still room for improvement in how we speak of Her when She is the Mother of all women. Here I will suggest ways to overcome these four obstacles within the LDS theological tradition.

LDS theology puts a strong emphasis on theosis—the idea that humans are to become gods. According to Joseph Smith, we must learn to become gods the same as all other gods who came before us.[5] From this perspective, Latter-day Saints are polytheists. There is a potentially infinite number of gods who dwell in worlds without end. Some might claim this theology is strictly monotheistic in that Latter-day Saints only worship one god, God the Father, but this is problematic for a few reasons. Though some Latter-day Saints only worship one male anthropomorphized god,[6] the idea that other infinite gods exist is not controversial. If God became God through evolutionary means, God is not a singleton. The status of God's godhood is intimately connected with the other gods who collectively become gods together, with their respective wives, Heavenly Mothers. Furthermore, when Latter-day Saints worship God the Father, they are also implicitly worshiping Heavenly Mother and the multitude of gods who also made God's godhood possible. In LDS theology, God the Father is sealed to God the Mother[7]—though it is also worth mentioning some past prophets have claimed we have many heavenly mothers through the practice of polygyny.[8] According to Latter-day Saint doctrine, God is not God unless They are composed of both man and woman, for God is both man and woman, and all are made in the image of God.[9] However, if the

---

5. See Joseph Smith's King Follett sermon, www.churchofjesuschrist.org/study/ensign/1971/04/the-king-follett-sermon, accessed Apr. 10, 2020.

6. "They acknowledge the Father as the ultimate object of their worship." *LDS Gospel Topics,* s.v. "Godhead," www.lds.org/topics/godhead, accessed July 30, 2018.

7. *LDS Gospel Topics,* s.v. "Mother in Heaven," www.lds.org/topics/mother-in-heaven, accessed July 30, 2018.

8. "The only men who become Gods, even the sons of God, are those who enter into polygamy." Brigham Young, Aug. 19, 1866, *Journal of Discourses,* 26 vols. (London and Liverpool: LDS Booksellers Depot, 1855–86), 11:269.

9. See Gen. 1:26–27; Rom. 8:16–17; and Ps. 82:6. According to Elder Erastus Snow, "if I believe anything that God has ever said about himself ... I must believe that deity consists of man and woman. ... There can be no God except he is composed of the man and woman united, and there is not in all the eternities that exist, or ever will be a God in any other way. We may never hope to attain unto the eternal power and the Godhead upon

standard narrative implies that God is both male and female sealed in a simplistic heterosexual union to produce spirit children, why is Heavenly Mother's role not a prominent as Heavenly Father's? What does this mean for women who are infertile, or do not desire motherhood? What does this mean for queer women? How can we emphasize the office of Heavenly Mother without perpetuating cisgender, heterosexual biases? Essentially, how is it possible for Heavenly Mother to be the trajectory for all women when Her esthetic is limited and neglectful of all women's experiences and desires?

MOTHERLY WOMEN

If theosis is the ultimate goal of Mormon theology,[10] Heavenly Mother is the most prominent feminine example of that trajectory. She is the deity Latter-day Saint women are to aspire to.[11] However, Her lack of presence in our communion and worship has caused many women to wonder why She is mostly absent in Her children's lives, or at least in their communal worship.[12] Is that a woman's trajectory in the heavenly eternities? For some Latter-day Saint women, the thought of deifying into Heavenly Mother is a terrifying disconnect between them and their potential spirit children. If Latter-day Saint families are to be sealed together as whole families, why is it our own Mother's presence is so essential, but simultaneously veiled? Many women have begun the search for more concerning Heavenly Mother, Her presence, and Her role in the theological narrative. Books such as *Dove Song: Heavenly Mother in Mormon Poetry, Mother's Milk: Poems in Search of Heavenly Mother* and communities like *Feminist Mormon Housewives, Exponent II,* and the *Finding Heavenly Mother Project* are a direct product of this aspiration to find our feminine trajectory in an androcentric religion. So what can we do to enrich our vision of Heavenly Mother?

First, our language could more fully reflect the richness of Latter-day Saint doctrine and theology. If God is man and woman combined in a

any other principle ... this Godhead composing two parts, male and female." Mar. 3, 1878, *Journal of Discourses,* 19:269–70.

10. Smith, "King Follett Discourse."

11. "Our theology begins with heavenly parents. Our highest aspiration is to be like them." Elder Dallin H. Oaks, "Apostasy and Restoration," *Ensign,* May 1995, 84.

12. Gordon B. Hinckley, "Daughters of God," *LDS Conference Report* (Salt Lake City: Church of Jesus Christ of Latter-day Saints, Oct. 1991).

sealed eternal union, instead of using the pronoun *He*, the plural *They* pronoun could be used. The gender of our God, our Heavenly Parents, is far more inclusive than exclusive, yet our semantics fall short. How we talk about God matters, and the shift from *He* to *They* is more inclusive of diverse gender experiences, including non-binary[13] identities and intersex[14] anatomies. *They* also reflects the potentially infinite plurality of God.

Following a shift in language could be a shift in our literature, music, vernacular, and, by extension, our worship. Policy could be extended to include the worship of a feminine deity with feminine pronouns and prominence. Latter-day Saints could be offered the opportunity to submit literature and music to be included in our Sunday worship about Heavenly Mother. Our language, worship, rituals, vernacular, and esthetics can include so much more than a male singleton. If we so choose, we can free our Mother and ourselves from the prison of thoughtless repetition. Her role is directly reflected in the roles of the women who worship Her in a symbiotic and literal process of becoming.

INDEPENDENT WOMEN

Being a lifelong Latter-day Saint, I say with confidence that one of the most common justifications for the exclusion of women from priesthood ordination may be summarized in one brief sentence: "Women have motherhood and men have priesthood." Motherhood is of such importance for Latter-day Saint women that is it often compared to a man's priesthood ordination—not in his participation in parenthood as a father, but in his divine right to act in the name of God through priesthood authority. As Elder John A. Widtsoe argues in *Priesthood and Church Government,* God the Father gave his sons priesthood power through ordination and gave women motherhood—"of equal importance and power."[15] It is strange that Widtsoe suggests it is God

---

13. Non-binary is a term used to describe genders that do not fit neatly into a "man" or a "woman" category. There is a spectrum of genders between these two poles, and within that spectrum is the non-binary experience.

14. Intersex persons have an anatomy that is composed of both "male" and "female" characteristics. They are born with an atypical biology that is typical of an assigned "man" or a "woman."

15. John A. Widtsoe, *Priesthood and Church Government* (Salt Lake: Deseret Book Co., 1954), 84.

the Father and not God the Mother who gave women motherhood. It would seem more fitting that motherhood is gifted by the Mother and fatherhood is gifted by the Father, or parenthood gifted by our Heavenly Parents. Even still, Widtsoe continues, "That grave responsibility [of motherhood] belongs, by right of sex, to the women who bear and nurture the whole race. Surely no right-thinking woman could crave more responsibility nor greater proof of innate powers than that!"[16] According to this prominent LDS apostle, a woman who craves a role or desires responsibility outside motherhood could not be a "right thinking woman." The critical underlying assumption Widtsoe is projecting is that women would inherently desire motherhood as the source of godly power and glory. This excludes the experiences of women who do not desire motherhood or even marriage as their divine purpose or trajectory.

This idea is not exclusively limited to Widtsoe. In my work in the Mormon feminist communities, it has been condescendingly explained to me by critics that women who desire ordination risk shirking their responsibility of motherhood and are neglectful of their children. However, what many fail to acknowledge is that a man can be ordained to the priesthood without shirking his responsibility of fatherhood or being neglectful of his children. The double standard is that men use their priesthood authority to bless the lives of others, while a woman would be using priesthood authority selfishly or at the expense of her children. Why is this assumption necessarily different for women than men? Furthermore, if a woman does not desire motherhood as her primary way of exemplifying godhood, why can she not seek after her godly potential by entering into the priesthood to serve and bless the lives of those around her? Her power and service may not need to include nor be limited to motherhood or marriage. Priesthood ordination is one way to empower women who strive after a godly potential—by acting in the name of God. By broadening the offices women may hold in religious practice, we also broaden the offices women may hold in the eternities, such as with Heavenly Mother. In this sense, Heavenly Mother is only one office a woman might hold in the eternities. Heavenly Mother may be the bearer of all spirit children, but that is

16. Widtsoe, *Priesthood and Church Government*, 85.

only one office, role, or responsibility a female deity might have. There are countless ways women serve and participate in their communities beyond motherhood or marriage. I don't see why this would necessarily be different in the next life.

INFERTILE WOMEN

Another problem with the Heavenly Mother concept of godhood is that Her power and glory is predicated on her ability to produce offspring. It is in her title Heavenly *Mother*. I can say from personal experience that worshiping deified motherhood is extremely painful for some, not all, women who struggle with infertility. In the church, it is as if womanhood is tantamount to motherhood, functionally speaking. The Latter-day Saint essentialist position of womanhood is to produce offspring to build up the Father's kingdom. Before I continue, I should clarify that my experience is not every woman's experience. Many Latter-day Saint women struggle with infertility and do not share my criticisms. Some take comfort in Heavenly Mother when it offers a trajectory which she may eventually be able to conceive children in the eternities. On the other hand, others may become resistant to Heavenly Mother when She feels like an unreachable trajectory for the infertile Latter-day Saint woman on earth. Every woman's experience is different, and I honor and respect those diverse experiences, just as I hope other women would honor and respect my experience.

For me, the Heavenly Mother concept of godhood has been both a friend and foe in my efforts toward motherhood. Motherhood and biological reproduction have been a personal struggle for me.[17] Being raised in a religion that puts a heavy emphasis on motherhood may be very difficult for women with a gender variant biology, like myself. I wanted to be a woman, even when my body did not comply. My womanhood was dependent upon my uterus. Since my uterus was faulty, I saw myself as faulty. Comments like Widtsoe's only perpetuated the problem. In his commentary on how priesthood is comparable to motherhood, Widtsoe continued, "Such power [reproduction] entrusted to women proves conclusively that they have been

---

17. Blaire Ostler, "How a Mother Became a Transhumanist," *Queer Mormon Transhumanist*, www.blaireostler.com/journal/2015/6/6/how-a-mother-became-a-transhumanist, accessed July 31, 2018.

recognized and trusted. Our Father even chose a Daughter of Eve to be the earth-mother and guide of His Only Begotten Son, and thus honored womanhood for all time and eternity!"[18] If this comment is to be taken seriously, it implies that women who cannot reproduce are not recognized, honored, and trusted by God the Father. Why would God the Father trust the woman sitting next to me in the pews, but not me? Am I even a woman if I'm not a mother? It can be incredibly painful for women with fertility issues or gender variant[19] anatomies like mine to internalize ignorant sentiments like these. I cannot help but feel like the constant barrage of messages about motherhood being the importance of a woman's existence is a way to maintain the patriarchal order of the church structure and narrative, not to comfort the women who need it most.

Similar to women who do not desire motherhood, infertile women should not be bombarded with messages of motherhood being their only or most valuable contribution to eternal glory. Women could be honored in other accomplishments to their religious community, just as men are, without overly emphasizing the role of mother. It would also help if women were granted access to all offices through priesthood ordination. It is also worth mentioning the most obvious way to help infertile women who desire motherhood is to support medical and scientific advancements which would allow safe reproduction for all gender variant anatomies. I have greatly benefitted from these technologies, and trust there are many more inspiring possibilities for the future of biological reproduction and creation.

QUEER WOMEN

Queer women are of particular concern when it comes to godly representation. Heavenly Mother offers a feminine template, but queer women are often neglected from the narrative. Is it possible for Heavenly Mother to know a transgender experience? Are transgender women also made in the image of God? If so, shouldn't the esthetics of our worship reflect that?

---

18. Widtsoe, *Priesthood and Church Government*, 85.

19. Gender variant is a label used to describe the broad spectrum of diverse gender experiences. In the specific sentence, "gender variant anatomies" refers to a person with an anatomy or biology that is not typical of the average "male" or "female."

Despite the ignorance of Widtsoe's comments concerning women, he leaves open a very intriguing possibility—motherhood by proxy or vicarious means. Widtsoe continues under the subheading *The Spirit of Motherhood* to clarify: "Women who through no fault of their own cannot exercise the gift of motherhood directly, may do so vicariously."[20] If motherhood may be accomplished vicariously, then why must motherhood be accomplished by cisgender women? Could motherhood be accomplished vicariously via transgender men or transgender women? New reproductive technologies are changing the landscape of both gender and procreation.[21] Soon, uterus transplants may allow transgender women the ability to carry children. If this is the case, a transgender woman who gestates her own offspring through technological means is not significantly different from her cisgender sister who gestates her own offspring through technological means. According to bio-essentialist claims, functionally, a transgender woman would be the child's biological mother. The primary difference between the two is that the cisgender mother is a mother by assignment and the transgender mother is a mother by affiliation. In time, we will see our Heavenly Parents have granted the *Spirit of Motherhood* to a diversity of genders.

It seems fitting for individuals who were assigned a male sex at birth to aspire to motherhood. Latter-day apostles teach "the highest and noblest work in this life is that of a mother"[22] and motherhood "is the highest, holiest service to be assumed by mankind."[23] Please note that motherhood is to be assumed by *man*kind. The semantics implicitly leave room for transgender mothers. Not only that, it is her highest, holiest service. Why shouldn't someone who was assigned male aspire to motherhood, especially if it is her noblest work?

Mormon theology also embraces the notion of proxy work—the idea that we can each fulfill the role of each other when the occasion

20. Widtsoe, *Priesthood and Church Government*, 85.

21. Blaire Ostler, "Sexuality and Procreation," *Queer Mormon Transhumanist*, www.blaireostler.com/journal/2016/3/22/broadening-our-understanding-of-sexuality-and-procreation, accessed July 31, 2018.

22. Russell M. Nelson, "Our Sacred Duty to Honor Women," *LDS Conference Report* (Salt Lake City: Church of Jesus Christ of Latter-day Saints, Apr. 1999).

23. James R. Clark, ed., *Messages of the First Presidency of The Church of Jesus Christ of Latter-day Saints*, 6 vols. (Salt Lake: Bookcraft, 1965–75), 6:178. In 1935, the First Presidency stated, "The true spirit of the Church of Jesus Christ of Latter-day Saints gives to woman the highest place of honor in human life."

calls for it. If this is the case, transgender women who desires motherhood could attain motherhood via proxy for cisgender women who do not desire motherhood. Likewise, transgender men who desire fatherhood could be bearers of children as gestational dads.[24] Consider a heterosexual couple composed of a transgender man and transgender woman. The transgender man could use his uterus to carry the child, while the transgender woman could assume the role of mother once the child is born. Consider a gay couple in which one of the fathers wants to assume what is traditionally thought of as the motherly role. Any couple, queer or not, might be able to benefit from surrogacy with a willing, consenting woman as a proxy gestational parent.[25] Even traditional adoption could be a form of proxy parenting. There are many possibilities as to how families might be composed of people doing "proxy work" for one another according to their needs and desires in a system of love, respect, and cooperation. As Widtsoe suggests, the *Spirit of Motherhood* includes many possibilities through vicarious participation.

CONCLUSION

The sealed union between Heavenly Mother and Heavenly Father may not strictly be a cisgender heterosexual experience. According to Latter-day Saint doctrine and theology, God is composed of both man and woman. In Hebrew, Elohim is a plural noun. His godhood is dependent on Her, just as Hers is dependent on Him. I see this sealed union as a representation of partnership between the sexes, not a necessary mandate for heterosexual copulation. Heavenly Mother and Heavenly Father represent two offices a person may hold, but under the infinite plurality of God, there is room for every gender, race, orientation, experience, and benevolent desire. Our Heavenly Parents, *They*, do not

---

24. "Gestational dad" is a term used to describe transgender men or intersex men with functioning ovaries and uterus that allow him to carry, deliver, and even nurse his offspring.

25. I acknowledge that surrogacy is fraught with controversy, especially around gay dads who participate in overseas surrogacy. The bodies of women of color are often exploited and misused in the underground network of overseas surrogacy. It is unacceptable for advancements in queer parenting to come at the expense of women of color, their bodies, their healthcare, and economic position. They deserve our love, care, and consideration to their volition, consent, and autonomy. Methods of surrogacy need to be radically revised to benefit and respect women of color and other economically disadvantaged women.

even mandate a necessary binary for our non-binary and genderqueer[26] siblings. The broad all-encompassing plurality of God leaves no one behind, and our esthetics, language and pronouns should reflect the doctrine that we are all made in the image of God. There's room for everyone in the pantheon of Gods!

If anyone has the potential to be a god in Mormon theology, Godly esthetics should reflect the image of all Their children. Likewise, Heavenly Mother, as the Mother of all women, holds multitudes under Her wings. Hers is the face that is reflected in the motherly woman, the independent woman, the infertile woman, and the queer woman. We need not restrict Her esthetics and by extension, her love, on account of our ignorance. Her image is the image of all those that choose the label "woman" with as many faces, variations, and expression that are manifested on earth and in the heavens. She truly is the Mother of all women.

---

26. Genderqueer, like non-binary, is a label used to signify a gender experience that is not exclusively masculine or feminine, or even outside the binary.

SEVEN

MORMONISM AND THE PROBLEM OF HETERODOXY

KELLI D. POTTER

According to the teachings of the Church of Jesus Christ of Latter-day Saints (hereafter, LDS Church or LDS Mormonism[1]), Joseph Smith's motivation to start a new religious movement begins with a particularly difficult epistemological problem. In his history, Smith writes,

> Some time in the second year after our removal to Manchester, there was in the place where we lived an unusual excitement on the subject of religion. It commenced with the Methodists, but soon became general among all the sects in that region of country. Indeed, the whole district of country seemed affected by it, and great multitudes united themselves to the different religious parties, which created no small stir and division amongst the people, some crying, "Lo, here!" and others, "Lo, there!" Some were contending for the Methodist faith, some for the Presbyterian, and some for the Baptist. ...
>
> ... What is to be done? Who of all these parties are right; or, are they all wrong together? If any one of them be right, which is it, and how shall I know it? (JS-H 1:5, 10)

Clearly, Smith is concerned with which of the above-mentioned denominations, if any, is correct. This is the concrete problem. But this concrete problem is also an instance of a more general *epistemological* and *semantic* problem concerning the nature and status of religious

---

1. Although I focus on the LDS tradition (i.e., the Church of Jesus Christ of Latter-day Saints), I sometimes mention two other Mormon denominations: Community of Christ (formerly Reorganized Church of Jesus Christ of Latter-day Saints) and the Fundamentalist Church of Jesus Christ of Latter-day Saints (FLDS). These three institutions disagree about who counts as an authority to speak for the Joseph Smith tradition. For a discussion of these and other schisms within Mormonism, see Newell Bringhurst and John Hamer, eds., *Scattering of the Saints: Schism within Mormonism* (Independence, Missouri: John Whitmer Books, 2007). I use "Mormon" and its cognates to refer to all the various Mormon sects, and I use "LDS" to refer to the Church of Jesus Christ of Latter-day Saints. "Latter-day Saints" refers to the members of the latter organization.

belief.[2] To see this, first note that Smith mentions only Christian denominations and does not mention Islam, Hinduism, etc. Given the time and location, Smith would have known about these religions, but none of them would have been a *live option* for him, to use William James's famous phrase.[3] It seems apparent that Smith had already decided that Christianity was correct and that his problem was to figure out which denomination had the correct interpretation of Christianity. So, Smith's concrete problem is not best understood as an instance of the problem of *inter*religious diversity (i.e., the existence of disagreement between distinct religious traditions). Instead, Smith's concrete problem is better understood as an instance of a problem concerning *intra*-religious diversity, or what I herein call "the problem of heterodoxy." Whereas the problem of interreligious diversity deals with how one should respond to the fact that there exists disagreement between religious traditions, the problem of heterodoxy deals with how one should respond to the fact that there exist different interpretations of the same religious tradition. That is, the problem of heterodoxy asks not "which religion is true?" but "which interpretation of X is the correct interpretation?", where *"X"* is the name of one of the religious traditions in question (e.g., Christianity, Buddhism, Islam, etc.). I submit that the latter, and not the former, is Smith's question.

The problem of heterodoxy is an underappreciated problem in the epistemology of religion. Usually, when philosophers deal with epistemological issues relating to religious disagreement, they focus on disagreement *between* and *among* traditions and not *within* traditions. This is a serious lacuna in the philosophical literature, since (as I argue below) the problem of heterodoxy is more fundamental. Moreover, since Smith put this problem at the center of his explanation of the need for a restoration of true Christianity, it is important to explore to what extent Smith offered a plausible response to the problem. In this essay, I offer a reconstruction of LDS Mormonism's theology as a response to the problem of heterodoxy. However, in the end, I argue that the response fails to solve the problem and provides a basis for the

---

2. Epistemology is the study of the nature of knowledge; semantics is the study of meaning, reference, and truth.

3. William James, *The Will to Believe and Other Essays in Popular Philosophy* (New York: Dover Publications, 1956).

ecclesiastical authoritarianism manifested in the present-day Church of Jesus Christ of Latter-day Saints.

INTERRELIGIOUS DISAGREEMENT VS. HETERODOXY

As mentioned, it is clear that there are two types of religious disagreement: *external* and *internal.* External religious disagreement occurs when two people from different faiths disagree. For example, Buddhists claim that everything is impermanent and Christians claim that God and the soul are eternal. This appears to be a case where the beliefs of Christians and Buddhists cannot both be true. This type of religious disagreement has been the focus of the discussion of religious diversity in contemporary philosophy of religion.[4] By contrast, internal religious disagreement is usually ignored or mentioned merely in passing.[5] Internal religious disagreement occurs when two people from the same faith disagree on some matter pertaining to the faith. There are two types of such disagreements. First, there are disagreements about what the doctrines of the faith are. Second, there are disagreements about how to interpret the doctrines. I call the first *doctrinal disagreements* and the second *interpretative disagreements.* An example of a doctrinal disagreement between Protestants and Catholics is whether the doctrine of the immaculate conception is Christian doctrine. An example of an interpretative disagreement is between Social Trinitarians and Latin Trinitarians over the doctrine of the trinity. These categories are not necessarily mutually exclusive. In this essay, I focus on interpretative disagreements.

The existence of interpretative disagreements suggests that we need to distinguish between the language used to express beliefs and the beliefs themselves. Indeed, the existence of interpretative disagreements indicates that two believers might utter the same sentence and yet mean something quite different. So, I refer to these utterances or written expressions as *doxastic expressions.*[6] For example, most Latter-day Saints would be happy to utter "God has a body," but they often mean

---

4. For example, see Philip Quinn and Kevin Meeker, eds., *The Philosophical Challenge of Religious Diversity* (Oxford, England: Oxford University Press, 2000).

5. William Christian mentions the problem of heterodoxy in passing but does not give a thorough treatment of the problem in his *Oppositions of Religious Doctrines: A Study in the Logic of Dialogue among Religions* (New York: Herder and Herder, 1972).

6. The word "doxastic" means having to do with belief. It is based on the Greek word for belief.

radically different things by this expression. The expression is the same, but the belief is different. This gives us the illusion that all Latter-day Saints believe the same thing, when, in fact, they do not. As Arne Naess puts it, Latter-day Saints are in *pseudo-agreement*.[7]

External and internal religious disagreements pose different philosophical problems. External disagreements raise an *epistemological* question: which belief is true (if any) and how do we know? Internal (interpretative) disagreements raise a *semantic* question: what *are* the beliefs of the faith? The first is an epistemological question because it requires that we figure out how to adjudicate between incompatible claims. The second is a semantic question because it requires that we determine the meaning of the doxastic expressions of the language. In other words, external disagreements threaten the epistemic status of one's belief whereas internal disagreements threaten the identity or content of one's belief. This is the first reason that the problem of heterodoxy is more fundamental than the problem of interreligious disagreement.

Moreover, the problem of heterodoxy is logically prior to the traditional problem of external religious disagreement. Indeed, every external religious disagreement depends on how the respective religious faiths are interpreted. On some interpretations, they do indeed disagree and on other interpretations they do not disagree. For example, Latter-day Saints could accept Social Trinitarianism but not Latin Trinitarianism. Whether Latter-day Saints and creedal Christians disagree on this matter depends on what the right interpretation of Christianity is. Hence, the problem of heterodoxy must be solved first.

JOSEPH SMITH'S SOLUTION

The LDS understanding of the apostasy and the restoration, as based on the now-canonized account of the first vision in Joseph Smith's official history, is presented as an answer to the problem of heterodoxy. That is, Smith—according to the current LDS understanding—was not concerned with which major religious tradition (Buddhism, Islam, Judaism, Christianity, Hinduism, etc.) was correct. He already "knew" that Christianity was correct. He was concerned, instead, with which

---

7. *Interpretation and Preciseness* (Oslo: I Kommisjon Hos Jacob Dybwad, 1953), 123–24.

interpretation of Christianity was the correct interpretation and with which Christian organization represented God's will.

Of course, the first source to go to in trying to determine which version of Christianity is correct is the Bible. And Smith did look to the Bible for an answer to his question. But instead of finding a direct answer in the Bible; he found out *how to get an answer* to his question (a "meta-answer") in James 1:5.[8] In fact, Smith seemed to recognize that the Bible could not really answer his question. He says,

> [T]he teachers of religion of the different sects understood the same passages of scripture so differently as to destroy all confidence in settling the question by an appeal to the Bible. (JS-H 1:12)

He understands that the Bible itself cannot settle the issue. But it does say (in James 1:5) that there are other ways to find answers to such questions, namely by asking God. Perhaps there are other interpretations of this passage, but that is clearly how Smith understood it, since that is what he did.

Given that the first vision[9] is the response that Smith received to his question, not only is the first vision the medium whereby the problem of heterodoxy is answered, it *constitutes* an instance of the type of event that is central to the answer as well. To be sure, the answer to the question about which church is true is "none." But the answer to the more general problem of heterodoxy is that we need revelation and the first vision itself is an instance of the kind of revelation required. In other words, Smith's answer to his quandary was that there should be communication between God and humanity.

Latter-day Saints believe that the traditional Christian churches had all deviated from the truth and that, as a result, God was no longer in contact with humanity. They call this *the great apostasy* or, more simply, *the apostasy*.[10] Smith initiated a new dispensation in which God would be in communication with humanity through prophets. And this answers the problem of heterodoxy because God can settle disputes about how to interpret Christianity by speaking to prophets. In other words,

---

8. James 1:5 reads, "If any of you lack wisdom, let him ask of God, that giveth to me liberally, and upbraideth not; and it shall be given to him."

9. For more on the first vision, see James B. Allen, "The Significance of Joseph Smith's 'First Vision' in Mormon Thought," *Dialogue: A Journal of Mormon Thought* 1, 3 (1966): 29–46.

10. James E. Talmage, *The Great Apostasy* (Salt Lake City: Deseret Book Co., 1983).

the only way to preserve orthodoxy would be to re-initialize contact between God and humankind (i.e., the restoration) and have that contact continue into the future (i.e., continuing revelation).

Let us be clear about what is implied by this approach to the problem of heterodoxy. Recall that the problem of heterodoxy is the problem of how to determine which interpretation of a particular faith tradition is correct, given competing interpretations. In particular, members of the same faith might accept the same doxastic expressions (e.g., "the Father, the Son and the Holy Spirit are one God"), and yet interpret those expressions differently. One major factor that leads to the problem of heterodoxy is that the religious leader in question is dead. And so if a question about what he or she meant by a certain doxastic expression arises, we cannot ask him or her.[11] The first aspect of Smith's solution to the problem is simple: Jesus is not really dead and so, in effect, we *can* ask him.[12] And we can use this method to settle all disputes about the content of the faith.

Of course, even if they do believe that Jesus lives, not all Christians believe that you can ask Jesus directly what he meant by a given expression in the New Testament (assuming that he did, in fact, utter some of what appears in the New Testament). So, some Christians must have a different answer to the problem of heterodoxy. One reasonable answer would be to go with the interpretation that best fits the whole body of data associated with Jesus: the extant texts, the historical background, linguistic analysis, archeological evidence, etc. However, given the state of scriptural interpretation in the nineteenth century, it would also seem plausible that more than one interpretation could fit with the relevant data. This observation seems even more accurate in light of contemporary biblical scholarship. In other words, it is plausible that the publicly available evidence concerning what Jesus taught *under-determines* the best interpretation of Jesus' teachings. Surely, several different approaches to Jesus' teachings are compatible with the evidence that we can accumulate.

If the available evidence concerning what Jesus taught does not

---

11. Although, even if the religious leader were not dead, there could still be disputes about whether she is interpreting her earlier statements accurately. We can, after all, misinterpret what we have said in the past.

12. It is true that, for Mormons, one should pray to Heavenly Father rather than to the Son. But this does not make a philosophical difference.

favor a unique interpretation of those teachings, then this *intersubjective* approach to solving the problem of heterodoxy (in the particular case of Christianity) does not work. Indeed, taking this approach leads to skepticism, given the assumption that the correct interpretation is underdetermined by the available evidence. Moreover, as cited above, we know that Smith had considered different interpretations of the texts in an attempt to figure out who was correct (JS-H 1:12). These considerations did not satisfy him. So, for Smith, the problem is not solved by the intersubjective approach. Instead, Smith turned to revelation. And it is important to see that using revelation to solve the problem of heterodoxy contrasts with the intersubjective approach insofar as it appeals to content that is not intersubjective, but rather is private or subjective.

To make this clear, it is helpful to be explicit about the distinction between intersubjective and subjective evidence. Intersubjective evidence is evidence for *every*body if it is evidence for *any*body. A mathematical proof is a proof for you as well as for me, once we both understand it. Subjective evidence, by contrast, is *non-transferrable,* to use van Inwagen's term.[13] If I have subjective evidence, there is no procedure that I could follow that would be sufficient for making that very same evidence available to you. An example of subjective evidence is memory. I recall that the bird that I saw on my hike yesterday was a finch. Since I did not take a photograph and am basing my claim on memory, I cannot show you my evidence. If you believe me, it is because you trust me.

The LDS concept of revelation is essentially the same as the concept of religious experience discussed in recent philosophy of religion.[14] As such, revelation is subjective evidence. This is true of most, if not all, religious experiences, including what Latter-day Saints call the witness of the Holy Ghost. Of course, some might claim that Smith's first vision was a publicly available experience of the Father and the Son— that is, if anyone else had been present in the forest on that day, such a person would have seen and heard exactly what Smith saw and heard.

---

13. Peter van Inwagen, "We're Right. They're Wrong," in *Disagreement*, ed. Richard Feldman and Ted Warfield (Oxford, England: Oxford University Press, 2010), 26.

14. William Alston, *Perceiving God: The Epistemology of Religious Experience* (New York: Cornell University Press, 1993).

But granting that an eavesdropper would have seen personages floating above Smith, it is not clear that such an eavesdropper would have seen the Father and the Son. Perhaps such an eavesdropper would have seen something else entirely—two people, two ghosts, two demons, two extra-terrestrials, two clouds, etc. That is, even if a religious experience is simultaneously an ordinary perceptual experience, the religious content goes beyond the publicly available content.[15]

Given that Smith's solution to the problem of heterodoxy invokes subjective content and evidence, it avoids the underdetermination problem faced by the intersubjective approach. Despite there being more than one interpretation of the faith that fits with the intersubjective evidence, it might seem that there would be only one that fits with one's own subjective evidence. Since Smith's solution involves reference to subjective experiences that cannot be transferred to others, I refer to this view as *interpretative gnosticism*. Interpretative gnosticism is the view that one can settle the question as to which interpretation of a religious tradition is correct by subjective religious experiences.

Also, since we are discussing the epistemology of religious belief, it makes sense to point out that Smith's solution to the problem of heterodoxy has similarities with the approach called *reformed epistemology*.[16] Advocates of reformed epistemology argue that certain religious beliefs are properly basic. This is because it is assumed that they are formed by a reliable belief forming process, even if the believer is not in a position to say why it is reliable. Religious experience fits into this category, according to reformed epistemologists. If it is from God, then it is reliable and can be trusted. Of course, people do have contrary

---

15. An early reviewer of this essay raised the following point: some claim that the experience of the Holy Ghost is fundamentally practical rather than cognitive and that, hence—given that the practical is intersubjective—the Holy Ghost is intersubjective. My response is that we may grant that the experience of the Holy Ghost is embedded in religious practices and that it has no meaning independent of those practices. In that sense, it *is* intersubjective. For example, it is agreed that the experience of the Spirit is calming and warming. But the doxastic content conveyed by these religious experiences is not intersubjective, since people disagree about this. And it is the doxastic content of religious experience that matters at this point in the argument. The response that there is no doxastic content in such religious experiences undercuts the argument being considered. It is, of course, not entirely irrelevant here that some people engage in the practices and never experience the Holy Ghost at all.

16. See, e.g., Alvin Plantinga and Nicholas Wolterstorff, eds., *Faith and Rationality* (Notre Dame, Indiana: University of Notre Dame Press, 1983).

basic beliefs on occasion. When they do, the question of justification might arise. And the reformed epistemologist would have to admit that her justification is non-transferrable. I say more about this below.

PROBLEMS

Despite being initially plausible, there are problems with Smith's approach to the problem of heterodoxy. The first problem arises from the fact that the content of religious experience is subjective. To be sure, there are such things as subjective justifications for beliefs (memory is the example given above). But Smith's use of religious experience as an answer to the problem of heterodoxy is not just an attempt to justify a particular belief over other competing beliefs; it is an attempt *to determine the propositional content that goes with certain doxastic expressions.* This move from the epistemological to the semantic changes the game. Indeed, given that Smith's solution employs a subjective religious experience to determine the proper content of a doxastic expression, then it seems clear that Smith's solution involves an appeal to subjective content to determine the correct meaning for certain expressions in a language. In other words, Smith's solution assumes that there is a *private* language.

Many philosophers of language have argued that a private language is impossible. It is not clear that there is a common core to these various private language arguments. Ludwig Wittgenstein's argument (or arguments) is the most famous; but its interpretation is a matter of great contention.[17] I want to avoid the controversies associated with interpreting Wittgenstein since I am afraid that my interpretation of him would be considered heterodox by many of his disciples. So, instead, I will explain Otto Neurath's private language argument.

Neurath's private language argument is stated in several places, but it can be found in its fullest form in his article entitled "Protocol Sentences."[18] Protocol sentences in this context may be understood as expressions that make basic observations about objects in the

---

17. See Ludwig Wittgenstein, *Philosophical Investigations* (New York: MacMillan, 1953).
18. Otto Neurath, "Protocol Statements," in *Philosophical Papers, 1913–1946*, trans. and ed. Robert S. Cohen and Marie Neurath (Dordrecht, Neth.: D. Reidel Publishing, 1983), 91–99.

experiential environment. He writes, using the names of characters from Daniel Defoe's *Robinson Crusoe,*

> If Robinson wants to join what is in his protocol of yesterday with what is in his protocol today, that is, if he wants to make use of a language at all, he must make use of the 'inter-subjective' language. The Robinson of yesterday and the Robinson of today stand in precisely the same relation in which Robinson stands to Friday. … If, under certain circumstances, one calls Robinson's protocol language of yesterday and today the same language then, under the same conditions, one can call Robinson's and Friday's the same language. …
>
> In other words, every language as such is "inter-subjective"; it must be possible to incorporate the protocols of one moment into the protocols of the next moment, just as the protocols of A can be incorporated into the protocols of B.[19]

It seems that Neurath argues as follows. First, he assumes that a language requires constancy of use over time. I believe that this is the point of Neurath's talk of "incorporation" of one moment's protocols into those of the next moment. And constancy of use implies that sometimes the expression is used correctly and other times incorrectly (if every use were correct, there would be no constancy of use). But then to check correct usage, Robinson stands to his earlier self the way he stands to Friday. If this is the case, then the only way that he can check the correctness of his own usage is in a way similar to how he checks Friday's. So, any language is intersubjective.

There is a problem with this argument as it stands. The problem is that Robinson is connected to his earlier self in a way that he is not connected to Friday—namely by memory. Robinson remembers his own earlier usage of the expression in question—call it E. Moreover, Robinson also remembers the mental state M that accompanied his previous usage of E. But to decide whether to use E in this new case, Robinson must interpret his own past usage of E, and the fact that his usage was determined by M at that time does not determine whether E should be used now. Even if subjective content can determine correct usage at one time, once that content has passed, there is still an issue about how to interpret the expression.

Neurath's considerations lead to a problem for Smith's interpretative

---

19. Neurath, "Protocol Statements," 96.

gnosticism. As soon as the religious experience that is intended to fix the content of the faith has passed, then the question of how to interpret that experience arises again. Suppose, for example, that Smith receives a revelation that F is the right interpretation of the doxastic expression E. By supposition, he knows what he means by the words in F at the time because he has a private mental state that determines their meaning. But as soon as that mental state is gone, the question of how to interpret the words arises again.

Given Smith's approach, this problem may only be solved by having another religious experience. And so, it would seem, interpretative gnosticism leads to the conclusion that one must be in a constant state of receiving revelation from God to fix the content of one's beliefs. This objection to interpretative gnosticism leads to the necessity of having continuous revelation. At any moment, when a question arises about how to interpret a doxastic expression, one must appeal to religious experience. Thus, we see that it is reasonable that the doctrine of continuing revelation accompanies the doctrine of the restoration in LDS theology.[20]

Another problem with Smith's approach arises from its subjectivism. The problem is that someone besides Smith might have a religious experience that confers a belief that disagrees with Smith's conclusions about the proper interpretation of the doxastic expressions in question. If a fourteen-year-old boy with little education and no training in theology can settle theological questions by asking God, then anyone should be able to do so. But, of course, this opens a Pandora's box. One person can receive a revelation that determines the content of belief E to be F and another can have a revelation that determines the content of E to be G, where F and G are not only distinct, but incompatible.

Notice that this leads back to the problem of heterodoxy. So, it seems that interpretative gnosticism does not really solve the problem after all. Similarly, reformed epistemology must also appeal to interpretative gnosticism in order to solve the problem of heterodoxy. Reformed epistemologists, such as Plantinga, believe that they have a special epistemic status that others do not possess. Speaking of the Christian believer's reaction to non-believers, Plantinga writes,

---

20. For more on the LDS doctrine of continuing revelation, see Henry Eyring, "Continuing Revelation," Oct. 2014, www.churchofjesuschrist.org/study/general-conference/2014/10/continuing-revelation.

She may agree that she as those who dissent are equally convinced of the truth of their belief, and even that they are internally on a par, that the internally available markers are similar, or relevantly similar. But she must still think that there is an important epistemic difference: she thinks that somehow the other person has made a mistake, or has a blind spot, or hasn't been wholly attentive, or hasn't received some grace she has, or is in some way less epistemically fortunate.[21]

First, it is important to note that Plantinga is discussing external religious disagreement rather than internal religious disagreement. Given this, he believes that if the Christian God really exists and is the cause of his religious belief, then he has important knowledge that people from other religious traditions lack. He believes that his tradition possesses a path to knowledge that is not available in the other traditions. Even if the believers of those traditions have some kind of religious experience as well, it is not sufficiently similar to the experiences of Plantinga's own tradition to be taken authoritatively. It seems that Latter-day Saints say the same thing as Plantinga. For the purposes of argument, let me grant that this move works as a response to the problem of external religious disagreement. Even so, it is clear that this response does not work once you apply it to the problem of heterodoxy. Heterodox Latter-day Saints might claim that the Holy Ghost witnesses to them that orthodox Latter-day Saints are wrong. One cannot dismiss this heterodox claim on the grounds that it is formed in the wrong way. It is one thing to say to outsiders that they are missing something important (as Plantinga does) and quite another thing to say this to one's fellow religionists.

LDS doctrine has an answer to this problem as well. The answer is to privilege the religious experiences of some over others. This leads to a hierarchy, where those at the top have the power to interpret the faith for everyone else. And this would help to explain LDS Mormonism's focus on the central role of priesthood authority (that is, power) in the restoration.[22]

If you grant all the assumptions that are made in Smith's solution

---

21. Alvin Plantinga, "Pluralism: A Defense of Religious Exclusivism," in *The Philosophical Challenge of Religious Diversity*, ed. Phillip Quinn and Kevin Meeker (Oxford, England: Oxford University Press, 2000), 182.

22. For more on the concept of authority in Mormonism, see Mario S. De Pillis, "The Quest for Religious Authority and the Rise of Mormonism," *Dialogue: A Journal of Mormon Thought* 1, 1 (1966): 68–88.

to the problem of heterodoxy, the solution *seems* to work. And since reformed epistemologists (who are, as the name suggests, usually protestants) do not accept the kind of authority that is required for this solution, I believe that the LDS solution is more initially promising than the reformed approach. We might call the LDS approach "restored epistemology," which amounts to reformed epistemology plus (what we might call) "epistemic authoritarianism," namely the view that the religious experiences of some are more authoritative than the religious experiences of others.

Despite its initial plausibility, I believe that restored epistemology fails as well. One of the assumptions here is that the religious experiences of some trump the religious experience of others. This assumption of epistemic authoritarianism is itself problematic, from an epistemological point of view. The problem is that there cannot be any good reason for accepting the claim that the religious experiences of some trump the religious experiences of others. To see this, let us consider the following scenario:

> Josephine lives in a town with three "Mormon" churches: the LDS Church, Community of Christ, and the FLDS Church. Josephine considers herself a Christian but wonders which denomination is truly Christian. Moreover, given where she lives, she has learned a little about Joseph Smith, has read the Book of Mormon, and wonders about Smith's claim to having restored Christianity. But in her investigation of Smith's restoration movement, she has discovered that these Mormon denominations disagree about how to interpret Smith's restoration. She wants to discover what Smith really taught in order to assess his claims to having restored Christianity. How can she know what Smith really claimed, given the sometimes wildly different interpretations of his teachings?

Clearly, Josephine's quandary is formulated to be analogous to the situation in which Smith found himself. If Smith's quandary were similar to Josephine's, and Smith's restoration were an answer to this quandary, then Smith's answer should work for Josephine as well. What is she to do? Restored epistemology tells her to go with whatever the authorities say when it comes to matters of internal disagreement. But which authorities should she listen to? LDS, FLDS, or Community of Christ?

The LDS approach is that she should attempt to have her own religious experience to figure out which Mormon denomination truly represents Smith's approach. So, let us imagine that Josephine does this and concludes that Community of Christ gets it right. Now, it seems clear that there are plenty of LDS Mormons and FLDS Mormons who would claim that her experience conflicts with their authorities and that, hence, they can dismiss her experiences as being incorrect. She cannot use her own religious experience to adjudicate the issue of whether she should trust the leadership of one denomination over the others, since those who adhere to the other denominations are in the same situation as she is with respect to the denomination that she chooses. Indeed, if she gets it wrong, then she is actually violating the epistemic authoritarianism of Smith's approach. Perhaps she can just privilege her own religious experience over everyone else's. This would solve the problem of disagreement with the authorities of the other denominations; but this would be to take the *reformed* approach rather than the *restored* approach to the epistemic quandary. Of course, it is obvious that Josephine's quandary cannot be resolved by an appeal to the authorities of one of the denominations since that is the very question at issue. Finally, there does not seem to be any intersubjective way of settling the dispute about who interprets Smith most faithfully.

But without a subjective or intersubjective justification for believing in the epistemic authority of the LDS (or Community of Christ, or the FLDS, etc.) leadership, there is no justification for this assumption. If you are an outsider, to accept one version of Mormonism, you must trust its authorities without any substantial reason to do so. But, now, notice that everyone starts out as an outsider, even if one is born into the LDS Church, one must still be converted.[23] Therefore, it follows that even life-long Latter-day Saints have no real basis for trusting their leaders. Restored epistemology amounts to epistemic "boot-strapping" and thus fails.

Mormonism's epistemic authoritarianism requires that I trust another's religious experience more than my own. And it requires that I do this without any independent check on the other person's testimony. Indeed, there are cases in which it is rational for me to trust another's testimony more than my own. For example, I should trust my doctor's diagnosis of my medical condition more than my own

---

23. See Grace Jorgensen, "Every Member a Convert," *Ensign,* Apr. 1980, www.lds.org/ensign/1980/04/every-member-a-convert.

diagnosis or the scientific community's nearly unanimous verdict on anthropogenic climate change over my own judgment about it. But these are cases where there is an objective way to determine who the *experts* are. In a way, religious authorities count as experts, of course. But there are different groups claiming to be the experts on Mormon doctrine. They each deny the expertise of the other groups. And the only way to determine who the real experts are is to settle the problem of heterodoxy in the first place (namely to know which denomination gets it right). So, unless we have a solution to the problem of religious experts (i.e., an objective criterion for determining who they are), we do not have a solution to the problem of heterodoxy. And unless we have a solution to the problem of heterodoxy, we do not have a solution to the problem of experts. The upshot, I believe, is that we are not in a position for us to defer rationally to experts on matters of religious belief. In fact, it is irrational to do so. So, it is irrational for us to accept the orthodox LDS solution to the problem of heterodoxy.

THE "A-THEOLOGICAL" APPROACH

Perhaps there is an alternative approach to the problem of heterodoxy available to Latter-day Saints. One debate within the LDS intellectual community deals with the role of theology in the faith. Some LDS theologians, such as David Paulsen and Blake Ostler, have taken an approach to Mormon theology that does not differ methodologically from such theologies in traditional Christian circles.[24] However, other LDS thinkers, such as Brian Birch, James Faulconer, and Adam S. Miller, eschew systematic theology entirely or, at least, claim that it plays no substantive role in the faith.[25] Here is Miller on the role of theology:

> Theology is a diversion. It is not serious like doctrine, respectable like history, or helpful like therapy. Theology is gratuitous. It works by way of detours. Doing theology is like building a comically circuitous Rube Goldberg Machine: you spend your time tinkering together an unnecessarily

---

24. See Blake Ostler, *Exploring Mormon Thought: The Attributes of God,* vol. 1 (Salt Lake City: Greg Kofford Books, 2001).

25. Brian Birch summarizes previous LDS *a-theological* approaches in "Faith Seeking Understanding: Mormon Atheology and the Challenge of Fideism," in *Mormonism at the Crossroads of Philosophy and Theology: Essays in Honor of David L. Paulsen,* ed. Jacob T. Baker (Salt Lake City: Greg Kofford Books, 2012), 47–68.

complicated, impractical, and ingenious apparatus for doing things that are, in themselves, simple.[26]

So, Miller takes theology to be superfluous. Faulconer goes farther and argues that (systematic) theology is *dangerous*:

> [T]he absence of official rational explanations or descriptions of beliefs and practices, and the presence of differing and inconsistent explanations for and descriptions of belief within the membership of the church, suggests that we have little if any official systematic, rational, or dogmatic theology. (I use those three terms, systematic theology, rational theology, and dogmatic theology, as synonyms.) We are "a-theological"—which means that we are without a church-sanctioned, church-approved, or even church encouraged systematic theology—and that is as it should be because systematic theology is dangerous.[27]

Following Faulconer, I call this the *a-theological* approach.[28] If we take this approach, we might tell a different story about the apostasy, restoration, and continuing revelation. LDS a-theologians might argue that the apostasy arises not from interpreting the doctrines the wrong way but from interpreting them at all. Perhaps the problem is not that we have the wrong theology, but that we do theology at all. Doing theology leads to disagreement and, eventually, schism, thus dividing the Christian community over trivial issues. Furthermore, LDS a-theologians could argue that the restoration is a return to the basic doctrines plus an imperative to stick to these alone. Indeed, in the above quotation, Miller contrasts "doctrine" with "theology," considering the former "serious" and the latter superfluous. The first problem with this approach arises from the concept of "doctrine" that Miller uses. What is doctrine? Perhaps, given the definitions offered above, doctrine consists of the set of basic doxastic expressions that every believer affirms. Of course, it is not entirely clear that such a set would not be very small. Nevertheless, it is plausible that there are some very basic doxastic expressions that every Latter-day Saint would affirm, such as "God exists," "God loves his children," etc. But there are

---

26. Adam S. Miller, *Rube Goldberg Machines: Essays in Mormon Theology* (Salt Lake City: Greg Kofford Books, 2012), xiii.

27. James E. Faulconer, "Rethinking Theology: The Shadow of the Apocalypse," *FARMS Review* 19, 1 (2007): 175–99.

28. "A-theological" means *without theology* and not *without God.*

a lot of other doxastic expressions that some Latter-day Saints would affirm and others would not (e.g., "marriage in the Celestial Kingdom will be plural marriage"). Certainly, these disagreements make a big difference to the nature of the belief held by the adherents of the faith. And very often these disagreements hinge on how the basic doxastic expressions (i.e., the "doctrines") are interpreted. But, then, one might define theology as *the interpretation of the basic doxastic expressions of the faith*. And, if so, then it follows that doing theology would be necessary for adjudicating the disputes about doctrines other than the basic doxastic expressions that everyone agrees with. In other words, to use the terminology introduced above, even if the a-theological approach solves the problem of internal interpretative disagreements, it does not solve the problem of internal doctrinal disagreements.

The LDS a-theologian might respond by claiming that anything above and beyond the set of basic doxastic expressions (i.e., the "doctrine") is not part of the faith. Instead, one should keep those disputes out of the community entirely. An example of this approach is seen in the LDS approach to the theory of organic evolution, in which the church neither endorses nor denies the truth of the evolution of species.[29]

This extra-doctrinal agnosticism comes at a price. One of the important features of religious belief is supposed to be that it gives us a good guide about how to live morally. But the moral implications of LDS doctrine are a matter of dispute among Latter-day Saints. For example, although the majority believes that it was right for the LDS Church to campaign against gay marriage, there are heterodox Latter-day Saints who reject this.[30] The different views on this issue depend on the interpretation of LDS doctrine. And so, extra-doctrinal agnosticism has the problem of undercutting one of the main functions of religious belief. Religious belief is supposed to have consequences for our practical and moral lives. Of course, most would argue that religious belief does not merely reduce to beliefs about morality,[31] but few would argue that religious belief does not have

---

29. See William Evenson and Duane Jeffery, eds., *Mormonism and Evolution: The Authoritative LDS Statements* (Salt Lake City: Greg Kofford Books, 2006).

30. For a heterodox approach to homosexuality in LDS Mormonism, see Taylor Petrey "Toward a Post-Heterosexual Mormon Theology," *Dialogue: A Journal of Mormon Thought* 44, 4 (2011): 106–41.

31. Cf. Ludwig Feuerbach, *The Essence of Christianity*, trans. George Elliot (New York:

moral implications. The problem with the a-theological approach to Mormonism is that it disconnects doctrine from moral practice. Without an interpretation of the basic doxastic expressions, it is not clear what they imply with respect to morality. And once we begin to interpret the basic doxastic expressions, we are doing theology in the sense addressed in this essay.

The a-theologian might respond by insisting that it is only systematic theology that is being rejected. Indeed, note that in the above quotation from Faulconer, he does not castigate all theology, only systematic, rational, or dogmatic theology. So, there might be some other kind of non-systematic, non-rational, and non-dogmatic way of doing theology that would suffice to bridge the gap between the basic doxastic expressions and moral imperatives. Perhaps Faulconer has something like narrative theology in mind. Yet, if this is all there is to the a-theologians' point, it seems that the problem of heterodoxy is not avoided by a-theology. Presumably, even non-systematic theologians may disagree with each other about how to interpret the basic doxastic expressions. If this is all there is to Mormon a-theology, it does not help with the problem of heterodoxy.

A final attempt to save the a-theological solution to the problem of heterodoxy might be to argue that I have separated questions about belief from questions about practice, and that they cannot be so separated.[32] This is a common point to make if you are an a-theologian. But I do not think the charge sticks in this case. Indeed, just above, I emphasized the need to get the beliefs right due to the fact that they have implications for what we should do. This is not to separate belief from practice, but quite the opposite.

Perhaps the problem is that I prioritize belief over practice and practice is actually more fundamental. So, let us suppose that practice determines belief and not the other way around (I grant this only for the sake of argument). How does this help with the fact that the religious tradition is doxastically indeterminate? Presumably, what matters is that the practices are *not* indeterminate. But this helps only

Harper Row 1957), and R. B. Braithwaite, *An Empiricist's View of the Nature of Religious Belief* (Cambridge, England: Cambridge University Press, 1955).

32. This point was suggested by an early reviewer of this essay. Ironically, note that I have *just* finished arguing that this is, in fact, true of the a-theological position.

if the practices help us to adjudicate between and among the different doxastic interpretations. And it is obvious that they cannot; there are different sets of beliefs that are consistent with any given set of religious practices.

Perhaps, instead, only orthopraxis matters; maybe orthodoxy is beside the point. That is, you can believe whatever you like as long as you engage in correct behavior. However, this approach would be to *separate* belief from practice and this was rejected above. Surely, the fact that LDS theology includes the claim that gender is eternal matters to how the LDS Church behaves. Moreover, even if practice could be so separated from belief, there might be divergences in practice and, then, the problem of heterodoxy (heteropraxy?) arises again.

CONCLUSION

Many Latter-day Saints discuss "Mormon doctrine" as if it involves a set of transcendent propositions. They distinguish what Mormons actually *believe* from *doctrine*. That is, they use the concept of doctrine in a normative way. This language presupposes a determinate set of propositions that are the *true* doctrines of Mormonism. They believe that part of the restoration of the gospel is the identification of these doctrines. The problem of heterodoxy leads us to wonder, with Joseph Smith, whether we can know what that determinate set is. Latter-day Saints believe that Smith's restoration does indeed solve this problem and that anyone who wonders which Christian denomination is correct can follow Smith's example to know the truth. I argue that Smith's approach is problematic, since it asks us to trust religious authorities without any reason to do so.

EIGHT

WOMEN AT THE GATES OF MORTALITY
RELIEF SOCIETY BIRTH AND DEATH RITUALS

SUSANNA MORRILL

Since the founding of the Relief Society in Nauvoo, Illinois, in 1842, LDS women have participated in the communal life of their community through this women's auxiliary of the Church of Jesus Christ of Latter-day Saints. On the surface, much of the work of the Relief Society was practical and charitable. Local units of the Relief Society were expected to assist the ward bishop in looking after community members who were poor, sick, or in despair. This work took many forms, but Relief Society women regularly assisted at the birth beds and deathbeds of friends and neighbors. As revealed by contemporary women's diaries, journals, and Relief Society publications for the period I studied (1870s–1920s), these were important duties in the LDS women's world in Utah and other LDS core cultural areas.

However, on a deeper level, this seemingly practical work of Relief Society women had profoundly religious meaning. Even though they were not part of the church-sponsored rituals performed in the ward house or the temple, these birth and death rituals were part of the expected social "mothering" administered by women of the community. The rituals gave women immense, multifaceted religious authority within the daily experience of LDS lived religion. Historian of religions Robert Orsi has described lived religion as "religious practice and imagination in ongoing, dynamic relation with the realities and structures of everyday life in particular times and places."[1] This concept is a way to describe how members of any given religious community make meaningful and workable for themselves the institutional, ritual,

---

1. Robert Orsi, *The Madonna of 115th Street: Faith and Community in Italian Harlem, 1880–1950* (New Haven, Connecticut: Yale University Press, 2002), xiii. For a more detailed description of "lived religion," see xix–xxiv.

and theological structures within which they live. Lived religion usually intersects in important ways with what might be called official, or institutional, manifestations of religion perpetuated by religious authorities. However, lived religion also can fill in the gaps of meaning that institutional religions inevitably leave. Scholars often use the concept of lived religion to find and interpret women's roles in religious communities because women have historically been excluded from the institutional and theological structures of most Judeo-Christian religions and, thus, from narratives of religious history.

Birth and death rituals were vital in the lived LDS religion of this era, but they were not commonly discussed by church officials in sermons or church publications. They became important to the community as women performed these actions repeatedly and consistently—in some cases, as directed by bishops or other church officials. They were expected and comforting rituals in the daily religious lives of Latter-day Saint men and women—an essential element in how the Saints dealt practically and religiously with the joyful and searing realities of birth and death.

In performing these rituals, women became, in essence, managers of the transition from the premortal spirit world to mortality upon birth and from the mortal world to the spirit world at death. According to LDS theological logic, they assisted spirit children in making the transition from the premortal to earthly existence, then at the end of life eased the passage of spiritually tested souls back to the divine presence. I have argued elsewhere that, in doing this work, Relief Society women acted as mediators of liminality because they were instrumental in helping human spirits negotiate the transition between the divine and mortal realms at times of birth and death.[2] Because of the LDS belief in a premortal existent state, for the LDS community, these times were especially dangerous, uncertain, and anxious—when the worlds of mortality and divinity briefly connected. These birth and death rituals placed women at the theologically crucial points of entrances to and exits from the spirit world. Women stood at the gates of mortality in the context of the lived, if not the institutional, religion of the LDS Church.

It makes theological sense in the LDS tradition that Latter-day Saints of this era understood women to be at the gates of mortality.

2. Susanna Morrill, *White Roses on the Floor of Heaven: Mormon Women's Popular Theology, 1880–1920* (New York: Routledge, 2006), 121–23.

Women's physical bodies served as the literal gates by which human souls entered the next stage of existence in the plan of salvation.[3] In many ways, this LDS theological view conforms to larger American Victorian popular understandings that God sent children to mothers, whose divine mission included an inescapable responsibility for shaping their moral and religious lives.[4] But in the LDS community, this idea had clear theological grounding. In LDS theology, the birth process started with the Mother in Heaven. In the nineteenth and early twentieth centuries, LDS theology held that God the Father was a physical, embodied being who paired with a divine Mother in Heaven to produce spirit children in a premortal spirit world.[5]

This concept is theologically important for two reasons. First, in LDS theology of this era, the divine birth of spirit children directly

---

3. This idea also appears in the contemporary LDS women's literature. An article from the *Woman's Exponent* argues: "Our girls must have a better knowledge of themselves, know how to take care of their own bodies how to dress, eat, exercise, work and study for the highest development of themselves, and then they will be in a condition to furnish bodies worthy of the noble spirits that are to roll on the work in this Last Dispensation, to make ready for the coming of our Lord and Savior, Jesus Christ." R.S.D., "The Economy of Women," *Woman's Exponent* 24, 5 (Aug. 1, 1895): 40. Laura Louisa Smith, "A Short Sketch of the life of Laura Louisa Smith," 35, Church History Library, Church of Jesus Christ of Latter-day Saints, Salt Lake City (hereafter CHL), expressed the same idea: "I felt devinely called, that I was in partnership with god in bringing into the world bodis [sic] for the spirit children of god to dwell in while here on the Earth."

4. For the religious roles of mothers in mainstream Protestant traditions, see Marilyn J. Westerkamp, *Women and Religion in Early America, 1600–1850: The Puritan and Evangelical Traditions* (New York: Routledge, 1999), 131–41. Popular literature also expressed the concept that babies were heaven-sent and that motherhood was a sacred power—for example:

In our home, where light and longing / Struggle sore thro' toil and strain, / Comes a presence, sweet and holy, / Thro' Life's sacrament of pain; / And a tender awe is blended / With our love's protecting balm, / As we kiss the baby features, / Nearest Heaven's immortal calm.

Elaine Goodale and Dora Read Goodale, "Nearest Heaven," *Apple-Blossoms: Verses of Two Children* (New York: G. P. Putnam's Sons, 1879), 130–31.

5. Joseph Smith also described God's embodiment in his King Follett Discourse in April 1844: "First, God Himself who sits enthroned in yonder heavens is a Man like unto one of yourselves—that is the great secret." Stan Larson, "The King Follett Discourse: A Newly Amalgamated Text," *BYU Studies* 18, 2 (1978): 7. Apostle John A. Widtsoe later talked about the divine pair: "Since we have a Father who is our God, we must also have a mother, who possesses the attributes of Godhood." John A. Widtsoe, *Rational Theology: As Taught by the Church of Jesus Christ of Latter-day Saints* (Salt Lake City: General Priesthood Committee, 1915), 65. For the development of the Mother in Heaven concept in LDS thought, see Linda P. Wilcox, "The Mormon Concept of a Mother in Heaven," *Sunstone* 5 (Sept./Oct. 1980): 9–15.

paralleled the later physical birth of these children into mortality. In the process of giving these children physical bodies and then giving birth to them, mortal mothers mirrored the work of the Mother in Heaven who gave them spiritual bodies and gave birth to them in the spirit world. Perhaps the parallel is even closer, given that there was no clear dichotomy between the spiritual and material in the early LDS Church. LDS founder Joseph Smith famously declared in revelation: "There is no such thing as immaterial matter. All spirit is matter, but it is more fine or pure, and can only be discerned by purer eyes" (LDS D&C 131:7). In both cases, mothers served as the literal gates of existence for these pre-mortal and mortal beings. The gates into spiritual existence and the gates into mortality were female in substance. It makes symbolic and logical sense that those assisting spirit children into mortality would be similarly female.

Second, those women assisting at birth beds and death beds—standing at the gates of mortality—were following the precedent of their Mother in Heaven. Nineteenth-century church leaders rarely mentioned the female divine figure in their sermons or publications. The figure of the Mother in Heaven was most clearly enunciated in the poem/hymn "O My Father," written by Eliza R. Snow in the 1840s. This hymn was extremely popular into the twentieth century and was used to open religious and secular meetings from surprise birthday parties to churchwide gatherings.[6] Perhaps most strikingly, on one occasion the hymn was sung at the moment of a young girl's passing.[7]

---

6. For instance, on June 19, 1890, the afternoon session of the Salt Lake Stake Relief Society meeting opened with the hymn. "Salt Lake Stake," *Woman's Exponent* 19, 1 (July 15, 1890): 31. The general Relief Society conference held on October 7, 1891, closed with it. "Relief Society Conference," *Woman's Exponent* 20, 8 (Oct. 15, 1891): 62. The Relief Society jubilee opened with "that Grand Invocation by Eliza R. Snow." "Relief Society Jubilee: Exercises at the Tabernacle," *Woman's Exponent* 20, 19 (Apr. 1, 1892): 140. At a party for the remembrance of deceased poet Hannah Tapfield King, the hymn was sung after the "ice cream and sweetmeats were served." "Memorial Day: Hannah T. King," *Woman's Exponent* 22, 1 (July 1 and 15, 1893): 6. The Tabernacle Choir sang the hymn at a public performance in Independence, Missouri, in the fall of 1893. "Salt Lake Tabernacle Choir," *Woman's Exponent* 22, 5 (Sept. 15, 1893): 37. On November 20, 1893, it was also sung at the surprise birthday party of Relief Society leader Mary Isabella Horne. "Three Quarters of a Century," *Woman's Exponent* 22, 9 (Dec. 1, 1893): 69.

7. "Death of a Sweet Child," *Woman's Exponent* 21, 6 (Sept. 15, 1892): 46. The death notice of Grace Victoria Winn records: "Often, she would request those who were around her to sing for her; and at the time when her last breath was drawn, they were singing her favorite hymn, 'O! my Father, Thou that dwellest,' she opened her eyes for a moment and

Latter-day Saints, then, most frequently encountered the Mother in Heaven in their communal ritual life. Snow's hymn describes the reality of premortal life and the last verse puts in the mouths of its singers the longing to return to this happier state and the first, divine parents:

When I leave this frail existence,
When I lay this mortal by,
Father, Mother, may I meet you
In your royal courts on high?
Then, at length, when I've completed
All you sent me forth to
With your mutual approbation
Let me come and dwell with you.[8]

In this one outstanding and oft-repeated description of her, the Mother in Heaven, paired with God the Father—the most prominent figure in the hymn—nurtures, sends off her spirit children to mortality, and then welcomes them back to the spirit world where they will continue to work and improve and wait for the end of time and the final resurrection.

This image, at least, is the way in which contemporary LDS women writers extrapolated the role of the Mother in Heaven from the hymn. Sometimes directly echoing the words of Snow's hymn, in LDS women's religious literature of this period, authors most often mention the Mother in Heaven when they describe spirit children leaving or re-entering the spirit world.[9] Jane Kartchner Morris's hymn, "Oh! My

---

smiled upon her friends, last of all, her mother, then closed them as if in peaceful sleep." The hymn was sung again after the dedicatory prayer was given at her grave.

8. George D. Pyper, *Stories of Latter-day Saint Hymns* (N.p., 1939), 1. This hymn is no. 292 in the current *Hymns* (Salt Lake City: Church of Jesus Christ of Latter-day Saints, 1985). See also Jill Mulvay Derr, "The Significance of 'O My Father' in the Personal Journey of Eliza R. Snow," *BYU Studies* 36, 1 (1996–97): 84–126.

9. Emily Hill Woodmansee quotes Snow's hymn in her poem, "Apostrophe … ," *Woman's Exponent* 16, 15 (Jan. 1, 1888): 113:

Free from this most "frail existence"— / Free to lay "this mortal by"— / Free to span the starry distance / To the "royal courts on high." / Ransomed spirit! deathless essence! / Hie thee hence to realms so fair; / Gain thy "Father's radiant presence;" / Greet thy noble "Mother there."

Louisa Lulu Greene Richards, "A Thread of Thought," *Woman's Exponent* 29, 6–7 (Aug. 15 and Sept. 1, 1900): 27, adds details to the less explicit departing scene in the hymn:

We were there, with God, our Father, / And voted "Thy will be done," / And our Mother, Queen in Heaven, / Smiled on us every one[.]

Mother," rewrites Snow's hymn to focus on the Mother in Heaven at center stage as she sends her spirit children off into mortality and welcomes them back to the spirit world after death.[10] In a short story published in the *Relief Society Magazine* in 1916, for instance, author Laura Moench Jenkins, in a fictional depiction, describes how the Mother in Heaven meets with and gives gifts to two of her spirit daughters before they leave for mortality. She is also the first to greet one who returns prematurely to the spirit world when the child's earthly mother has an abortion.[11]

As articulated in LDS women's writings of the time, one of the Mother in Heaven's most salient characteristic was that she sent off her loved ones to the journey of mortality and then welcomed them back to her and her consort's presence. When women assisted at the birth beds and deathbeds of their neighbors, they were mirroring in reverse the work of their divine mother. As the Mother in Heaven sent her children into mortality, Relief Society women stood ready to welcome them, just as the Mother in Heaven stood ready to welcome back her matured spirit children sent out from mortality by their Relief Society caretakers. Apparently, in the lived religion of the LDS Church, the gates into mortality were female and so were attendants who stood immediately on either side of them.

HISTORICAL CONTEXT

Relief Society women did not create LDS birth and death rituals from nothing; rather, within the context of distinctive LDS theology, they adapted practices common in mainstream American society. Historically, the function of women who attended their neighbors at times of birth and death is well known.[12] Women-driven birth and death practices were part of the lived religion of most American communities. Martha Ballard, a Maine midwife who kept a diary from 1785 to 1812, routinely documents the assistance of the mother's female relatives, friends, and neighbors during the delivery. For example, on October 3,

---

10. Jane Kartchner Morris, Journals and Reminiscences, Oct. 1916–Feb. 1971, 3:148, MS 14399, CHL.

11. Laura Moench Jenkins, "Beyond the Portals," *Relief Society Magazine* 3, 6 (June 1916): 325–34.

12. Carroll Smith-Rosenberg, *Disorderly Women: Visions of Gender in Victorian America* (Oxford, England: Oxford University Press, 1986), 60–71.

1789, Ballard describes one such communal scene: "Mrss. Goffs illness increased & shee was safe delivered at 11 hour & 30 minute morn a daughter. Her marm, Mrs Bullin, Mrs Ney were my assistants. Mrs. Jacson Came back at 1 h p.m."[13] Laurel Thatcher Ulrich, who edited the diary, terms this concept "social medicine" in which the midwife had a distinctive role as "the most visible and experienced person in a community of healers who shared her perspective, her obligations, her training, and her labor."[14] Ballard also recorded that women nursed the sick, attended the dying, and laid out bodies for burial.[15] In an example that shows the cross-fertilization between LDS and wider practices, Nancy Peirson, a first-generation LDS convert who was living with her non-LDS family in Massachusetts in the 1840s, also describes watching at the beds of dying friends and relatives and helping to make burial clothes, noting on one occasion that she "went to Mr Griffins and helped Mrs. Sharp make his shroud."[16] Women like Peirson brought these common American cultural practices with them when they converted to the LDS Church.

In the LDS community, however, female-identified birth and death rituals came to be associated specifically with the Relief Society and took on LDS theological meanings.[17] Relief Society leaders in the 1870s, most prominently Eliza R. Snow herself, could draw on the explicit encouragement of Joseph Smith in Nauvoo for the organization's combined practical and spiritual focus, including work around birth and death. According to the version of the Relief Society minutes of June 9, 1842, that were incorporated into the church's official history, Smith admonished Relief Society members that their work, properly performed, had vital significance: "you must repent and get the love of God. Away with self-righteousness. The best measure or principle to bring the poor to repentance is to administer to their wants—the

---

13. Laurel Thatcher Ulrich, *A Midwife's Tale: The Life of Martha Ballard, Based on Her Diary, 1785–1812* (New York: Alfred A. Knopf, 1991), 103.

14. Ulrich, *Midwife's Tale*, 64.

15. Ulrich, *Midwife's Tale*, 39, 72.

16. Nancy Peirson, Diary, Oct. 27, 1848[?], mssFAC 554, Huntington Library, San Marino, California. See also Jan. 7, 1849; Feb. 13, 1847.

17. Linda King Newell, "Gifts of the Spirit: Women's Share," in *Sisters in Spirit: Mormon Women in Historical and Cultural Perspective*, ed. Maureen Ursenbach Beecher and Lavina Fielding Anderson (Urbana: University of Illinois Press, 1992), 117.

Society is not only to relieve the poor, but to save souls."[18] Two months earlier in April 1842, Smith had explicitly assured members of the Relief Society that they were authorized to bless the sick in a manner parallel to priesthood blessings: "if the sisters should have faith to heal the sick, let all hold their tongues, and let every thing roll on."[19]

In the mid- to late nineteenth century, women engaged in the kind of social medicine Ulrich describes, combining the Relief Society's practical and spiritual work as they developed a distinctive LDS version of birth and death rituals. In Nauvoo in 1847, Patty Sessions, a well known and respected midwife, was set apart by Brigham Young and Heber C. Kimball to attend to the medical needs of the women of the LDS community.[20] Throughout her life, she delivered hundreds of infants following the practices of midwives across the country and, like them, carefully recorded payments for her services.[21] Interestingly, Sessions recorded that the patriarch who bestowed her patriarchal blessing upon her also "ordained" her to lay hands on the sick for healing, and her diary includes many examples of washing and anointing women for their health.[22]

In the St. George Stake in the late nineteenth and early twentieth centuries, the Relief Society presidency had responsibility for taking care of the sick, assisted at births, attended the dying, comforted the survivors, washed and laid out bodies, and attired them in burial clothing they had made. They routinely called on other Relief Society members to help perform these tasks, a pattern that was typical of most LDS Relief Societies.[23] Clothing for the dead who had been temple endowed also included temple-related clothing such as the apron or veil.

18. Minutes, June 9, 1842, *Joseph Smith Papers*, www.josephsmithpapers.org. Compare B. H. Roberts, ed, *History of the Church of Jesus Christ of Latter-day Saints*, 7 vols., 2nd ed. rev. (Salt Lake City: Deseret Book Co., 1976 printing), 5:24–25.

19. Minutes, Apr. 28, 1842, *Joseph Smith Papers*. Compare Roberts, ed., *History of the Church*, 4:603. For a discussion of this point, see Jill Mulvay Derr, Janath Russell Cannon, and Maureen Ursenbach Beecher, *Women of Covenant: The Story of Relief Society* (Salt Lake City: Deseret Book, 1992), 66.

20. Patty Sessions, *Mormon Midwife: The 1846–1888 Diaries of Patty Bartlett Sessions*, ed. Donna Toland Smart (Logan: Utah State University Press, 1997), 7.

21. Smart, ed., *Mormon Midwife*, 402.

22. Smart, ed., *Mormon Midwife*, 349; for examples, see 359, 360, 362, 368, 379.

23. Verna L. Dewsnup and Katharine M. Larson, comps., *Relief Society Memoirs: A History of Relief Society in St. George Stake, 1867–1956* (St. George Stake Relief Society, 1956), 39, 76, 157–60.

By at least the 1890s, one local Relief Society began to sell pre-made burial robes that presumably met the proper temple requirements.[24] In 1912, the Temple and Burial Clothing Department was established by the central Relief Society leadership to provide ready-made temple and burial garments to the entire church, though in some areas Relief Society women still sewed these garments on their own.[25] Ritualized death and birth care, in short, took on characteristic elements of LDS culture as they became integral parts of women's religious duties in the Relief Society.

The work of Eliza R. Snow offers a window into this process of development. Snow was an authoritative model for women to follow because of her vital role in the first Nauvoo Relief Society, for which she acted as the secretary. She was also considered to be a prophetess in her own right; the hymn "O My Father" was ranked as a revelation by her contemporaries.[26] Long after Snow's death in 1887, a 1916 article in the *Relief Society Magazine* highlighted Snow's active work at both birth beds and deathbeds along with her supervision of temple work for women: "She made many temple robes and other garments for the clothing of the dead. She was never idle." Furthermore, "no night was too dark, no distance too great, for her to go out and administer to the sick child or to the discouraged mother. She has waited upon thou-

---

24. According to Salt Lake Stake Relief Society leaders Mary Isabella Horne, Maria Young Dougall, and Gladys Woodmansee, "Our Shopping Department," *Young Woman's Journal* 2, 6 (1891): 289, their cooperative store was offering burial suits for sale, noting: "We make a specialty of temple clothing and burial suits." This function eventually became a full-fledged business, taken over by Beehive Clothing, with temple clothing, including burial raiment appropriate for endowed deceased members available through church-maintained distribution centers. The current *General Handbook* (Salt Lake City: The Church of Jesus Christ of Latter-day Saints, 2020), 27.3.9, provides detailed instructions for burial in temple clothing, including who may or may not be eligible, the recommendation that stake presidents "in areas where temple clothing may be difficult to obtain" should keep a complete set of temple clothing for a man and another for a woman on hand and, that "where cultural traditions or burial practices make this [being buried in temple clothing] inappropriate or difficult, the clothing may be folded and placed next to the body in the casket." The responsibility of dressing the deceased is now assigned to the family unless no one of the same gender is an endowed member. In that case, "the bishop asks the Relief Society president to invite an endowed woman to dress the body" and assigns an endowed man the parallel responsibility.

25. Derr, Cannon, and Beecher, *Women of Covenant*, 197. In 1938, Caddie Neilson, president of the Washington Ward Relief Society in the St. George Stake, reported that Relief Society women still made burial clothes. Dewsnup and Larson, *Relief Society Memoirs*, 79.

26. Derr, Cannon, and Beecher, *Women of Covenant*, 30.

sands and has washed and anointed multitudes of prospective mothers for their future confinements." [27] Snow modeled the essential role of women at the entrance into and exit from mortality; Relief Society women similarly accepted among their duties to minister at the childbeds and deathbeds of their friends, neighbors, and family members.

In mainstream American culture, especially urban Protestant culture, the concept of social medicine began to recede with the increasing professionalization of medicine. By the mid-nineteenth century, though at first with mixed success, medical leaders began to standardize medical education; they attempted to marginalize those, including midwives, whom they saw as falling outside of these standards.[28] Patients increasingly looked to male doctors associated with local medical schools or hospitals. By the early twentieth century, women often chose to have their children in hospitals assisted by doctors, nurses, and the latest in medical technology.[29] Exceptions to these trends occurred, especially in rural or immigrant communities.[30] Yet as the twentieth century progressed, most women preferred hospital births assisted by doctors.

Similarly, undertakers followed the example of the medical establishment as they self-consciously sought to become more professionalized. As historian James Farrell has documented, the National Funeral Directors Association was founded in 1882. This group pressed to take over the management from the family of the body and the funeral. After the 1880s, morticians encouraged embalming, the use of mass-produced caskets, and moving the funeral from the home parlor to the funeral parlor.[31]

However, LDS women continued to perform birth and death rituals well into the twentieth century. No doubt one reason was the lack

27. "The Mother of the Mothers in Israel: Eliza R. Snow," *Relief Society Magazine* 3, 4 (Apr. 1916): 186.

28. Geoffrey Marks and William K. Beatty, *Story of Medicine in America* (New York: Scribner, [1973]), 199; Smith-Rosenberg, *Disorderly Women*, 230–31.

29. Judith Walzer Leavitt, "'Twilight Sleep:' Technology and the Medicalization of Childbirth," in *Major Problems in the History of American Medicine and Health*, ed. John Harley Warner and Janet A. Tighe (Boston: Houghton Mifflin, 2001), 373.

30. For instance, Robert Orsi, *Madonna of 115th Street*, 132, notes that, even into the late nineteenth and early twentieth centuries, Catholic Italian immigrants in New York City often felt more comfortable calling to sickbeds older Italian women who were skilled in treating medical conditions, rather than opting for an American male doctor.

31. James J. Farrell, *Inventing the American Way of Death* (Philadelphia: Temple University Press, 1980), 152, 146, 157–60, 169–73, 172–75.

of qualified doctors in frontier Utah.[32] Yet from the founding of the Relief Society as encouraged by Joseph and Emma Smith, Snow, and other LDS leaders, this women's practical, charitable work also had great religious significance. The LDS community may have preserved these rituals longer precisely because they expressed deeply LDS religious meaning and identity for the men, women, and children of the community—meaning that developed over time and through lived experiences. And, in fact, after 1880, while other Americans increasingly deferred to funeral directors in caring for the corpse, Relief Society women continued to perform these last rites as an integral part of the burial process.[33] Even today women still dress the bodies of deceased loved ones.

Men were not absent during these critical times of entrance into and departure from mortality. However, nineteenth-century diaries, journals, poetry, and stories most often note and express appreciation for the presence of women. In their capacity as priesthood holders, men gave blessings to women before childbirth, to the ill, and to the dying.[34] During regular and special ward meetings, they led community members in prayers for the health, safety, and sometimes even welcome

32. The lack of medical care for women was a consistent concern for male and female church leaders. They encouraged women to obtain formal medical training at Eastern colleges and also established nursing and obstetrical courses in Utah under the auspices of the Relief Society. Derr, Cannon, and Beecher, *Women of Covenant*, 106–07.

33. Farrell, *Inventing the American Way of Death*, 147–50. There is a clear connection between the Relief Society's diminishing authority and autonomy and the increasing restrictions placed on women washing, anointing, and giving blessings to other women. The central leadership of the church had banned these practices by the mid-twentieth century as part of a larger process of standardizing church practices and repositioning the Relief Society as an auxiliary rather than an institution that was seen to be somewhat parallel to the priesthood. See D. Michael Quinn, "Women Have Had the Priesthood since 1843," in *Women and Authority: Re-emerging Mormon Feminism*, ed. Maxine Hanks (Salt Lake City: Signature Books, 1992), 365–409; Newell, "Gifts of the Spirit: Women's Share," 111–50. Other aspects of birth and death rituals seem to have gradually fallen away in the twentieth century as Latter-day Saints increasingly followed wider American culture in using the services of doctors and morticians.

34. Midwife Patty Sessions records numerous blessings from priesthood holders when she was ill. Smart, ed., *Mormon Midwife*, 302, 328, 330. A dramatic example is President Lorenzo Snow's administering to Ella Wight Jensen, a young woman in her twenties, on her deathbed and reportedly calling her back from "the other world." Jensen said she had already crossed the threshold into the next world when she heard Snow inform her: "Sister Ella you must come back as your mission is not yet finished here on this earth." Ella Wight Jensen, Statement 1934, Feb. 5, Salt Lake City, 3, MS 374, CHL.

death of terminal sufferers.[35] They blessed babies and dedicated graves.[36] In some communities, certain men had the assignment of washing and dressing male corpses.[37] Men were present and important actors at times of birth and death, exercising their priesthood power to smooth over these difficult times. Yet in the lived religion of the community, it was women who dominated at the moments of birth and death.

The assumed presence of women is vividly demonstrated in a fictional story from the *Young Woman's Journal,* a publication of the Young Ladies Mutual Improvement Association (now succeeded by Young Women for girls ages twelve to eighteen). The protagonist, Inid, describes waking up, at first unable to speak or move, but gradually realizes that she is in a coffin, the apparent victim of a drowning. Though Inid requires three pages to put the pieces together, the reader instantly grasps the situation because Inid is aware of a group of women friends and relatives who are speaking in hushed tones and working on a white garment. "Gradually her sight grew clearer, and she could distinguish the people in the room— one of them a neighbor, Mrs. Burbidge, the others her mother and Aunt Julia. They were sewing on some filmy white material, edged with delicate lace and it seemed to Inid that it looked like a wedding garment."[38] The author, well-known LDS writer Josephine Spencer, was tapping into an easily recognized element of her readers' lived religion and using it as a literary device to juxtapose their awareness against Inid's increasingly annoying obtuseness and denial of her "death." What else would a group of women speaking in hushed, mournful tones and sewing beautiful white robes be doing but making burial garments for a corpse?

BIRTH RITUALS

In the diaries and journals of LDS women and men from the 1870s through the 1920s, women are the constant, background presence at

---

35. Anna Griffiths, Diary, June 10, 1923, MS 9618, CHL, notes that her family was instructed to dedicate their Aunt Lillie to the Lord because someone with great faith was holding her to the earth.

36. Elder Joseph H. Felt dedicated the grave of Victoria Grace Winn. "Death of a Sweet Child," *Woman's Exponent* 21, 6 (Sept. 15, 1892): 46.

37. Juliaetta Bateman Jensen, *Little Gold Pieces: The Story of My Mormon Mother's Life* (Salt Lake City: Stanway Printing Co. & Hiller Bookbinding Co., 1948), 143, reports that her father washed and dressed deceased men in their community. He also provided this service to President John Taylor (120–22).

38. Josephine Spencer, "Cross Lines," *Young Woman's Journal* 10, 9 (1899): 395–96.

these difficult times. Though multiple Relief Society women usually assisted at births and deaths, often the central figure was the midwife who helped at times of birth and death, because, all too often, the times of birth became times of death for either the mother or infant. In his diary, Allen Frost, for instance, describes the harrowing scene of the death of his wife, Elsie, after she gave birth to a daughter in January 1880. She had not expelled the afterbirth; the local midwife and her assistants, desperately "wished me to call in Sister Judd, who is also a midwife, to see if she can remove the afterbirth."[39] Though the afterbirth was finally expelled two days later, Elsie, after another three days, died with much suffering. On each of these agonizing days, Frost lists the presence of three or four women in constant attendance, trying to help Elsie, relieve her pain, and make her more comfortable.[40] Similarly, in his diary in February 1902, Osmer D. Flake described how eight local women assisted his family when his young son died after an extended illness: "Mary sees to the clothes. Pearl Turley sat up the after part of the night. Sisters West, Sarah Hunt, Bell Flake, Nellie Hunt, Blanck [Blanche?] Flake & Pearl McLaws are helping Mary."[41] Women were the assumed, collective presence at these times; they were the quiet supporters of the central actors who were coming into or leaving the mortal world. Women also encouraged and comforted family members and made sure that the daily round of chores and meals continued, despite the upset of events.

The assistance that Relief Society women provided at childbirth was vital because these moments involved great psychological upheaval: joy, anticipation, and anxiety. Relief Society women were essential for providing emotional support and physical comfort at these times. Indeed, motherhood was the main religious role that women were expected to play in the LDS community. Throughout the writings of this time period, priesthood and Relief Society leaders consistently expressed the centrality of motherhood for women. At the funeral of Catherine Perkes McAllister, the stake president, Nephi L. Morris, proclaimed in tribute: "I sometimes feel in the presence of a woman who has filled the full measure of her being as a mother, and has done so acceptably

39. Allen Frost, Diary, Jan. 23, 1880, MSS MFilm 00130, Huntington Library.
40. Frost, Diary, Jan. 23–28, 1880.
41. Osmer D. "Oz" Flake, Diary, Feb. 28, 1902, MSS MFilm 00096, Huntington Library.

to those to whom she owed such sacred obligations, that I stand in the presence of the most sacred life conceivable."[42]

Most women of this era communicate great eagerness for motherhood. In her autobiography, Edna Richardson, originally of West Jordan, joyfully compares the anticipated birth of her first child to the arrival of an angel: "My little angel, that God in his goodness was sending to me to love, and to cherish and to care for as long as he should see fit to leave her with me."[43] On the birth of this first child, she noted: "My darling baby—I wish I could put into words my feeling for this little bit of Heaven that had come into our home."[44] Richardson and her contemporaries looked forward to welcoming, as they saw it, those visitors from heaven whom they were assigned to guide, nurture, and protect through their early journeys on earth.

Yet because of still-high rates of infant and maternal mortality, these times of birth were also fraught with anxiety and real danger. Jane Hindley, just past her own child-bearing years, noted in her journal in March 1874 that one of her friends had died in childbirth, another terrible blow to Hindley who had already suffered through the painful process of having her husband take a plural wife (she was the first wife), the death of an infant son whom she never forgot, and at least two miscarriages. She wrote: "Today a Dear frie[n]d of [mine?] Died in child Bed the boy is all right but the Mother is gon and left Eight children. ... I spent a day with her just before she was taken ill it has caused me to have very solemn thoughts."[45] Perhaps because of her own experiences and her friend's death, Hindley was "quite anxious

---

42. Nephi Morris "Beautiful Tribute to Motherhood," *Woman's Exponent* 35, 8 (Mar. 1907): 57. Mothers were seen as having great power for good or ill. Aunt Ruth, "Our Children," *Woman's Exponent* 15, 24 (May 15, 1887): 189, quoted Brigham Young as saying: "I will tell you the truth as you will find it in eternity. If your children do not receive impressions of true piety, virtue, tenderness, and every principle of the holy Gospel, you may be assured that their sins will not be required at the hands of the father, but of the mother." Apostle Rudger Clawson, "Birth Control," *Relief Society Magazine* 3, 7 (July 1916): 364, took the position that women could safely have eight to ten children, perhaps more: "The law of her nature so ordered it, and God's command, while it did not specify the exact number of children allotted to woman, simply implied that she should exercise the sacred power of procreation to it utmost limit."

43. Edna Rae Cummings Richardson, "Down Memory Lane," [1965?], 114, MS 9962, CHL.

44. Richardson, "Down Memory Lane," 115.

45. Jane Charters Robinson Hindley, Journal 1855–1905, Mar. 17, 1874, MS 1764, CHL.

about My [daughter] Ester she Expects to be confined soon I Pray God that all will be well with her. I shall be so thankfull when it is over and she is well again."[46]

Interestingly, like Hindley, in their personal writings, LDS women rarely expressed concern for their own safety. Rather, they focus on the health and well-being of husbands, children, family, and friends—as their community expected.[47] If they had felt differently, it seems unlikely that they would have recorded these feelings since these diaries and journals were usually written to be histories and salutary tales for future generations.[48] Writers tend to present themselves in the best light possible. Still, judging from the anxious reflections of Hindley and others on the birthing process of loved ones, women must have

---

46. Hindley, Journal, May 18, 1874. More than twenty years later, another daughter, Minnie, lost a child, and Hindley could not bear to witness the scene just a few days before the infant boy's death: "I have been at Minnies this afternoon her Baby is very ill, and Minnie is frantic for fear it will die I tried all I possably could to comfort her but could not. ... I was so upset that I had to leave[.]" Ibid., Nov. 8, 1898.

47. A repeated theme in LDS women's literature of this period was that an important part of being a mother was to suffer and sacrifice oneself on behalf of loved ones. During the height of the US government's campaign against polygamy, Relief Society general president Zina D. H. Young argued that it was women's duty to suffer while caring for the well-being of the community: "Isaiah says the daughters of Zion shall be polished after the similitude of a palace, and this will be brought about by all doing their duty, and may all have the gift of wisdom with power to overcome that we may have faith to feed the flocks that they faint not." Z. D. H. Y., "Letter to the Sisters," *Woman's Exponent* 19, 7 (Sept. 15, 1890): 54. Morris, "Beautiful Tribute," 57, praised Catherine Perkes McAllister for her self-sacrifice: "She was, like many other women, a sufferer. It seems to me that the apotheosis of woman is through her suffering, and in her destined sorrows she nearest approaches the Son of Man, the greatest of sufferers. ... He is approached, I say, more nearly by woman in her sufferings for others, than by anyone else."

48. There is internal evidence that women such as Martha Cragun Cox, Elizabeth Ramsay Fraser, and Marie M. C. Jensen intended even their private writings to be read. Cox titled her autobiography, now housed in the Church History Library: "Biographical Records of Martha Cox. Written for my children and my children's children, and all who may care to read it." Similarly, she opens her work with the explanatory note: "There are few lives so uneventful that a true record of them would not be of some worth—in which there are no happenings that can serve as guide or warning to those that follow. It is to be hoped that in the pages that follow there will be somethings found that may be taken as good lessons to those who read." MS 1661, CHL. Elizabeth Ramsay Fraser, Diary, July 2, 1887, MS 149, CHL, opened her diary noting that thirty years had passed since her birth had begun "a life of joy and sorrow of which I intend showing forth on these pages. Praying that the Lord will strengthing me, and bring to my mind or cause me to think correctly and write the same." Marie M. C. Jensen, Diary, Jan. 1, 1900, MS 14155, CHL, echoed similar themes in her opening entry: "I have decided to [write?] me a journal that my children can have when I am no more."

feared for their own safety as well since childbirth was still all too often fatal for mothers and infants.[49]

As a result of these hard realities and the resulting fears, Relief Society members, as well as male priesthood holders, would often bless expectant mothers before childbirth. Relief Society women took an active role in attempting to stabilize these joyful but dangerous times of birth, providing reassurance and comfort with overtly religious rituals. As Linda King Newell has shown, the practice by women seems to have often involved a detailed ritual of washing the expectant mother in water while speaking blessings and then repeating the process with consecrated oil.[50] These blessings bear some formal similarity to washings, anointings, and blessings performed during temple ceremonies.[51]

From the relatively scanty evidence, it appears that the women who gave these blessings were often (though not always) midwives—a logical extension of their practical work in attempting to bring mothers and infants through the process in a healthy state. For instance, Susannah Fowler, a midwife and folk doctor, was also "called" by local church officials to wash and anoint women in connection with childbearing. In June 1900, she noted: "Called to assist in washing and anointing three sisters. Ettie Norton and Laurie Wimmer preparatory to confinement, and Mary Brasher for barrenness. Took part with all."[52] This brief mention of her participation underscores that these rituals were part of the fabric of everyday life even as it obscures their power and meaning for the women administering and receiving them.

WASHINGS, ANOINTINGS, AND BLESSINGS

Those giving the blessings pronounced in association with washing and anointing were generally middle-aged or older, respected women.

---

49. Laurel Thatcher Ulrich, *Midwife's Tale*, 170, comments: "But as late as 1930, there was one maternal death for every 150 births in the United States; the major gains in obstetrical safety have come in the past fifty years." According to Derr, Cannon, and Beecher, *Women of Covenant*, 231, in 1922, Relief Society general president Clarissa Smith Williams urged spending more on infant and maternal care because of what she saw as an unacceptably high death rate among mothers and infants in the church that year: 58 mothers and 751 babies.

50. Newell, "Gifts of the Spirit," 131.

51. David John Buerger, *The Mysteries of Godliness: A History of Mormon Temple Worship* (San Francisco: Smith Research Associates, 1994), 11, 23, 36–40, 78–81, 105.

52. Mary Susannah Fowler, Diary, June 4, 1900, MS 0318, Special Collections, Marriott Library, University of Utah, Salt Lake City.

If they were not midwives, like Patty Sessions and Susannah Fowler, they held other positions of responsibility and respect. For instance, Ruth May Fox, eventually the general president of the Young Ladies Mutual Improvement Association, regularly washed and anointed local women before childbirth and, more generally, for their health. On March 6, 1900, when she was in her late forties, she noted in her diary that she attended a Relief Society meeting in Salt Lake City and "from their went with Sister Elisabeth Stephenson to wash and anoint Sister Edith [Smith?] Pendleton previous to her [confinement?] My first time."[53] Just two years later in Spring City, Utah, Marie M. C. Jensen, then in her mid-forties, also made particular note of her first time: "Been called to assist in washing an anointing Antomine Larsen for her confinement. Ellen Julegren[,] Stina Acord[,] Maria Larsen it was our first attempt an we felt very weak an humble but I pray the Lord will ecnolech [acknowledge?] our work, an she may recived the bennefit."[54] Women like Fox and Larsen felt privileged and humbled to step in at these delicate times. They felt the weightiness of their work and the importance and danger of the transitional times that they were attempting, at some level, to control.

We can see some of the emotional and spiritual results of these blessings for the recipients in one of the few extended descriptions of the process written from the point of view of a woman receiving the blessing. In this case the blessing was for illness, rather than pregnancy. Anna F. Griffiths of Salt Lake City had a chronic condition, diabetes, of which she eventually died. In hopes of improving her health when she was a teenager, two local, older, respected women washed and anointed her for her health. She was so moved by her experience that she included an in-depth description of the event. As she expresses, the prayers of such rituals put women and their ailments in the hands of God, provided the physical comfort of tender touch and the spiritual sustenance of prophetic blessings by friends who knew the afflicted intimately. Preparatory to the blessing, Griffiths bathed and then lay in a gown on her couch:

> The sisters had a word of prayer offered by grandma Eardley. In that
> prayer she asked for the Lord to be with them that day in their work and

53. Ruth May Fox, Diaries, 1894–1931, Mar. 6, 1900, MS 6348 1–2, CHL.
54. Marie Jensen, Diary, Nov. 12, 1902.

to bless me his handmaid. To look over our faults and imperfections, and if there was anything standing that day, between us & God, to forgive and make me well. Then they started their blessed work. Sister Burnham washed me with water to cleanse my whole body. Sister Eardley followed drying. First sister Burnham washed my forehead, asking as she washed it, for my pain to be [cleared?], that I would be able to discern right from wrong, then my eyes that I may always have my natural sight, my cheeks that I would have the glow of health and purity in them, my nose that I would always be able to smell, my lips that I would always praise God, my ears that I could hear the still small voice and heed its warning. Then she washed my back and shoulders and asked for blessings upon them, my chest that I would not catch colds in it or anything of any evil nature come to it, also washed my stomach and then my legs, and lastly my feet, so I could run and not be weary and be able to go into the Lord's house and perform dutys and praise the Lord all my days.[55]

The women "sealed" the washings with a prayer and then "Grandma Eardley" followed the washing by anointing Griffiths's body with oil and repeating almost the same prayers and in the same order. Again, the procedure was "sealed" with a prayer and the women left with assurances that she would get well. Indeed, Griffiths felt great confidence in their work, noting: "When sister Eardley was set apart of this work, she was promised by one of the presi[?]e[?]dents of our church who set her apart, that never a case would be lost, where she had helped to wash & anoint them, but they would get well."[56]

By ritually invoking the power of God upon Griffiths, this ceremony had beneficial psychological and spiritual effects for the young woman. During the blessings, she was overwhelmed with the power of the work, reflecting: "When the dear soul [Eardley] had knelt at my feet and was rubbing them with her hands, I couldn't help but let a few tears fall, to think of those dear sisters being so humble, that they could even wash peoples feet. It reminded me also of the savior and the lesson taught by him." In their actions, the women were recapitulating the words and actions of Jesus Christ as he demonstrated his authority through humble service to others. In these difficult times of transition,

55. Anna F. Griffiths, Diary, Mar. 20, 1926. Newell, "Gifts of the Spirit," 130, notes that Relief Society women seem to have formulated standardized forms of prayers given during washings and anointings, although these forms were not required by church leaders.
56. Griffiths, Diary, Mar. 20, 1926.

women sought to tap into the spiritual power of their—according to LDS theology—elder brother, Jesus Christ. This blessing brought great peace to Griffiths who felt a positive sense of calm and peace as a result: "It has been about an hour since those sisters left, and I feel well, my head has stopped aching, and I am thrilled beyond words. I have something to live for and my body is clean."[57] In birth and healing rituals women provided spiritual and physical comfort. Indeed, it is hard to see where the physical ends and the spiritual begins.

DEATH RITUALS

Although Anna Griffiths's record is unusual in its detail, it was not an unusual experience for women suffering from various ailments; its logical connection to the experience of childbirth is obvious. Washing was also associated with the deathbed—the second major transition between immortality and mortality. Just as Relief Society members cared for women and their babies, so they were prepared the bodies of their sisters in the faith for death and burial, both processes that required cleanliness and appropriate clothing. Susannah Fowler, who had helped in washing and anointing Ettie Norton for childbirth, also attended the birth and had the responsibility to "wash and dress the baby."[58] Similarly, the main death rituals in which women participated were attending the dying, making the burial clothes, washing and dressing the corpse, laying out the body, and attending and sitting up at night with the body until the actual funeral.

Throughout public and private women's literature, the two functions—assistance at childbed and deathbed—are linked. A history of the Gunlock Ward in southern Utah in the late nineteenth century makes this common link: "During these early years, the Relief Society sisters, especially in the small isolated wards, were called upon to assist in caring for the sick and needy, acting as midwives, and preparing bodies for burial. They went day or night, through storm or sunshine, heat or cold, to help in these activities."[59] On a more personal level, Julina L. Smith paid tribute to one of her plural sister wives: "Though you [the deceased plural wife] have left us sorrowing I know your five

---

57. Griffiths, Diary, Mar. 20, 1926.
58. Fowler, Diary, June 25, 1900.
59. Dewsnup and Larson, *Relief Society Memoirs*, 120.

SUSANNA MORRILL

precious ones, and Aunt Edna's [another plural wife] four, and my one who preceded you, are rejoicing in this reunion. As we stood by each other to assist and welcome the new-born, so we stood side by side when the angel of death visited our home."[60] Smith associated these exits and entrances as parallel inversions of each other and also, significantly, as places where women "stood by each other," forging strong, deep bonds with each other.

Similar to experiences in blessing and assisting in births, those who participated in preparing the bodies saw it as a sacred duty and were often overwhelmed at their first experience with it. Added to the fears of mismanaging a sacred moment were fears associated with handling the dead. In the mid-1860s, St. George teenager Martha Cragun Cox was sent by her mother to sit up with a sick infant in a neighbor's home during an epidemic. In this case, the baby died when Martha Cragun Cox was on watch. "When it was all over, the mother asked me if I would not perform the next sad rights [sic]," meaning to wash, dress, and lay out the baby's corpse. "I could not refuse as there was no other way," Martha recorded, adding even after the recollection of years: "I did the best I could but suffered under the ordeal and when I had washed the little fellow and wrapped him in a piece of and an [sic] old white window curtain I laid him out on the flat top of an old chest."[61] While death in LDS theology was seen as a gateway to another, better realm, its physical reality was unsettling and uncomfortable. This young woman was unsure, frightened, and even repelled the first time that she performed these burial preparations.

It was unusual for such a young woman to take part in the death rituals, and no doubt it was primarily the epidemic that pressed Cox

---

60. Julina L. Smith, "A Loving Tribute to Sarah Ellen Richards Smith," *Relief Society Magazine* 2, 5 (May 1915): 216.

61. Cox, Autobiography, 112. A slightly later account from the 1940s shows that even older, experienced women felt ambivalent about these duties, although they also saw them as bonding experiences. Pauline A. Mathis, South Ward Relief Society, St. George Stake, wrote: "In this kind of service, trying to relieve the sick and bereaved, facing the serious side of life so much of the time, we girls grew very close. I learned to appreciate the keen sense of humor, both Eola and Fern had. We always went to the mortuary to dress the female and children members, and one morning while dressing a sister, in the dead silence a chicken squaked [sic] outside the mortuary window, Eola flinched and said, 'Oh, what's that?' She was so frightened, but after we decided what it was we enjoyed a good laugh." Dewsnup and Larson, *Relief Society Memoirs*, 188.

into service. Most women who performed the rituals were midwives or active members of the Relief Society who had sometimes been formally appointed to the roles. Olive Woolley Kimball, president of her local Arizona Relief Society, often sat up with the sick and dying and made countless burial outfits, but it was not until October 1901, over six months after she became ward Relief Society president, that she assisted in the washing and dressing of a corpse. Though Kimball typically wrote in a straightforward manner and with little overt emotion or commentary, this event had a strong impact on her: "Before breakfast I went and took the clothes to the Bishops and helped dress their boy first time in my life that I ever helped dress a corpse but we got it done alright and then I went home got my breakfast washed and dressed baby, got myself ready and then went to the funeral."[62] No doubt because of the inevitable intensity of the experience, most women who formally or informally managed these death experiences were, like Kimball, middle-aged or older and of calm, steady temperament.[63]

On the surface, these death rituals were simply practical. One of the reasons that women sat up with the dying was the possibility of an unexpected rallying or of an unusual happening at the moment of death. Similarly, sitting up with body had the practical purposes of watching for signs of life. People feared being buried alive, a fear legitimated by enough instances (and even more reports) about a "dead" loved one who revived.[64] Another practical consideration was the condition of the corpse. In warm weather, watchers might change bottles

---

62. Olive Woolley Kimball, Journal, Oct. 18, 1901, MS 2136, CHL.

63. For instance, Patty Sessions, who was a midwife, also washed and dressed corpses for burial. Smart, ed. *Mormon Midwife*, 22. She was in her late thirties when she joined the church. Midwife Susannah Fowler, Diary, Mar. 25, 1900, recorded in her late thirties that she helped to prepare the dead for burial. The short, straightforward entries in the diaries of all three women—Kimball, Sessions, and Fowler—demonstrate that other women looked to them as experts and leaders in times of trouble because of their pragmatic, level-headed personalities.

64. An obituary notes that Elizabeth Timpson was apparently dead about fifteen minutes, reviving only when the family was about to begin preparing her body for burial. Sadly, Timpson did die shortly afterward. "In Memoriam: Elizabeth Timpson," *Woman's Exponent* 27, 18 and 19 (Feb. 15 and Mar. 1, 1899): 110–11. Harriet O. Lee recorded an extended description of her experiences in the spirit world when she appeared to be dead for forty-eight hours. She awoke to find a coffin in her room and funeral preparations underway. She lived for many decades after this incident. Harriet O. Lee, "A Remarkable Vision," (recorded 1901), MS 6282, CHL. One family delayed their mother's burial for four days because she feared being buried alive. M. E. Bond, "Extracts: Letters to Mrs. H. M. Whitney," *Woman's Exponent* 11, 19 (Mar. 1883): 151.

of ice packed around the body to slow its decay and to protect it from insects and rodents.[65]

There were also psychological aspects to the rituals—people wanted their loved ones to look their best for their burial. An endowed person would be clothed in white temple apparel. Even those who were not endowed were customarily clothed in white.[66] As reported in the spring 1901 edition of the *Woman's Exponent,* a publication associated with the Relief Society, "Elder Arnold Giaque" of the Sixth Ward in Salt Lake City praised the Relief Society sisters for "the magnitude of the work which had been done by the sisters. When the angel of death enters into a family, they are ministers of peace to cheer and comfort the bereaved, to clothe our dear ones who are called home in suitable robes. 'I have received of their kindness at a time of this kind. I appreciate it more than I can express.'"[67] As a vital part of this work of comforting, women strove to make the dead attractive to their relatives. In accounts of burials, the bereaved record vivid memories of the last glimpses of their loved ones in their coffins. These descriptions functioned as memory snapshots for the mourners. Jean Brown Fonnesbeck in 1917 article recorded such a moment about her grandmother: "I shall never forget how beautiful she looked on her burial day. She was robed all in the purest white with a shimmering, gauzy veil like a halo about her head." Relatives noticed how lovely and calm she looked. A friend exclaimed: "'How beautiful she is! She looks like a bride.'"[68] Fonnesbeck leaves the reader with the image of her grandmother as a bride a second time to her husband, whom she would soon meet in the higher realm.[69] Such descriptions obviously comforted family members.

---

65. Jensen, *Little Gold Pieces,* 143, describes how her father obtained ice to delay deterioration of bodies. Relief Society women in southern Utah also used ice. Dewsnup and Larson, *Relief Society Memoirs,* 188.

66. E. Gordon Erickson, "A Sociological Study of Funeral Customs and Legal Burial Requirements in Utah" (master's thesis, University of Utah, 1939), 19–20.

67. "Sixth Ward Anniversary," *Woman's Exponent* 29, 22 and 23 (Apr. 1 and May 1, 1901): 100.

68. Jean Brown Fonnesbeck, "Grandmother Middleton," *Young Woman's Journal* 28, 3 (1917): 142. Similarly, in an obituary of Louisa Larsen, her husband noted: "She was beautiful even in death and she was laid away neatly in a nice white coffin, and the children will hold this in dear remembrance." Lauritz Larsen, "Obituary," *Woman's Exponent* 21, 11 (Dec. 1, 1892): 88.

69. Fonnesbeck, "Grandmother Middleton," 142.

Such details were not only comforting observances of the community's conventions but also, apparently, set in motion vital religious
consequences. Writings of this period, though not articulated as formal
doctrine, seem to communicate the expectation that the deceased would
enter the afterlife garbed in his or her burial apparel and that omitting
customary rituals would impact the deceased spirit's reception in the
afterlife. In an article in the *Young Woman's Journal,* Mary B. Crandal
of Springville, Utah, described a dream about her youngest daughter,
Eliza.[70] In the mother's dream, Eliza, robed in beautiful white garments
and holding a bouquet of flowers, ascended toward heaven as Crandal
begged God to spare her daughter. Crandal interpreted the dream as
predicting her daughter's death, and, in fact, teenaged Eliza died one
year later. Crandal averred that the dream had been a true prophecy
since the Relief Society women, without any suggestions from Crandal,
made Eliza a white cashmere burial dress that looked exactly like the
clothing in which Eliza had been attired in Crandal's dream.

Another motivation for providing proper cleanliness, clothing, and
laying out of the deceased was the possibility that the deceased might,
when the caregivers themselves died, reproach them with neglect. At a
meeting of the Granite Stake Relief Society in Salt Lake City in 1904,
members were encouraged to give all dead meticulous care to avoid
such postmortal rebukes: "The topics touched on were in relation to
our traveling sister missionaries, the special missionary work and the
Temple work, also that the dead should be laid away in a proper manner, that the poor as well as the rich should be clothed in the best
material, that they should have no cause to reproach us when we meet
them, that the sick, the poor and needy are tenderly cared for."[71] Such
explanations are perhaps best explained as ways to enforce appropriate
observances of conventions regarding the dead, though they also suggest anxiety about a loved one's transition to the spirit world if she or
he were not properly clothed.

This anxiety resurfaces repeatedly in women's writings of this era.
Rhoda Smith Allred of Lewiston, Utah, expressed the dual anxiety
about handling the dead and the proper preparation of the dead when

---

70. Mary B. Crandal, "A Dream and Its Fulfillment," *Young Woman's Journal* 7, 3
(1895): 127–31.
71. "R. S. Reports. Granite Stake," *Woman's Exponent* 32, 10 (Mar. 1904): 77.

she and a neighbor attended a dying neighbor, then prepared her body for burial. "My neighbor lady and myself fixed her for burial and put her in the casket and carried it out of doors. When we got to the door two of the handles came off. There wasn't a man brave enough to take the lid off so I did it myself and straightened her in place and put the lid back on."[72] Allred's characterization of the action as "brave" confesses her own fear but also her powerful motivation to open the coffin and be sure that the corpse presented a seemly appearance.

Fears about the proper arrangement of the dead even manifested in the dreaming unconscious of one woman. In 1887, Elizabeth Ramsay Fraser was deeply disturbed by a dream in which Ruth Hunt Fraser's body (apparently her deceased sister wife) would be moved to another burial spot. Some of her anxiety stemmed from the dedicatory blessing that had been given at the grave ten years earlier. This blessing promised that "the body of Ruth Hunt Fraser was to rest there untill the morning of the resurrection unless removed by friends and I dreamed that I had not one friend in Richfield."[73] Because of this warning, in her dream she feared that the blessing's promise would be invalidated and would not let anyone touch the grave until she got Ruth Hunt Fraser's father to accompany her to the graveyard.

An even keener anxiety surfaced when Fraser dreamed that they opened the coffin and viewed Ruth Hunt Frazer's body: "I smoothed my hand over her forehead and hair and found that she was warm and had no vail nor apron on I run to town and got a vail and apron from Martha [Horne?] and put them on her and We had such a time to get the coffin lid to stay on after we had taken it off and when it was shoved off to eather side I could see the Robe and under clothing all drawn up and seen her bare feet and legs and I fixed them several times befor I could get them to lay all right but I replaced new what was lacking and left her laying in peace and in good order[.]"[74] Fraser's report of her

72. Rhoda Luann B. Smith Allred, Oral History, 7, Utah State Historical Society, Salt Lake City.

73. Fraser, Diary, Aug. 23, 1887.

74. Fraser, Diary, Aug. 23, 1887. Mary Harding's husband, George, shielded her from a similar, but real-life situation when her brother's body was moved to another burial place. Still, Harding suffered anxiety even after she had found out about it—her feelings had not been totally spared. Nonetheless, she was assured that the body was indeed that of her brother. George, "with the help of other men attended to this without my knowledge of the time it was to be accomplished for he thought it would grieve me too much if I knew

dream expresses no fear of the corpse, only concern in the seemliness of the body's appearance. Fraser's anxiety focuses on the general disarray of Ruth Hunt Fraser's burial clothing and the two missing items. She struggled to cover the bared legs and finally successfully arranged the apparel, leaving the corpse lying "in peace and in good order."

It was critical in Fraser's dream that Ruth Hunt Fraser be attired properly in a temple veil and apron, perhaps signifying her postmortal status as someone who had received the temple ordinances essential to salvation.[75] As David Buerger shows, early Latter-day Saints believed that the pattern of temple garments was revealed from heaven and that authoritative heavenly messengers such as Peter, James, John, and Jesus wore such garments when they visited Joseph Smith and other early church leaders. Specific items of clothing associated with the temple endowment were important in ceremonies during which faithful members were given names, signs, and tokens that would allow them to reach the highest state of exaltation in the afterlife. This apparel thus was part of a constellation of knowledge and behaviors that helped propel the initiate to the highest rank of eternal life—and church leaders directed that only those who had gone through the proper temple ceremonies should be buried in them.[76] Fraser was determined that her loved one would be dressed for the afterlife in raiment that symbolized her high spiritual state.

In the end, this coalescence of hope and fear also demonstrates Fraser's potential agency as she properly dressed this particular corpse. Hope is seen in the promise of the resurrection as symbolized by the still preserved corpse.[77] More importantly, at this time of psychological

they were doing it. After the body had been reburied he told me about it. I asked him if he were positive he had taken up the right body. When he told me the foot bones had been separated from the leg bones I knew he had made no mistake and was comforted." Mary Jones Harding, "Diary and Reminiscence," 99, MS 14358, CHL.

75. Erickson, "A Sociological Study of Funeral Customs," 19–20, confirms that temple-endowed Mormons were customarily buried in their temple clothes.

76. Buerger, *Mysteries of Godliness*, 39, 78, 82–83, 130, 142–45, 150.

77. Oliver Boardman Huntington explicates the idea that apparently miraculously preserved bodies symbolized the promise of the final resurrection. Huntington was the brother of Zina D. H. Young, who was a plural wife in turn of both Joseph Smith and Brigham Young and president of the Relief Society after Eliza R. Snow's death. He was present in Nauvoo when the city cemetery was moved to the outskirts of the settlement. One of the corpses that needed to be moved was Zina Baker Huntington, his mother, who had died over three years before in 1839, apparently of malaria, when Oliver was almost sixteen. In an article for the

and emotional confusion—even danger—signified by the disarranged clothes that could be straightened only by great effort, Elizabeth Ramsay Fraser and Rhoda Smith Allred stepped in. Allred literally smoothed down the clothes, as did Fraser in her dream. In the process, both women clarified and smoothed this transitional moment—Allred literally and Fraser in her dream world. They were the last humans to touch and ready these cherished bodies as the spirits made their transition to the spirit world; they also readied the bodies for their resurrection in glory. It seems likely that Fraser's belief community shared the seriousness, which manifested itself in this dream, of observing the proper rites connected to death for all corpses. These women held the power to ease these transitions for the dying and the grieving by assuring that the proper rituals had been observed.

The power of women to ease the transition of death is the theme of a 1917 article in the *Relief Society Magazine* by Annie D. S. Palmer. Titled "A Morning Reverie," it recounts a detailed dream. Palmer had awakened, thinking about her outstanding local Relief Society president, Tena Jensen, and the many faithful Relief Society members who were serving their communities. Thinking thus, Palmer dreams—perhaps a waking dream or directed imagination—the description makes it unclear: "I dreamed, and in my mind hurried: and, with almost the quickness of thought, I was carried some seventy-five or a hundred years into the sunlight of future joy."[78] Here, Palmer sees Jensen engaged in the same kind of duties that she had as an earthly Relief Society president and follows her on her rounds. Everywhere the president is greeted with great happiness:

> As we drew near to another mansion, a grim, gaunt figure approached whom I knew as Death. From the splendid house came two sisters hurrying

---

Young Woman's Journal, Oliver, many years later, describes that his mother's body, when examined, was miraculously preserved, "full and plump as ever in life," though the coffin itself was in a state of decay. Huntington took the body's remarkable preservation as a promise of the final resurrection of the faithful: "[It?] was a strange sight to see [our?] mother again in perfect form [and?] feature, giving us a foretaste [of?] the resurrection of the dead, as [spoken?] of by Isaiah and John [the?] Revelator." The family made sure that the body was laid away again in proper order, even putting between the feet two toes that had broken off during the investigation of the corpse before reluctantly and reverently reburying her. O[liver] B[oardman] Huntington, "Resurrection of My Mother," *Young Woman's Journal* 5, 7 (1894): 347.

78. Annie D. S. Palmer, "A Morning Reverie," *Relief Society Magazine* 4, 3 (Mar. 1917): 138.

down the path and laughing as they ran. They, too, clasped Sister Jensen in fond embrace.

"We feared yon apparition once," said the younger woman, "and well we might. Do you remember the night he carried sister away? I shudder even now as I think of the cruel poverty, and the agonizing pain. But you comforted sister for the lonely journey and cared for me when she was gone. He has no power here; we laugh at his weakness. 'Oh grave, where is thy victory; oh death, where is thy sting?'"[79]

Further cementing the idea that these duties were primordially and essentially women's, Tena Jensen assures Palmer: "There is so much joy in it! I often wonder why we ever thought it hard when on the earth. I am going now to meet a sweet old sister who is dreading to die. The dear old soul has suffered so much and is so weary of life—oh, she will be so glad when it is over!"[80] In short, a Relief Society worker in the spirit world prepares to welcome a woman who is, presumably, being ushered out of mortality by Relief Society sisters on that side of the veil. As this story tells, Relief Society women help those transitioning from one phase of life to the next, abolish the fear of death and, in essence, conquer death. Death, who is significantly gendered as male, can only lurk around the edges of a female-centered celebration.[81] As the two sisters recollect, he is the central, menacing actor for those making the transition to the spirit world without the powerful help of Relief Society women. In their presence, he is banished to the periphery—becoming only a brief moment in an increasingly happy, divine, and eternal life.

Palmer's dream-story cements the strong connection between the physical work of cleaning and clothing bodies and the seemingly more psychological and spiritual work of comforting the dying and their loved ones. Death rituals transcended comforting the living and respecting the dead, significant though those roles were. In their work,

---

79. Palmer, "A Morning Reverie," 138–39.

80. Palmer, "A Morning Reverie," 139.

81. Death is gendered as male throughout LDS women's literature of this period. See Hannah T. King, "Autumn, 1883," *Woman's Exponent* 12, 9 (Oct. 1, 1883): 65; Millicent, "Nellie's Child," *Woman's Exponent* 17, 24 (May 15, 1880): 185; Mrs. Deborah Billings, "Lines in Memory of Sister M. J. Tanner ... ," *Woman's Exponent* 18, 20 (Mar. 15, 1890): 157. This gendering of death as male was also common in popular nineteenth-century American literature. See, for instance, Habington, "Dead Leaves," in *The Language of Flowers*, ed. Henrietta Dumont (Philadelphia: H. C. Peck & Theo. Bliss, 1852), 218.

Relief Society women attempted to ease fears and anxieties surrounding birth and death. That they continued in these roles from generation to generation shows that these struggles were never fully won. When Relief Society women were successful, however, it was because they and their community believed that these rituals assisted loved ones in moving from mortality to the postmortal world and, ultimately, to the final resurrection.

CONCLUSION: AT THE GATES OF MORTALITY

In the lived religion of the LDS Church during the 1870s to the 1920s, women stood at the gates of mortality, usually being the first human beings to ease the passage of spirit children into earthly life and welcome them. At the same time, they were the last humans to ease the passage of the, ideally, matured human back into the spirit realm. Both times of transition were made easier by the comfort and rituals offered by women in the Relief Society—comfort and rituals that had deep religious meaning for participants and recipients. In this work, Relief Society women lived and even helped to create some theological realities of their faith. Mirroring the life and work of their divine Heavenly Mother, women, assisted by other women, became the literal gates into mortality as they provided spirit children with the bodies that served as passports into earthly existence. In assisting these women in childbirth and, more generally, their community members in death, Relief Society women mirrored some of the most prominent characteristics of the Mother in Heaven. They lingered at the gates of mortality, welcoming and bidding farewell to the faithful at two of the more critical junctures of the plan of salvation—those times when the earthly and the divine briefly connected—so that those living within the plan could successfully advance to the next phase of existence.

NINE

"SHAKE OFF THE DUST OF THY FEET"
THE RISE AND FALL OF MORMON RITUAL CURSING

SAMUEL R. WEBER

In July 1830, just three months after the formal organization of the Mormon Church, Joseph Smith dictated a revelation that promised, "[I]n whatsoever place ye shall enter in & they receive you not in my name ye shall leave a cursing instead of a blessing by casting off the dust of your feet against them as a testimony & cleansing your feet by the wayside."[1] Subsequently, the historical record is replete with examples of ritual cursing being performed up through the 1890s. While many of Smith's revelations and doctrinal innovations continue to be practiced by the LDS Church today, cursing has fallen into disuse. Despite this ritual's unique status as an act of formally calling down God's wrath upon others, it has received little attention in scholarly studies.[2]

The first objective of this essay is to examine ritual cursing within Mormonism: how ritual cursing began, who performed curses, who was cursed, and how the ritual was performed. Factors that contributed to an environment conducive to ritual cursing are also explored. Cursing arose during a period of bold innovation within Mormonism, as Joseph Smith unveiled a seemingly endless stream of new doctrines and practices. Although ritual cursing may be appropriately described as new to the religious world in which Mormonism was born, it had ancient roots. Ritual cursing was an expression of Christian primitivism

---

1. Revelation, July 1830 (D&C 24:15), *Joseph Smith Papers*, www.josephsmithpapers.org.

2. See Gregory A. Prince, *Power from On High: The Development of Mormon Priesthood* (Salt Lake City: Signature Books, 1995), ch. 3: Ordinances, 1829–1830, and Grant Underwood, *The Millenarian World of Early Mormonism* (Urbana: University of Illinois Press, 1999), ch. 4: The Bible, the Mormons, and Millenarianism. See also David Golding, "The Foundations and Early Development of Mormon Mission Theory" (master's thesis, Claremont Graduate University, 2010); and Daniel L. Belnap, "'Those Who Receive You Not': The Rite of Wiping Dust Off the Feet," *International Journal of Mormon Studies* 5 (2012): 81–127.

among Mormons, an attempt to recapture an ancient biblical rite that had been lost over time. The most common practitioners of ritual cursing were Mormon missionaries who faced rejection in their efforts to proselytize. Mormonism began as a small sect with many religious and political enemies, and Mormons used ritual cursing as a means of holy retaliation against their enemies. The manner in which the ritual was performed varied, typically including the dusting or washing of feet, but at times involving the shaking of one's garment. Cursing was considered part of a missionary's duty to prepare the world for the imminent Millennium. The ritual designated unbelievers as such, marking them as separate from believers for the day of judgment. The ritual was fluid and developed over time, cross-pollinating with other rituals from the School of the Prophets, the Kirtland, Ohio, endowment, and the prayer circle. The combination of doctrinal innovation, Christian primitivism, and millenarianism, set against a backdrop of proselytizing efforts, disbelieving masses, and persecuting mobs, provided fertile ground for ritual cursing to flourish in the early days of the church.

The second objective of this essay is to examine the decline and discontinuation of the cursing ritual. This discontinuation resulted from a reduction in prominence of several aforementioned influences present during the formative years of the church. Over time, Mormonism transitioned from a small, young, persecuted minority to a stable, sizeable economic power in the western United States.[3] With the transition to stability, pressures and priorities within Mormonism changed. As Mormons removed themselves geographically from their tormentors, violence and persecution lessened. Generations passed without Jesus' return, and Mormonism's millenarian impulse began to fade. Missionaries no longer sealed unbelievers up to the day of judgment, but returned to the homes of potential converts again and again and gave multiple chances to hear the gospel message. Cursing was advised against and eventually dropped from church discourse and publications. Doctrinal innovation gave way to the routinization necessary for Mormonism to endure as an institution, and practices viewed as nonessential to the church's mission were eliminated. Without persecutors

---

3. For an analysis of an important period of transition within Mormonism, see Thomas G. Alexander, *Mormonism in Transition: A History of the Latter-day Saints, 1890–1930* (Urbana: University of Illinois Press, 1986).

tormenting them, the Millennium around the corner, and an environment favoring innovative ritual practices, the impetus to curse was lost for most Mormons. With the church stable and persecution minimized, the practice was discontinued.

BIBLICAL PRECEDENTS AND JOSEPH SMITH'S REVELATIONS

The Bible was a fertile source of inspiration for Joseph Smith's revelations. Doctrinal innovations such as baptism for the dead, post-mortal degrees of glory, and plural marriage resulted from Smith's poring over the pages of the Old and New Testaments. Similarly, Smith's pronouncements on curses had biblical precedents. Jesus himself told his disciples: "And whosoever shall not receive you, nor hear you, when ye depart thence, shake off the dust under your feet for a testimony against them. Verily I say unto you, it shall be more tolerable for Sodom and Gomorrah in the day of judgment, than for that city" (Mark 6:11, see also Matt. 10:14, Luke 9:5). Similar instruction is repeated in his commission to seventy others (Luke 10:10–12). This act of retribution was performed by Jesus' followers elsewhere in the New Testament, as when Paul and Barnabas "shook off the dust of their feet against [the Jews] … [and] were filled with joy, and with the Holy Ghost" (Acts 13:51–52).

Bible scholars have offered various interpretations of the New Testament dust-shaking gesture. Some have drawn parallels to rabbinic literature in which Jews traveling in gentile lands are expected to remove the dust of an impure foreign nation from their bodies before returning to the holy land. Others have suggested that the act was intentionally humorous. Still others have ignored the subject entirely. T. J. Rogers argues convincingly that these biblical passages should be read in the context of ancient hospitality customs. Guests in the ancient world could expect their hosts to provide water to wash their feet, symbolizing a transition from stranger to guest in the home of their host. To shake the dust from one's feet would therefore serve as evidence that this custom had not been observed, and hospitality had been refused to the apostles. It is implied that God would notice this testimony and execute punishment on those who had refused hospitality to his servants.[4]

---

4. T. J. Rogers, "Shaking the Dust off the Markan Mission Discourse," *Journal for the Study of the New Testament* 27, 2 (2004): 169–92. Thanks to Jared Anderson for directing me to this article.

The founding prophet of Mormonism offered his own take on the biblical dust-shaking gesture by advocating its renewed practice by Mormon proselytizers as a cursing ritual. With ample biblical examples (another doctrinal innovation, baptism for the dead, had only a single New Testament verse as precedent), Smith's scribes recorded a revelation in July 1830 instructing missionaries for his new church to "[cast] off the dust of your feet" as a testimony against the disbelieving.[5] One year later, on August 8, 1831, the doctrine reappeared in a new revelation: "shake off the dust of thy feet against those who receive thee not not in their presence lest thou provoke them but in secret & wash thy feet as a testimony against them in the day of Judgement."[6] Smith produced three revelations on curses in 1832. In the first of these, he stated that those who performed curses would "be filled with joy and gladness," likely alluding to Paul and Barnabas's dusting of feet in Acts 13:51–52. Smith's revelation also declared that "in the day of judgment you shall be judges of that house and condemn them."[7] In his second 1832 revelation on cursing, it was implied that water could be used to "cleanse your feet in the secret places by the way for a testamony against them."[8] The final 1832 cursing revelation specified that this ritual should be performed "alone" and that "pur[e] water" should be used to cleanse the feet.[9] As with other Mormon ordinances, the actions of biblical figures became imbued with special status and ritualized.

After the initial revelations on ritual cursing were received by Smith, discourse on the subject continued in official church publications. In November 1835, Smith wrote on the subject in the *Latter-day Saints' Messenger and Advocate*. In cases where a man forbade his wife and children from joining the church, the responsibility for their sins would be answered upon him as head of the house. "[T]he guilt of that house is no longer upon thy skirts: Thou art free; therefore, shake off the dust of thy feet, and go thy way."[10] The January 1, 1842 edition of the *Times and Seasons* included a letter from Orson Hyde discussing his travels in

---

5. Revelation, July 1830, *Joseph Smith Papers*.

6. Revelation, Aug. 8, 1831 (D&C 60:15), *Joseph Smith Papers*.

7. Revelation, Jan. 25, 1832 (D&C 75:20–22), *Joseph Smith Papers*.

8. Revelation, Aug. 29, 1832 (D&C 99:4), *Joseph Smith Papers*.

9. Revelation, Sep. 22–23, 1832 (D&C 84:92–95), *Joseph Smith Papers*.

10. Joseph Smith, Letter to the Elders of the Church, Kirtland, Ohio, *Latter-day Saints' Messenger and Advocate* 2 (Nov. 1835): 211.

the Holy Land. He noted that by journeying during the dry season, his feet and legs were completely coated with dust. "I then thought how very convenient it must have been for the ancient disciples to fulfill one injunction of the Saviour, 'shake off the dust of your feet.'"[11] An 1842 epistle from the Nauvoo Stake high council to be read in "all the branches of the church" admonished members to bear their afflictions "as becometh saints," and that when they were unable to obtain justice they should "shake off the dust off your feet."[12] Smith's authority to curse was reemphasized in an 1843 revelation with the following language: "whomsoever you Curse I will Curse Saith the Lord."[13] Continual discourse on cursing published through official church channels created an environment in which Mormon proselytizers were prepared to curse those who rejected their message.

WHO PRONOUNCED CURSES

Smith's revelations on ritual cursing were given primarily to Mormon missionaries. Those who rejected the message of the Mormon preachers were to be cursed. The earliest recorded performance of cursing by a Mormon elder preceded Smith's aforementioned revelations. According to his mother's reminiscence, Samuel Smith, brother of the prophet and the church's first missionary, reported that on June 30, 1830, he "washed his feet in a small brook" as testimony against an innkeeper in Livonia, New York, who rejected the Book of Mormon and denied the missionary room and board.[14] Use of this ritual quickly caught on among Mormon proselytizers.

It was not always easy for missionaries to follow the command to curse. When Orson Hyde failed to convert his sister to Mormonism, he felt compelled to shake the dust off his feet. "[T]ears from all eyes freely ran, and we shook the dust of our feet against them but it was

---

11. Orson Hyde, Letter to the Editor, St. Louis, *Times and Seasons* 3 (Jan. 1, 1842): 848, 852; on Smith Research Associates, *New Mormon Studies: A Comprehensive Resource Library*, CD-ROM (Salt Lake City: Signature Books, 1998 ed.).

12. Nauvoo High Council, "Communications. An Epistle," St. Louis, *Times and Seasons* 3 (June 1, 1842): 809–10; on Smith Research Associates, *New Mormon Studies* CD-ROM.

13. Revelation, July 12, 1843 (D&C 132:47), *Joseph Smith Papers*.

14. Lucy Smith, *Lucy's Book: A Critical Edition of Lucy Mack Smith's Family Memoir*, ed. Lavina Fielding Anderson (Salt Lake City: Signature Books, 2001), 478–79.

like piercing my heart."[15] When Wilford Woodruff was followed by Mr. Pitt, a man "filled with the Devil" who was "shouting, hooting & yelling as though a part of hell at least had broke loose," he demonstrated humility in the pronouncement of his curse. "May the will of God be done conserning that man, I pray that we may ever be reconciled to his will in all things."[16] Woodruff consigned Pitt's fate to God.

Mormons rarely knew of any consequences of their curses. Generally, the elders had faith that if their curse had no direct effects during mortality, it would take effect in the afterlife. One exception occurred in the West Indies in 1853: "The Elders cursed the Mayor, Hector Michell, whose duty it was to have protected them in their person and position as ministers, in the name of the Lord Jesus Christ. Subsequently they learned that the mayor's toes and fingers rotted off and that he soon died with the rot and scabs."[17]

WHO RECEIVED CURSES

Early Mormon missionaries frequently encountered religionists who were equally enthusiastic about their own denominations. When Samuel Smith and William McLellin spoke to an assembly of Campbellites in 1831, the group "spoke out and said that they did not want to hear any more—They called a vote and I [McLellin] was requested to say no more. ... the[y] rejected all with disdain and desired us to depart out of their coasts. Which we did and wiped the dust of our feet against them."[18] It was not the last time religious disagreement resulted in ritual cursing.

At times curses were administered against individuals or groups who failed to support missionaries financially. Following the apostolic example of traveling without "purse, nor scrip" (Luke 10:4, also Mark 6:8), Mormon elders often had to rely on the generosity of others for

15. Orson Hyde, Journal, Sept. 16, 1832, qtd. in Leonard J. Arrington and Davis Bitton, *The Mormon Experience: A History of the Latter-day Saints*, 2nd ed. (Urbana: University of Illinois Press, 1992 printing), 193. Hyde counterbalanced the pain of cursing by blessing when he could. "[Traveled] on from House to H[ouse] shook off the dust against some and blest others." Hyde, Journal, Oct. 23, 1832, MS 1386, Church History Library, Church of Jesus Christ of Latter-day Saints, Salt Lake City, hereafter CHL.

16. Wilford Woodruff, Journal, June 19, 1840, MS 1352, CHL.

17. Report of Aaron F. Farr, Journal History of the Church of Jesus Christ of Latter-day Saints (chronological scrapbook of typed entries and newspaper clippings, 1830–present), Feb. 11, 1853, qtd. in Prince, *Power from On High*, 111.

18. Jan Shipps and John W. Welch, eds., *The Journals of William E. McLellin: 1831–1836*, (Urbana: University of Illinois Press; Provo: BYU Studies, 1994), 47.

food and lodging. Orson Pratt cursed those who would not render assistance "for the relief of our suffering brethren in zion," and washed his feet against a family that refused him lodging for the night.[19] William McLellin and David W. Patten cursed a schoolhouse full of congregants who refused their request for a donation at the conclusion of a meeting.[20] William McLellin, Brigham Young, and Thomas B. Marsh washed their feet against a man who refused to provide them "bread and milk for breakfast ... without money."[21]

Mormon missionaries sometimes faced overwhelming rejection from the communities they visited. In such instances, they followed Jesus' injunction to leave curses on entire cities where his followers were scorned (Luke 10:10–12). Detroit was cursed in 1831;[22] Chicago

---

19. "Feb. 27th. We left Painesville and came to Thompson. On the way we endeavored to obtain some assistance from the world for the relief of our suffering brethren in zion, but they refused to render any assistance. We therefore washed our feet against them. ... Mar. 20th. Brother John Murdock and I left Geneseo and came to the village of Dansville. About dark we called upon the family of a man by the name of Parkman for lodging during the night, but they refused to keep us. Therefore we washed our feet as a testimony against them." *The Orson Pratt Journals*, comp. Elden J. Watson (Salt Lake City: Elden Jay Watson, 1975), Feb. 27 and Mar. 20, 1834, unpaginated transcript online at www.boap.org/LDS/Early-Saints/OPratt.html (accessed Apr. 15, 2020); compare Orson Pratt, "History of Orson Pratt," *Utah Genealogical and Historical Magazine* 28 (Apr. 1937): 92–93.

20. "[A] Methodist priest arose and said that he had an app. here at five o clock and he wished to fill it and he wanted to know if I would get through so as to give place. I told him that I did not know how long I should speak but I desired to speak until I should get through— However I told him that we would leave it to the people. A vote was called. Three or four voted for me to close and for him to speak but a majority Voted for me to continue— consequently I continued until I had spoken about two hours on the plain simplicity of the Gospel and its spiritual gifts and powers. After which Elder Patten called for a donation but not a man moved his tongue or his finger to help us consequently we left them believing that we had done our duty as to delivering our message and we wiped the dust off our feet and we also clensed our feet in pure water as a testimony against them and we passed on toward old Oswego about 4 miles." Shipps and Welch, eds., *Journals of William E. McLellin*, 182–83.

21. "[W]e call at a Mr M. Hawley who kept tavern and told him that we were preachers of the Gospel and we wanted some bread and milk for breakfast and we asked for it without money but he abused us and after we had born testimony to him we came to a little brook and clensed our feet as a testimony against him—" Shipps and Welch, eds., *Journals of William E. McLellin*, 189–90.

22. "We left the boat immediately and took lodging in a tavern; we breakfasted and dined freely with a merchant's wife, a sister to Almira Mack. We four brethren labored from morning till noon endeavoring to get a chance to preach, but we were not successful. I was turned out of doors for calling on the woolcarder to repent. After dinner we took leave of the two ladies and the family with which we had dined and wiped our feet as a testimony against that city." John Murdock, Journal, Journal History, June 14, 1831, qtd. in Prince, *Power from On High*, 109.

was cursed in 1831;[23] Sinclairville, New York, was cursed in 1835;[24] Paris, Arkansas, was cursed in 1836;[25] Beach Hill, Connecticut, was cursed in 1837;[26] Collinsville, Connecticut, was cursed in 1837;[27] eight households in Belfast, Maine, were cursed in 1838;[28] and the Fox Islands, Maine, were cursed in 1838.[29] Sensing an urgency to their work, Mormons dusted their feet in these areas and moved on to other communities in the hope of finding more fruitful ground for proselytizing.

Mormons occasionally pronounced curses upon each other. In an 1840 meeting of the Kirtland, Ohio, elders quorum, Henry Moore was charged with false prophecy, deception, laziness, and "Trying to persuade a woman to promise to have him while his own wife is still living." Additionally, Moore was accused of "pronouncing curses upon Elder Charles Thompson because he would not uphold him in the above abominations and washing his feet against me [Thompson] for the same reason."[30] Seven years later, cursing was invoked in sentencing an unknown (possibly Mormon) perpetrator. When someone killed Albert Carrington's cow in 1847, the Salt Lake Stake presidency and high council met to discuss punishment of the unidentified wrongdoer. As traditional means of litigation were impossible against an anonymous

23. John Murdock, Journal, late 1831, Prince, *Power from On High,* 109.

24. "At 4 Oclock we attended in the village in order to fill our app. [in Sinclairville, New York] but the schoolhouse was locked and only One person who was an old lady attended—consequently we left them shaking the dust from our feet as a testimony against them." Shipps and Welch, eds., *Journals of William E. McLellin,* 174.

25. Woodruff, Journal, Oct. 12, 1836.

26. "We left Mr Bidwell and beach hill and repaired to a stream of pure water aside from the abodes of men and in company with my brethren Elders Stillman & Hale and myself we clensed our hands and feet in testimony against the inhabitants of beach hill who had rejected us and our testimony." Woodruff, Journal, July 3, 1837.

27. "Brother [Jonathan] Hale & myself repaired to a stream of pure water & we there cleansed our hands and feet and bore testimony before God against Mr Vanarsdalen a Prysbeterian priest who rejected our testimony & against the whole villedge who rejected our testimony." Woodruff, Journal, July 11, 1837.

28. "During the day we repaired to the sea shore & clensed our feet with pure water & bore testimony against eight housholds before God who had rejected us or turned us from their Doors the evening before." Woodruff, Journal, Feb. 23, 1838.

29. "[W]hile the Sun was sitting in the western horizon, I retired aside from the abodes of men by the sea shore alone by myself and clensed my feet with pure water and bore testimony before GOD against the inhabitants of those Islands of the Sea for rejecting my testimony while in their midst and were excedingly mad against me. ... This is the last night I ever spent or shall spend upon those Islands of the Sea." Woodruff, Journal, Aug. 12, 1838.

30. Lyndon W. Cook and Milton V. Backman, Jr., eds., *Kirtland Elders' Quorum Record, 1836–1841* (Provo, Utah: Grandin Book Co., 1985), 50–51.

criminal, a novel solution was settled upon. "After several remarks of <by> the counselors, Pres. John Smith sealed a curse upon the person or persons who killed Carrington's cow until they came forward and made restitution. The curse was sanctioned unanimously by the council."[31] These examples demonstrate that Mormons did not exclusively curse non-Mormons; at times they cursed their own or, in the case of Carrington's cow, those who were unknown.

Cursing was used as a means of coping with the mob violence and forced migration perpetually endured by the Mormons. Prior to their departure from Nauvoo, Illinois in 1845, the Saints spent a night dancing in the temple. This was not only for recreation: "when we danced before the Lord we shook the dust from off our feet as a testimony against this nation."[32] When they encountered forces they could not overcome, Mormons turned their enemies over to God and his judgments.

HOW CURSES WERE PERFORMED

In describing the cursing ritual, Mormons frequently wrote that they "bore testimony" against the disbelieving, echoing language from Smith's revelations. Joseph Coe, a Mormon missionary in New York in 1831, "washed his feet as a testimony" against those who "would not receive my doctrine" five times during a three-week period.[33] John

---

31. Journal History, Dec. 18, 1847, qtd. in Prince, *Power from On High*, 111. Note: < and > characters enclose shorthand text.

32. Historian's Office history of the Church, 1839–circa 1882, December 10, 1845; compare *History of the Church of Jesus Christ of Latter-day Saints*, ed. B. H. Roberts, 7 vols., 2nd ed. rev. (Salt Lake City: Deseret Book Co., 1948 printing), 7:557–58.

33. "On the 16th (Lord's day) Brother Thayer, by mutual consent, left me. I went to Foresville, (in the same county) and attended a meeting of Baptists and Presbytarians. In the evening I requested and obtained liberty to speak, but was stopped in a very few minutes; went to the tavern again and washed my feet as a testimony against the people in the schoolhouse. ... On the 19th I preached in Perrysburg, (Cattaraugus Co., N.Y.); the congregation was ignorant and unbelieving. On the 24th I preached in Lockport (lower town), but to no effect; I bore testimony against the people. On the 28th I settled some temporal concerns with J W. Colliers, and on the 29th went to the town of Royalton to see J. Turner, an old friend, but he would not receive my doctrine; therefore I bore testimony against him. On the 30th I left Lockport (Niagara Co., N.Y.) for Middleberry Newcombes, attended a Baptist meeting in the evening, spoke a few words and requested to make an appointment, which I did and preached in the evening of Nov. 1st. Some reviled; others were fearful and unbelieving, and I bore testimony against them. ... From [Warsaw] I went to the town of Portage (Wyoming Co.), where I tarried for some time, and preached there in several places. Some believed, but were not baptized; others were unbelievers, but their prejudices were fast giving way; thence I went by way of Yates county (N.Y.) to Springport and Scipio, in

Murdock encountered Dr. Matthews, "a very wicked man," in September 1832, who "reviled against us, the Book of Mormon, and the Doctrine we taught. We bore testimony according to the Commandment and the Lord helped us in tending to the ordinance."[34] Heber C. Kimball and Orson Hyde washed their feet and bore testimony against a Baptist priest who denounced them as false prophets.[35] Wilford Woodruff and Jonathan Hale "clensed our feet in the pure water of the Sea as a testimony against Gideon J. Newton for rejecting our testimony of the Lord & of the Book of Mormon."[36] William McLellin,[37] Samuel Smith,[38] and Orson Pratt[39] all used similar language in

---

Cayuga Co., N.Y., preached in a number of places in Cayuga county. I found the people there unbelieving, but willing to relinquish a part of their prejudice, but as they did not receive my doctrine, I bore testimony against them." Joseph Coe, Journal, Journal History, Oct. 12, 1831, CR 100 137, CHL.

34. John Murdock, Journal, Sept. 1832, qtd. in Craig J. Ostler, *The Doctrine and Covenants: A Book of Answers*, (Salt Lake City: Deseret Book Co., 1996), 132.

35. "At Mendon, his former home, Heber and his companion, Elder Orson Hyde, were confronted by a Baptist priest named Fulton, who withstood them harshly. Says Heber: 'He called us false prophets, and, rejecting our testimony, advised us to go home. We declared unto him that we should go forth preaching the Gospel, and no power should stay us. I told him if he did not repent of his sins and be baptized for the remission of them, he would be damned, which made him angry. We then passed on until we came to a pure stream of water, and there cleansed our feet, bearing testimony against him, as the Lord commanded.'" Orson F. Whitney, *Life of Heber C. Kimball, an Apostle* (Salt Lake City: The Kimball Family, 1888), 80.

36. Woodruff, *Journal*, 1:180. "[W]e went by ourselves by a pure stream of water and clensed our hands and feet and bore testamony before God against ... all that rejected our testamony." Jonathan Hale, Journal, July 11, 1837, qtd. in Arrington and Bitton, *Saints Without Halos: The Human Side of Mormon History* (Salt Lake City: Signature Books, 1981), 14.

37. "This morning we took breakfast with a Christian preacher (as he called himself). He charged us with being false prophets. Reason or Testimony had no influence on his mind ... and his heart seemed so hard and wicked that he would have struck us dumb if he had had it in his power, but we left him raging and when we came to a brook Bro. H[yrum] washed his feet for a testimony against him." Shipps and Welch, eds., *Journals of William E. McLellin*, 36–44. "We had an appointment at a schoolhouse. an assembly of Campbellites, Methodists Presbyterians and deists attended. I spoke 1 hour & ¾ but was called a liaar while speaking and interupted two or three times more by the wicked wretches. we dismissed and I shook the dust off my feet as a testimony against the rebellious." Shipps and Welch, eds., *Journals of William E. McLellin*, 72.

38. "Shook dust from our feet as a testimony against them." Samuel H. Smith, Diary, Mar. 1, 16, 18 and June 1, 1832, microfilm of holograph, L. Tom Perry Special Collections and Manuscripts, Harold B. Lee Library, Brigham Young University, Provo, Utah.

39. "We called at a house in Arkport village for the purpose of obtaining a meeting in that place, but the woman of the house rejected our testimony, and said that if the Book of Mormon was good she could not receive it. Therefore we washed our feet as a testimony against her." Orson Pratt, "History of Orson Pratt," *Utah Genealogical and Historical Magazine* 28 (Apr. 1937): 92–93.

their journals. In effect, testimony was borne twice: first, testimony of the restored gospel was borne for the benefit of those listening; second, testimony was borne to God (as feet were dusted or washed) that the missionaries' duty had been fulfilled.

In a particularly interesting case, a man was cursed more than once. A Methodist priest by the name of William Douglass was cursed multiple times by Wilford Woodruff, first in September 1837 "for rejecting the Book of Mormon & our testimony,"[40] and later in February 1838 for "rejecting our testimony & offending our little ones." Following the latter curse, Woodruff recorded in his journal that it was "the third witness borne to heaven against that man."[41] This is the only example I have found of an individual being cursed repeatedly.

The New Testament apostle Paul described a variant of shaking the dust off one's feet that involved the shaking of a garment. In Acts 18:6, Paul "testified to the Jews that Jesus was Christ. And when they opposed themselves, and blasphemed, he shook his raiment, and said unto them, Your blood be upon your own heads; I am clean: from henceforth I will go unto the Gentiles." Similar instances of garment shaking exist in the Old Testament (Neh. 5:13) and Book of Mormon (2 Ne. 9:44). As enthusiastic participants in a primitive church restoration movement, it is not surprising that early Mormons imitated biblical exemplars by occasionally shaking their garments instead of their feet as a variant of the cursing ritual.

In December 1837, Heber C. Kimball and Orson Hyde were encountering difficulties in the mission field. Mormon meetings were being disrupted by priests from other Christian denominations, which resulted in Kimball shaking his garments at them.

> After Brother Hide speking [spoke] to the people about one [h]our; I got up and bore testimony to the congration and shock [shook] my garments before them and told them that my garments ware clean of blo[o]d. Thare was menny preas [priests] that ware thare at that time but had Rejected our testimony and cold [called] us evy thing but good and shoock thare fist at us and sisced [hissed] at us and gnashed thare theth [teeth] at us and thretned us evry way that they could. The nex[t] day we felt by the Spirrite of the Lord that we would gow and wash our feet against them

40. Woodruff, Journal, Sept. 30, 1837.
41. Woodruff, Journal, Feb. 1, 1838.

and that we would not have now [any] more to dow with [them] for we was clean of thare blo[o]d and that we would have now [no] more to dow [do] with them hare after; then we went and washed our feet and hands and shuck our garments against them and bore testamony to our Father who art in heaven.[42]

Another example of garment-shaking was related by Ashbel Kitchell, the intended recipient of a curse. After a failed endeavor to preach to a group of Shakers (of which Kitchell was a part), Parley P. Pratt "arose and commenced shakeing his coattail; he said he shook the dust from his garments as a testimony against us, that we had rejected the word of the Lord Jesus." As this ritual was performed in front of an audience, it received an understandably negative response: "Before the words were out of his mouth, I was to him, and said;—You filthy Beast, dare you presume to come in here, and try to imitate a man of God by shaking your filthy tail; confess your sins and purge your soul from your lusts, and your other abominations before you ever presume to do the like again &c. While I was ministering this reproof, he settled trembling into his seat, and covered his face."[43] Such conflict may shed light on the necessity of following the scriptural injunction to curse "in secret," as Kitchell was not unique in taking offense at this Mormon practice.[44]

THE MILLENARIAN MINDSET OF EARLY MORMONISM

Most early Mormons shared the belief that Christ's second coming was nigh and that the Millennium would commence during their life-times.[45] One step in the process of cleansing the earth preparatory to its millennial state was the separation of the righteous from the wicked. In the parable of the wheat and the tares, Jesus said, "Gather ye together first the tares, and bind them in bundles to burn them: but gather the wheat into my barn" (Matt. 13:30). This parable was

---

42. Stanley B. Kimball, ed., *On the Potter's Wheel: The Diaries of Heber C. Kimball* (Salt Lake City: Signature Books/Smith Research Associates, 1987), 21.

43. Lawrence R. Flake, "A Shaker View of a Mormon Mission," *BYU Studies* 20, 1 (Fall 1979): 98.

44. "Sunderland found especially offensive the practice that Woodruff and other missionaries had of washing the dust from their feet as a ritual condemnation of those who rejected their message." Thomas G. Alexander, *Things in Heaven and Earth: The Life and Times of Wilford Woodruff, a Mormon Prophet* (Salt Lake City: Signature Books, 1993), 64.

45. Underwood, *Millenarian World of Early Mormonism.*

referenced in two of Joseph Smith's revelations. The first indicates the tares must be "bound in bund[l]es" before the field can be burned.[46] The other states:

> therefore I must gather to gether my people according to the parable of the wheat and the tares that the wheat may be secured in the garner to possess eternal life and be crowned with celestial glory when I come in the Kingdom of my fathe[r] to reward evry man according as his work shall be whilst the tares shall be bound in bundles and their bands made strong that they may be burned with unquenchable fire.[47]

Early Mormon missionaries were participating in this separation of good from evil. Performance of a ritual curse was, in effect, binding its recipients like tares preparatory to their burning. Orson Hyde performed at least six curses during his missionary travels during the spring of 1832.[48] His journal entry of March 19 echoes the language of Jesus' parable, "went on 3 or 4 Miles Sealed up many to the day of wrath, bound the tares in bundles."[49]

Another millenarian image from the scriptures that took hold in the minds of early Mormons was that of sealing.[50] Separate from but related to the LDS practice of temple sealings, high priests were authorized in 1831 to seal church members "up unto Eternal life," preparatory to "the coming of the Son of man."[51] Elsewhere, Joseph Smith wrote

---

46. Revelation, Dec. 6, 1832 (D&C 86:7), *Joseph Smith Papers*.
47. Revelation, Dec. 16, 1833 (D&C 101:65–66), *Joseph Smith Papers*.
48. "We journeyed early in the spring of 1832, eastward together, without 'purse or scrip,' going from house to house, teaching and preaching in families, and also in the public congregations of the people. Wherever we were received and entertained, we left our blessing; and wherever we were rejected, we washed our feet in private against those who rejected us, and bore testimony of it unto our Father in Heaven, and went on our way rejoicing, according to the commandment. ... went on from fairview 6 or 7 miles Shook off the dust of my feet against almost all [March] 2 went on to Mill Creek & found ... the people verry hard, seemingly no Salvation for them ... [March] 3rd left Mr. Longs & went on 2 miles Blest Some & Shook off the dust of our feet against others. ... [March] 15th ... sealed many over to the day when the wrath of God shall be poured out. ... [March] 18th. went on through a Presbyterian neighbourhood on Sunday shook off the dust of our feet against almost every house. ... [March] 19th. went on 3 or 4 Miles Sealed up many to the day of wrath, bound the tares in bundles, blessed some." Hyde, Journal, Feb. 1–Dec. 22, 1832.
49. Hyde, Journal, Feb. 1–Mar. 19, 1832.
50. David John Buerger, "'The Fulness of the Priesthood': The Second Anointing in Latter-day Saint Theology and Practice," *Dialogue: A Journal of Mormon Thought* 16, 1 (Spring 1983): 10–44.
51. Revelation, Nov. 1, 1831 (D&C 68:11–12), *Joseph Smith Papers*.

that priesthood holders have "power given to seal both on Earth & in Heaven the unbelieveing & rebelious yea verily to seal them up unto the day when the wrath of God shall be poured out upon the wicked without measure"[52] Mormons took part in the divine pre-millennial separation of righteous from wicked through ritual performance: one ritual sealed worthy individuals up to salvation, whereas the cursing ritual sealed others to destruction. Having shaken the dust from his feet, Orson Hyde wrote in his journal in 1832: "sealed many over to the day when the wrath of God shall be poured out."[53] Wilford Woodruff's journal entry for May 22, 1836, relates that by cursing those who rejected the Mormon gospel, "We delivered them unto the hands of God *and the destroyer.*"[54]

In August 1840, the role of cursing was questioned by British convert Joseph Fielding in the *Millennial Star* periodical. He described a prevalent belief that curses sealed their recipients to damnation, and then questioned that assumption. Parley P. Pratt provided an ambiguous response.

> Question 6th. — Ought the Elders and Priests, when their testimony is rejected, to wash their feet, &c., and is there no hope of those against whom they wash their feet? An idea has gone out that we consider such sealed up for destruction. Is the washing of feet, in this way, anything more than a testimony that we are clear of their blood, when we bear testimony of it before God?
>
> Answer. — Certainly ... when the Elders and Priests have borne a faithful testimony to any city, town, village or person, and that testimony is rejected, and they have fulfilled the revelation, that city, town, village or person is in the hands of a righteous God, who will do with them according to his own pleasure; we are clear from their blood. [55]

Whether priesthood was required to perform curses was never specified. It seems likely that when Fielding listed "Elders and Priests" in his question above, he did so not because of prerequisite priesthood office, but because they were the ones proselytizing. Smith's revelations on

---

52. Revelation, Nov. 1, 1831 (D&C 1:8–9), *Joseph Smith Papers.*
53. Hyde, Journal, Mar. 15, 1832.
54. Woodruff, Journal, May 22, 1836. The bold italicized portion is in shorthand.
55. Joseph Fielding, Letter to the Editor, Aug. 6, 1840, *Millennial Star* 1 (Aug. 1840): 95.

cursing were directed chiefly to Mormon missionaries, and it was they who most often put the ritual into practice.

INFLUENCE OF THE SCHOOL OF THE PROPHETS
AND THE KIRTLAND ENDOWMENT

In December 1832, Joseph Smith received revelation to organize a school for the instruction of church leaders. As part of the initiation into this "School of the Prophets," Smith dictated that "ye shall not receive any among you into this school save he is clean from the blood of this generation; And he shall be received by the ordinance of the washing of feet" (D&C 88:138–39). Elsewhere in the same revelation, a command was given to "clean your hands, and your feet ... that you, are clean, from the blood of this, wicked generation."[56] Orson Pratt indicated that his initiation ceremony in 1833 involved washing both hands and feet so that "my garments were clean from [the] blood [of this wicked generation]."[57] By 1836, Smith was preparing to administer special blessings to worthy participants in Kirtland. In a meeting of priesthood holders on January 21, Smith and others "attended to the ordinance of washing our bodies in pure water. We also perfumed our bodies and our heads." Once the Kirtland House of the Lord was dedicated in March of that same year, Smith emphasized the ordinance of washing of feet.[58] Six years later, a washing ordinance would form a portion of Smith's Nauvoo endowment ceremony.

Rituals and ordinances in these formative years were fluid, often inconsistent in their performance. Cross-pollination between simultaneously developing ordinances took place, as when the initiation ceremony for the School of the Prophets was adapted to fit the Kirtland endowment and later reframed in Nauvoo as a temple initiatory ordinance. Shaking the dust off one's feet was likewise influenced by these other washing ordinances.[59]

---

56. Revelation, Dec. 27–28, 1832 (D&C 88:74–75), *Joseph Smith Papers.*

57. "Washed my hands and feet as a testimony unto the Lord that I had warned this wicked generation and that my garments were clean from their blood, and on the same day I admitted into the School of the Prophets." *Orson Pratt Journals*, Feb. 18, 1833, 16. "We now feel that our garments are clean from you, and all men, when we have washed our feet and hands, according to the commandment." Orson Hyde and Hyrum Smith to Edward Partridge and Others, Jan. 14, 1833, Letterbook 1, *Joseph Smith Papers.*

58. Joseph Smith, Journal, Mar. 27–29, 1836, *Joseph Smith Papers.*

59. Thanks to Jonathan A. Stapley for insights which contributed to this section.

In 1836, after having received the washing rituals in the School of the Prophets, Wilford Woodruff recorded three separate occasions on which he cursed unbelievers by washing his hands and feet.[60] His journal entry for the last of these, dated October 12, describes the cleansing of his entire body with water and alcohol.

> 12th Retired in company with Elder A. O. Smoot unto the banks of Blood River aside from the abodes of men to spend some time in Prayer & Praise to God & to Perform a solemn duty that is rquired of all the Elders of Israel whose testimony is rejected by this generation while they are preaching the gospel of Jesus Christ & bearing testimony of his NAME. after we had Cleansed our Bodies with Pure water & also with strong drink or spirits this not by Commandment but from Choice we then according to Commandment cleansed our hands and feet and bore testimony unto God against the Benton County mob & also against Paris & many others who had rejected our testimony. We enjoyed a solumn, spiritual, & interesting Season.[61]

Woodruff's journal entries for 1837 (by which time he would have received the Kirtland endowment washings) include two more instances of washing hands and feet in conjunction with the performance of a curse.[62]

Often the injunction that invitees to the School of the Prophets

---

60. "Elder [David W.] Patten Preached three discourses. ... After the close of the last discours Mr Rose rejected the testimony given & called on Br Patten to rase the dead that he might believe. Br Patten rebuked him sharply for his infidelity & unbelief. We then communed with the Saints. I then retired from the scene with Elders Patten & Boydstun to a stream of pure water & cleansed our hands & feet & testified against that people who had threatened us & rejected our testimony. We delivered them unto the hands of God *and the destroyer. O God, thy will be done*." Woodruff, Journal, May 22, 1836. "We then returned to Mr Jacksons. Had an interview with him. He denied all his former faith & pretentions. He raged much. Was filled with the spirit of anger wrath *and the devil*. He rejected our testimony *and denied the revelations of Christ*. We left his house at 10 oclock at night & went to a stream of Pure water & clensed our hands & feet & testified against him that our garments might be clear of his blood." Woodruff, Journal, May 24, 1836. Bold italicized portions are in shorthand.

61. Woodruff, Journal, Oct. 12, 1836.

62. "We left Mr Bidwell and beach hill and repaired to a stream of pure water aside from the abodes of men and in company with my brethren Elders Stillman & Hale and myself we clensed our hands and feet in testimony against the inhabitants of beach hill who had rejected us and our testimony." Woodruff, Journal, July 3, 1837. "Brother [Jonathan] Hale & myself repaired to a stream of pure water & we there cleansed our hands and feet and bore testimony before God against Mr Vanarsdalen a Prysbeterian priest who rejected our testimony & against the whole villedge who rejected our testimony." Woodruff, Journal, July 11, 1837.

be "clean from the blood of this generation" (a phrase that was later included in temple rites) was echoed in descriptions of the cursing ordinance. Missionary companions Wilford Woodruff and David Patten cursed a dissenter John Jackson, "that our garments might be clear of his blood."[63] Joseph Fielding's question about curses to Parley P. Pratt asked, "Is the washing of feet, in this way, anything more than a testimony that we are clear of their blood, when we bear testimony of it before God?"[64] In August 1841, Woodruff related his missionary endeavors with Dr. Noah Porter:

> I bore testimony unto him of the work of God Book of mormon &c but he rejected my testimony in the Strongest term & evry thing in the form of Prophets Apostles, revelation, Inspiration or the gift of the Holy Ghost, Healings Miracles tongues &c. Seemed to be much stired up because the work had come to Farmington. But I done my duty answered my mind, bore testimony of the truth.
>
> After he left the house I prayed with the family & those present could see the spirit manifest in Dr Noah Porter was dictated by the powers of Darkness. I was glad to have this opportunity of bearing testimony to Dr Porter of the work of God that he might be left without excuse. I returned to my Fathers house but before retiring to rest I repaired to the river & cleansed my feet with water in testimony against Dr Noah Porter In obediance to the commandment of God that my garments might be clear of his blood & I say in the name of Jesus Christ that if he does not repent of the course he has persued in this thing, he will no longer Prosper but the judgments of God will be upon him.[65]

What it meant to these early Mormons to be clean from the blood of others is explained in the same revelation outlining the commencement of a School of the Prophets: "it becometh evry man, who hath been warned, to warn his neighbour, therefore they are left with<out> excuse, and there sins are upon your own heads."[66] A similar theology of divine responsibility is present in the Old Testament:

> Son of man, I have made thee a watchman unto the house of Israel: therefore hear the word at my mouth, and give them warning from me. When I say unto the wicked, Thou shalt surely die; and thou givest him not

---

63. Woodruff, Journal, May 24, 1836.
64. Joseph Fielding, Letter to the Editor, 95.
65. Woodruff, Journal, Aug. 6, 1841.
66. Revelation, Dec. 27–28, 1832 (D&C 88:81–82), *Joseph Smith Papers.*

warning, nor speakest to warn the wicked from his wicked way, to save his life; the same wicked man shall die in his iniquity; but his blood will I require at thine hand. Yet if thou warn the wicked, and he turn not from his wickedness, nor from his wicked way, he shall die in his iniquity; but thou hast delivered thy soul. Again, When a righteous man doth turn from his righteousness, and commit iniquity, and I lay a stumblingblock before him, he shall die: because thou hast not given him warning, he shall die in his sin, and his righteousness which he hath done shall not be remembered; but his blood will I require at thine hand. Nevertheless if thou warn the righteous man, that the righteous sin not, and he doth not sin, he shall surely live, because he is warned; also thou hast delivered thy soul. (Ezek. 3:17–21)

Here Ezekiel expounded the duty of the Israelites to warn others to repent. Should a member of the faith fail in this duty, God would hold him responsible for the evil doings of those he might otherwise have saved. A doctrinally analogous passage is present in the Book of Mormon: "answering the sins of the people upon our own heads if we did not teach them the word of God with all diligence … otherwise their blood would come upon our garments" (Jacob 1:19). Thus, when Mormon elders cursed, they did so not only to call down wrath upon their opponents, but also to free themselves from the burden of the sins of those around them. Only then could they "be filled with joy and gladness."

THE PRACTICE WANES

Despite repeated enjoinders to shake the dust from one's feet and the enthusiasm with which some followers embraced the cursing ritual, there emerged from early on a counter rhetoric warning against the flippant condemnation of others. Warnings were given to avoid "over-zealousness in declaring judgments against the wicked,"[67] and Mormons were cautioned to "Talk not of Judgment."[68] W. W. Phelps instructed church elders in 1832 to "Warn in compassion without threatening the wicked with judgments."[69] In 1835, church leaders explicitly stated, "Pray for

67. Underwood, *Millenarian World of Early Mormonism*, 51.
68. Revelation, June 22, 1834 (D&C 105:24), *Joseph Smith Papers*.
69. *The Evening and the Morning Star* 2, 2 (July 1832): 6.

your enemies in the Church and curse not your foes without; for vengeance belongs to God."[70]

Although cursing was initially embraced as a necessary ritual of Mormonism, over time the recorded instances of cursing became fewer and farther between. Part of this was due to the Mormons having removed themselves to a remote area of the continent. In the process, they left many of their enemies behind, and shifted their focus from proselytizing to community building. Orson Pratt mentioned cursing in passing in an address given in 1876,[71] but it appears that the Saints were not very concerned with cursing during the years 1850–80. The work of settling a new land, organizing a territorial government, and confirming church organization under the leadership of Brigham Young took precedence over the responsibility of cursing the occasional outsider.

Eventually, missionaries were sent out to preach the gospel and an increasing number of outsiders entered the Utah territory. With renewed exposure to the rejection of non-Mormons, the practice of shaking the dust off one's feet resurfaced, but never again with the same widespread performance as was seen during the early years of the church. B. H. Roberts recorded only a single instance from his 1880–82 mission to Iowa when he "felt at liberty" to curse someone. After receiving "rather rough treatment" in the home of a man he thought might help him obtain permission to preach at a nearby schoolhouse, Roberts departed and journeyed a mile eastward. Climbing over a fence for privacy,

> I stripped my feet and washed them in witness against this man and house for the rejection of me. This I recount as the only instance when I felt at liberty to attend to this ordinance of the washing of feet against one who had rejected me. I never returned to the house and never knew what became of it, but I left my testimony thus registered according to the commandments of the Lord.[72]

---

70. Joseph Smith, Oliver Cowdery, W. W. Phelps, and John Whitmer (Kirtland, Ohio), Letter to John M. Burk (Liberty, Clay County, Missouri), Journal History, June 1, 1835, qtd. in Prince, *Power from On High*, 110.

71. Aug. 20, 1876, *Journal of Discourses*, 26 vols. (London and Liverpool: LDS Booksellers Depot, 1854–86), 18:265.

72. Gary James Bergera, ed., *Autobiography of B. H. Roberts* (Salt Lake City: Signature Books, 1990), 90–91; on Smith Research Associates, *New Mormon Studies* CD-ROM.

By this time, mentions of cursing in discourses from church leadership were rare and generally made in passing. In an 1883 session of the reformed Salt Lake City School of the Prophets, Wilford Woodruff "gave instructions and stated the effects that have followed this ordinance. Spoke upon the shaking off the dust of the feet and washing the feet in pure water in summer or in winter and the judgements of God have followed."[73] George Q. Cannon cautioned that "[in] our prayers we should not condemn our enemies but leave them in the hands of God."[74]

USE OF THE PRAYER CIRCLE

Joseph Smith introduced a new temple endowment ceremony to church leaders in Nauvoo in 1842, and by 1843 this endowment included ritual prayer circles.[75] After the deaths of Joseph and Hyrum Smith in 1844, a prayer or oath was added to the endowment. Known as the "oath of vengeance" or "law of retribution," the ritual stipulated that the recipient of the endowment pray that God avenge the blood of his slain prophets.[76] By the 1880s, Mormons were accustomed to including a call to God's wrath upon their foes in their temple ceremonies. Although curses overall were becoming fewer in number, the 1880s saw a brief flourish in cursing and a new variant in its ritual performance. Cursing practice had been influenced in the past by the washing rituals of the School of the Prophets. In the 1880s, cursing would cross-pollinate with temple ordinances, influenced by the oath of vengeance and incorporating the prayer circle.

In 1880, Wilford Woodruff was president of the Quorum of the Twelve Apostles. The church was under immense pressure from the

---

73. Minutes (St. George), Dec. 24, 1883, School of the Prophets Salt Lake City meeting minutes, 1883, internally paginated, CR 390 5, CHL.

74. Dennis B. Horne, ed., *An Apostle's Record: The Journals of Abraham H. Cannon, Member of the Quorum of the Twelve Apostles, 1889–1896* (Clearfield, Utah: Gnolaum Books, 2004), 118–19.

75. D. Michael Quinn, "Latter-day Saint Prayer Circles," *BYU Studies* 19, 1 (Fall 1978): 79–105. The year 1843 also saw the introduction of the second anointing, a ritual that bestowed upon recipients the power to bind, loose, curse, and bless. See David John Buerger, *The Mysteries of Godliness: a History of Mormon Temple Worship* (San Francisco: Smith Research Associates, 1994), 87–90. Samuel Hollister Rogers, a recipient of the second anointing, "told the Lord that his anointed one had been violated," and invoked a curse upon his neighbor. See Buerger, *Mysteries of Godliness*, 104. Thanks to Amberly Dattilo for bringing this to my attention.

76. Buerger, *Mysteries of Godliness*, 133–36.

federal government to end the practice of plural marriage. Woodruff recorded that God spoke to him, promising plagues, wrath, and judgment against the church's accusers. God's anger was kindled against those in positions of government authority, such as:

> The Preside[n]ts of the United States, The Supreme Court, The Cabinet, The Senate & House of Conress of the United States The Governors of the States and Territor/ies\ The Judges & Officers sent unto you and all men & persons who have taken any part in persecuting you or Bringing distress upon you or your families or have sought your lives or sought to hinder you from keeping my Command[men]ts or from Enjoying the rights which the Constitutional Laws of the Land guarantee unto you.[77]

In an effort that bears striking resemblance to the oath of vengeance, a list was compiled of over 400 "Names of Persons, to be held in Remembrance before the Lord, For their Evil Deeds, and who have raised their hands against the Lord's anointed." The list included four U.S. presidents: Martin Van Buren, Ulysses S. Grant, Rutherford B. Hayes, and James Buchanan.[78] To secure God's judgments against those on the list, Woodruff was instructed to gather the Twelve and wash their feet as a testimony against their enemies.[79] The apostles were then to clothe themselves in temple robes and form a prayer circle.

Woodruff describes the eventual performance of this ordinance in solemn terms:

> O Pratt was vary feeble yet we all performed the ordinance of washing our feet against Our Enemies And the Enemies of the Kingdom of God according to the Commandmet of God unto us.
>
> W. Woodruff opened By Prayer And John Taylor was Mouth in the washing of feet. At the Prayer Circle Lorenzo Snow was Mouth at the opening And Presidet JOHN TAYLOR was mouth at the Altar, and Presented the Prayer written By W. Woodruff (By request of Presidet Taylor) And the names were presented before the Lord according to the Commandment.

---

77. Woodruff, Journal, revelation copied following Dec. 31, 1880.

78. Buerger, *Mysteries of Godliness*, unpaginated image and text.

79. Woodruff, Journal, revelation copied following Dec. 31, 1880 (originally given Jan. 26, 1880). This revelation was given a second time to Woodruff only days later, again emphasizing "the duty of the Apostles and Elders to go into our Holy places & Temples and wash our feet and bear testimony to God & the Heavenly hosts against the wickedness of this Nation. My pillow was wet with the fountain of tears that flowed as I Beheld the Judgments of God upon the wicked." See Woodruff, Journal, Jan. 27, 1880.

It was truly a solomn scene and I presume to say it was the first thing of the Kind since the Creation of the world. ... We were 3 hours in the Meeting & ordinances.[80]

The actual prayer, written by Woodruff and read by John Taylor, reads in part:

Now O Lord our God we bear our testimony against these men, befor Thee and the heavenly hosts and we bear testimony unto thee Our heavenly Father that we according to thy Commandments unto us we have gone alone by ourselves and Clensed our feet in pure water and born testimony unto Thee and thy Son Jesus Christ and to the heavenly hosts against these wicked men by name as far as the spirit has manifested them unto us. We have borne our testimony against those who have shed the blood of thy Prophets and Apostles and anointed Ones, or have given Consent to their death and against those who have driven thy saints and imprisoned them and those who are still ready to deprive us of Life, Liberty and the privilege of keeping the Commandments of God.

And now O Lord our God Thou hast Commanded us that when we have done this we should gather ourselves together in our holy Places and Clothed in the robes of the Holy Priesthood should unite ourselves together in Prayer and supplication and that we should bear our testimony against these men by name as far as wisdom should dictate.

... O Lord hear us from heaven thy Holy dwelling place and answer our Petions Sustain thine anointed ones and deliver us from the hands of Our Enemies. Overthrow the Evil designs of the wicked and ungodly against thy Saints and break Evry weapon formed against us.[81]

This episode is notable for a shift in the provocation to curse. In the past, curses had been performed primarily against those who rejected a proselytizer's message. Here the curse was called down upon the church's political enemies.

On one other known occasion, a prayer circle was formed with intent to curse. In 1889, a prayer circle was convened to curse R. N. Baskin, a non-Mormon lawyer who was actively engaged in the anti-polygamy crusades of the time.[82] According to the journal of new apostle Abraham H. Cannon, a group of nine church leaders convened on December 23, 1889. All but two of them were dressed in

80. Woodruff, Journal, Jan. 19, 1881.
81. Woodruff, Journal, revelation copied following Dec. 31, 1880.
82. "'Mormons' and Citizenship," *Deseret Weekly*, Nov. 23, 1889, 684–93.

their temple robes. Each member took a turn acting as mouth for the prayer circle. Joseph F. Smith "was strongest in his prayer and urged that Baskin should be made blind, deaf and dumb unless he would repent of his wickedness."[83] Diary entries from participants do not indicate that feet were dusted or washed in connection with this prayer circle. The church was struggling to beat Baskin in the courtroom, and church leaders expressed their frustration by requesting that God stop the trouble at its source.

DECLINE AND DISAPPEARANCE

With the beginning of the end of plural marriage in 1890, Mormonism continued its evolution from a small, persecuted sect toward a stable, respectable institution. As persecution declined, so too did the discourse and practice of ritual cursing. The last publicized endorsement of cursing by a general authority came from John W. Taylor in the April 1899 general conference. "[This] is the way Christ is going to Judge the world, for He gave a special commandment that . . . if they reject you shake the dust off your feet as a testimony against them, for it shall be more tolerable in the day of judgment for the city of Sodom or Gomorrha than for that city or household that rejecteth you."[84]

Around the time of Taylor's address, church discourse shifted toward ignoring cursing or mentioning it only with some degree of antipathy. In response to inquiries regarding shaking the dust off one's feet from President B. E. Rich of the Southern States Mission, George Reynolds of the Seventy was authorized by the First Presidency to write the following letter (dated March 11, 1899):

> I am directed by the First Presidency to say in reply to your favor that the business of the wholesale washing of feet, &c should not be indulged in by the elders. If an elder feels that he has just cause and is moved upon by the spirit of God to wash his feet against a person or persons who have violently or wickedly rejected the truth, let him do so quietly and beyond

83. Horne, *Apostle's Record,* 119.

84. *Report of the Semi-Annual Conference of the Church of Jesus Christ of Latter-day Saints,* April 1899 (Salt Lake City: Church of Jesus Christ of Latter-day Saints, semi-annual), 23 (hereafter cited as *Conference Report*); on Smith Research Associates, *New Mormon Studies* CD-ROM.

noting it in his journal let him not make it public. Nothing should be published in the "Southern Star" or else-where on this subject. Elders should be privately instructed and should let the matter rest between them, the Lord, and the persons concerned.[85]

Such a direct statement against the wholesale practice of cursing cast a shadow across the potential future of this ritual. Another mission president, Nephi Pratt, was recorded in the *Conference Report* for April 1906 as doubting the propriety of cursing. There had been "indifference manifested in the larger cities of [the Northwestern States mission], and we have some times thought that all had been done there that ought to be done there. ... Always we had a doubt whether we ought to shake off the dust from our feet against some of the cities in the northwest."[86]

Ritual cursing was not mentioned in general conference for the next sixty years. In April 1968, S. Dilworth Young spoke of the cursing ritual in a distinctly past tense.

> There have been times when we thought that if we approached a man and he, hostile because of stories he had heard about us, or suspicious because we were strangers, rebuffed us, then we had done our duty by shaking off the dust of our feet against him. We have not done that duty until we have given him a fair chance to learn that his prejudices are unfounded.[87]

In the sixty years of silence over the general conference pulpit, cursing was transitioning from a practiced ritual to a historical relic. Mormons had less cause to be interested in ritual cursing as they became more mainstream and less persecuted. The millenarian impulse that motivated early missionaries to shake the dust from their feet had waned. The 1946 edition of *The Missionary's Hand Book* included as one of forty-two rules, "Bless, but do not curse."[88] Any mention of the ritual in church publications referred to cursing as something

---

85. George Reynolds, Letter to Ben E. Rich, Mar. 11, 1899, typescript in Scott G. Kenney Collection, "People" series, box 2, folder 11, J. Willard Marriott Library Special Collections, University of Utah, Salt Lake City, qtd. in Golding, "The Foundations and Early Development of Mormon Mission Theory," 100.

86. *Conference Report,* Apr. 1906, 33.

87. *Conference Report*, Apr. 1968, 65.

88. *The Missionary's Hand Book* (Salt Lake City: Church of Jesus Christ of Latter-day Saints, rev. 1946).

done in the past, not as a practice to be engaged in the present.[89] An excerpt from the *Doctrine and Covenants Compendium* (published in 1960) is illuminating:

> Today it is not the general custom in the Church for our Elders on missions to shake off the dust of their feet against the people who do not receive them. In our time the Lord is giving men everywhere ample opportunity to receive the Gospel. Consequently, Elders may return to the same people time and time again, thus giving them every opportunity to receive the word of God before His judgments come unto them.[90]

J. Reuben Clark mentioned the biblical dusting of one's feet twice in his *On the Way to Immortality and Eternal Life* without ever discussing its parallel practice in the modern church.[91] Modern commentators have followed suit, mentioning cursing only as an interesting footnote in the church's history.[92]

The disappearance of this ritual from Mormon liturgy may be due to a number of factors. The tone of church discourse on cursing evolved from commandment and instruction to caution and discouragement. With passing generations, the sense of Christ's impending return lessened. When a missionary was rejected, it was no longer believed that the disbelieving parties had lost their one chance for

---

89. "The cleansing of their feet, either by washing or wiping off the dust, would be recorded in heaven as a testimony against the wicked. This act, however, was not to be performed in the presence of the offenders, 'lest thou provoke them, but in secret, and wash thy feet, as a testimony against them in the day of judgment.' The missionaries of the Church who faithfully perform their duty are under the obligation of leaving their testimony with all with whom they come in contact in their work. This testimony will stand as a witness against those who reject the message, at the judgment." Joseph Fielding Smith, qtd. in *Doctrine and Covenants Student Manual: Religion 324 and 325* (Salt Lake City: Church of Jesus Christ of Latter-day Saints, 2001), 130.

90. Sidney B. Sperry, *Doctrine and Covenants Compendium* (Salt Lake City: Bookcraft, 1960), 254.

91. J. Reuben Clark Jr., *On the Way to Immortality and Eternal Life* (Salt Lake City: Deseret Book Co., 1949), 357, 372.

92. Bruce R. McConkie, *Mormon Doctrine* (Salt Lake City: Bookcraft, 1958), 162–64. Sperry, *Doctrine and Covenants Compendium*, 332. Melvin R. Brooks, *LDS Reference Encyclopedia*, (Salt Lake City: Bookcraft, 1960–65), 111–12. Kent P. Jackson and Robert L. Millet, eds., *Studies in Scripture, Vol. 5: The Gospels* (Salt Lake City: Deseret Book Co., 1986), 234. Richard L. Bushman, *Joseph Smith and the Beginnings of Mormonism* (Urbana: University of Illinois Press, 1987), 165. Sherwin W. Howard, "Cursings," *Encyclopedia of Mormonism*, 4 vols. (New York: Macmillan Publishing Co., 1992), 1:352. Todd Compton, "The Spiritual Roots of the Democratic Party: Why I Am a Mormon Democrat," Sunstone Symposium speech, Summer 2001.

salvation. The missionary mindset shifted from one of binding wheat and tares up to the day of destruction to one of returning to homes again and again to give people multiple chances to accept the gospel. With the move to Utah and subsequent renouncement of plural marriage, Mormonism's enemies became fewer and the accompanying physical violence was reduced. As Mormons gained control of their lives and their surroundings, the apparent need to shake the dust off their feet lessened. The spirit of doctrinal and liturgical innovation that permeated early Mormonism waned over time, particularly with the rise of Correlation in the 1960s. Together with the loss of other non-salvific Mormon ordinances (e.g., female healing blessings, baptism for health), there may have simply been no place in modern Mormonism for cursing. The modern church's heightened awareness of national attention and public relations would likely make the continued practice of cursing an embarrassment.

Although anecdotes describing present-day episodes of shaking the dust off one's feet persist,[93] mission presidents do not receive instruction from general authorities regarding the performance of this ritual. According to one former mission president, it is generally understood that to curse someone in the mission field today would be inappropriate.[94] No current church handbook or manual lists cursing as an

---

93. After being rudely rebuffed by an investigator of European descent for bringing a native Guatemalan companion to a missionary discussion, John Dehlin recorded the following conversation with his mission president in his journal: "During my interview with President Romney, he told me that Barrios and Aston told him what had happened w/ the Colonel's wife. He said to me, 'Elder Dehlin, how important is that family to you?' I said that they were ok, and that mostly I was thinking of the future possibility of the kids becoming members, and not so much the mother. Then he sat silent for a second, looked down, and then looked up to me and said, 'I feel inspired to ask you to go to that lady's house and perform the ordinance'" John Dehlin, Journal, Mar. 26, 1990, qtd. in John Dehlin, Email to Samuel R. Weber, Apr. 10, 2007, printout in my possession. Dehlin later recounted from memory how the ordinance was performed. "A few days later, Elder Pivaral and I walked up to the Colonel's wife's house. We stood, quietly in front of the house. We looked at each other with a bit of bewilderment, and then we bowed our heads and gave the cursing, 'Heavenly Father. In the name of Jesus Christ, and by the power of the holy Melchizedek priesthood which we bear, we leave a curse upon this house, for the wicked, racist acts of the Colonel's wife. And we do so in the name of Jesus Christ, Amen.' Then we looked back up at the house, stomped our feet on the pavement several times (to dust off the feet), looked at each other again with some bewilderment, and then walked back home." John Dehlin, Email to Samuel R. Weber, Apr. 10, 2007, printout in my possession.

94. Thomas Cherrington, Interviewed by Samuel R. Weber, Nov. 16, 2006.

official ordinance.[95] Although no longer formally practiced, curses live on in the form of missionary folklore[96] and Mormon fiction.[97]

CONCLUSION

Mormon cursing flourished for a time, but by the 1900s it was extinct for all practical purposes. As the factors that had precipitated ritual cursing during the early days of Mormonism dissipated over time, performance of the ritual ceased. Modern Mormonism no longer consists of a small group of violently mistreated social outcasts as it once did. As the church has become more stable and prosperous, its goals appear to be more geared toward integration and contribution to the surrounding community rather than separation from and condemnation of unbelieving gentiles. While not denying cursing as part of its history, the church has experienced a paradigm shift to a more blessing-focused theology. President Joseph F. Smith's words from a 1904 general conference reflect on the practice of cursing while simultaneously looking forward to a future of love and redemption:

95. Gregory Prince has noted that "cursing is not considered an ordinance in the Latter-day Saint church today," and that "no church handbook or manual lists [cursing] among official ordinances." Prince, *Power from On High*, 108.

96. "In [some missionary] stories, when the opposition is keener, [the missionaries] are not equal to the task and are forced to bring the Lord in to fight the battle for them. In these accounts, following biblical example, the elders shake dust from their feet and thereby curse the people who have treated them ill. The Lord responds to the missionaries' actions in a dreadful manner. In Norway a city treats missionaries harshly; they shake dust from their feet, and the city is destroyed by German shelling during the war. Throughout the world, other cities that have mistreated missionaries suffer similar fates. Towns are destroyed in South America by wind, in Chile by floods, in Costa Rica by a volcano, in Mexico by an earthquake, in Japan by a tidal wave, in Taiwan and Sweden by fire. In South Africa a town's mining industry fails, in Colorado a town's land becomes infertile, and in Germany a town's fishing industry folds. Individuals who have persecuted missionaries may also feel God's wrath. An anti-Mormon minister, for instance, loses his job, or breaks his arm, or dies of throat cancer. A woman refuses to give missionaries water and her well goes dry. A man angrily throws the Book of Mormon into the fire only to have his own house burn down. In one story, widely known, two elders leave their garments at a laundry, and when the proprietor holds them up for ridicule, both he and the laundry burn, the fire so hot in some instances that it melts the bricks." William A. Wilson, *On Being Human: The Folklore of Mormon Missionaries* (Logan: Utah State University Press, 1981), 19. The last story quoted above was still circulated in the Germany Hamburg Mission where I served from 2002 to 2004.

97. "I better warn you, I'm getting mad. I'm getting ready to dust off my feet on you. … God's going to wipe his hindparts with you and flush you down a toilet, and I say good riddance to bad rubbish." Levi S. Peterson, "The Third Nephite," *Dialogue: A Journal of Mormon Thought* 19, 4 (Winter 1986): 170.

[I]f they cursed, in the spirit of righteousness and meekness before God, God would confirm that curse; but men are not called upon to curse mankind; that is not our mission; it is our mission to preach righteousness unto them. It is our business to love and to bless them, and to redeem them from the fall and from the wickedness of the world. ... We are perfectly willing to leave vengeance in the hands of God and let him judge between us and our enemies, and let him reward them according to his own wisdom and mercy.[98]

Without a powerful modern resurgence of liturgical innovation, Christian primitivism, millenarianism, or violent persecution, cursing is unlikely to reemerge as a practice within Mormonism. However, an appreciation of its role in the early restoration provides a fascinating window into the mindset of Mormonism's founding generations.

---

98. Joseph F. Smith, qtd. in McConkie, *Mormon Doctrine*, 163.

TEN

"SATAN MOURNS NAKED UPON THE EARTH"
LOCATING MORMON POSSESSION AND EXORCISM RITUALS IN THE AMERICAN RELIGIOUS LANDSCAPE, 1830–1977

STEPHEN C. TAYSOM

Joseph Smith believed in the Devil. His public ministry began with a dramatic case of possession and exorcism.[1] In April 1830, Smith, the twenty-four year-old founding prophet of Mormonism, entered a small log home in rural New York to find a young friend, Newel Knight, in agony. Knight's "visage and limbs [were] distorted & twisted into every possible shape and appearances." Knight then levitated and was thrown violently around the room. To Smith, it was clear that this was the work of Satan. Word of the strange happenings quickly spread, and a handful of neighbors and family members gathered in astonishment. Eventually Smith was able to get close enough to Knight to grasp his hand, at which point Knight "requested with great earnestness that I should cast the Devil out of him, that he knew that he was in him, and that he also knew that I could cast him out." Smith

---

1. The term translated "exorcism" in English comes from the Greek *exorkizō* (ἐξορκίζω) and means "to bind with an oath" or "to adjure" (e.g., 1 Thes. 5:27). From antiquity Christians have used the term to refer to rituals that drive evil spirits out of human beings. My use of the term in the context of Mormon ritual practice is potentially problematic and requires brief justification. "Exorcism" is something of a fraught term because, since the Middle Ages, it has been closely associated with the specific Roman Catholic ritual. Protestants typically use the term "deliverance" rather than "exorcism" to distance themselves from Catholic practice. Mormons have no term that is equivalent to either "exorcism" or "deliverance." A denominationally-neutral term for the practice of casting out devils and demons is "dispossession." I have elected, however, not to use the term "dispossession" when referring to such Mormon rituals and have chosen instead to use "exorcism" despite the particular association the term has with Catholicism. Because Mormonism does not have a term for this particular ritual act, there is no emic vocabulary upon which I can rely. My choice, then, is between two etic terms: "exorcism" and "dispossession." I have chosen the former because "exorcism" is a more widely-recognized and generally less awkward term than "dispossession."

"rebuked the Devil, ~~in~~ and commanded him ~~to leave him~~ in the name of Jesus Christ to depart from him." Knight then claimed to see Satan leave his body and "vanish from his sight."[2]

Satan did not vanish for long, however. From Smith's day until the present, Satan, and the belief that he and his "angels" can and do possess the bodies of human beings, have been regular fixtures in Mormon thought. Despite what one scholar sees as the "cooling of the demonic throughout Mormon culture" after the nineteenth century, the ideas remain alive and well.[3] In 2005, the LDS Church's official magazine, *The Ensign*, reprinted a talk from LDS Apostle Marion Romney reaffirming Smith's early teachings on the subject. "We Latter-day Saints need not be, and we must not be, deceived by the sophistries of men concerning the reality of Satan," Romney warned. "There is a personal Devil, and we had better believe it."[4] This is not to suggest that Mormon ideas have not changed in the nearly two centuries since the Knight exorcism. "Casting out evil spirits" was frequently spoken of by church leaders in the nineteenth century. Today the practice still exists, but it has dropped from official discourse. Eric D. Huntsman, a scholar of ancient history and member of BYU's department of ancient scripture who writes from a devotional LDS point of view, recently published a book by LDS-owned Deseret Book Company on the subject of the miracles of Jesus. Huntsman dedicates an entire chapter to the exorcisms performed by Jesus, and concludes that "demonic possessions occurred and Jesus had the power to deliver those who were held captive in that way. Although both can also occur today, Satan has other effective tools [such as addiction and abuse] adapted to our time to lead people into bondage and make them miserable."[5] Although, as Huntsman's work makes clear, possession and exorcism have taken a backseat to other explanations for certain

---

2. History, circa June–October 1839 [Draft 1], *Joseph Smith Papers*, www.josephsmith-papers.org.

3. Christopher J. Blythe, "Vernacular Mormonism: The Development of Latter-Day Saint Apocalyptic, 1830–1930" (PhD diss., Florida State University, 2014).

4. Marion G. Romney, "Satan, the Great Deceiver," *Ensign*, Feb. 2005, www.churchofjesuschrist.org/study/ensign/2005/02/satan-the-great-deceiver; accessed Aug. 3, 2020. The talk was originally given in the April 1971 general conference.

5. Eric D. Huntsman, *The Miracles of Jesus* (Salt Lake City: Deseret Book Co., 2014), 85.

behaviors, for Mormons they remain, to use William James's famous phrase, "live options" in the twenty-first century.[6]

Despite such a pervasive and enduring belief in the reality of the Devil and of his propensity for possessing human bodies, very little is known or understood about Mormon possession/exorcism events. Despite the existence of many such accounts, scholarly studies of Mormon exorcism are extremely scarce.[7] Most studies of Mormonism have focused on the official beliefs and practices as articulated and undertaken by leaders and other prominent Mormons. Casting out evil spirits, however, has no official ritual standing within Mormonism. In the nineteenth and early twentieth centuries, Mormon officials spoke openly about possession and exorcism, but there is no prescribed exorcistic ritual, nor is there any official guide to diagnosing a demoniac. In a religion that is has become as highly centralized and allows as little room for ritual innovation as does Mormonism, it is unusual to find a practice that is both practiced and not officially described.[8] The absence of any mention of possession or exorcism in official modern church materials accounts, in part, for how the subject of Mormon exorcism has eluded scholars. Despite official silence on the subject, Mormons have a long, and continuing, history of casting out evil spirits.

This essay looks beyond the official invisibility of possession and exorcism, and explores how Mormons in different times and places translated their diabological beliefs into ritual action. This is not an attempt to excavate the causes of possession. I agree with Fernando Cervantes's position that "for the historian ... the interest in [possession and exorcism] is not so much to be found in the way in which they point to pathological states or psychiatric complexes, but rather in the fact that they allow some understanding of the spirituality of the time [and] the contemporary ideological climate" and contexts in which the events

---

6. James discusses his theory of live options in his 1896 lecture "The Will to Believe." The category is explicated at length in John H. Whittaker, "William James on 'Overbelief' and 'Live Options,'" *International Journal for Philosophy of Religion* 14, 4 (1983): 203–16.

7. Blythe offered the first rigorous and interpretative exploration of exorcism and possession as a method of nineteenth-century Mormon identity formation in the first two chapters of his excellent dissertation. Blythe, "Vernacular Mormonism."

8. There are very few rituals that, particularly in the nineteenth century, evaded official description. Exorcism is one example; another is "deathbed dedication." For a recent treatment of some LDS rituals, see Jonathan A. Stapley, *The Power of Godliness: Mormon Liturgy and Cosmology* (New York: Oxford University Press, 2018).

occurred.[9] Following that philosophy, my essay has four main goals: (1) to build on ritual studies scholarship to develop a model for the study of ritual suited to the case of Mormon exorcism; (2) to situate Mormon belief and ritual practice dealing with possession and exorcism within the larger context of American culture and religion; (3) to examine the cultural work done by and the cultural implications of individual instances of possession and exorcism; and (4) to use exorcism as a window into the dynamics and characteristics of Mormonism more generally. I argue that several core Mormon beliefs coalesced to form a typology of possession and exorcism that led to an active belief in these phenomena at the same time that such belief was waning among American Evangelical Protestants. I further argue that instances of possession and exorcism functioned for Mormons as performances that accomplished a wide variety of cultural and religious goals, from supporting Mormon truth claims to providing an avenue for women to express themselves, to expressing late-twentieth century Mormon attitudes about the sacredness of hierarchy. Finally, I argue that exorcism accounts reveal in fine-grained detail the constant engagement with, and adaptation to, larger religious and cultural forces at work in the American context.

RITUAL TYPOLOGY

Whatever else they may be, exorcisms are culturally constructed performances in that they include the "deliberate, self-conscious 'doing' of highly symbolic actions in public."[10] Any cultural performances are particular enactments of a typological model. A typology sets the boundaries for what a group will accept as a legitimate instance of a particular phenomenon. In the case of possession, the typology informs the entire group about how possessed persons are expected to act. The same is true for the exorcistic ritual. In that case, the typological model will, first, determine whether exorcism is a recognized or approved category of action, and, if so, the model will indicate what ritual actions are efficacious and appropriate.

To anyone looking for a simple definition of ritual, Catherine Bell delivers bad news. "It becomes quickly evident," she writes, "that there

---

9. Fernando Cervantes, *The Devil in the New World: The Impact of Diabolism in New Spain* (New Haven, Connecticut: Yale University Press, 1994), 104.

10. Catherine Bell, *Ritual: Perspectives and Dimensions*, rev. ed. (New York: Oxford University Press, 2009), 159–60.

is no clear and widely shared explanation of what constitutes ritual or how to understand it."[11] If this is not sufficiently sobering, Brian Levack points out that "demonic possession is a methodological landmine for historians."[12] Possession is interesting from a scholarly point of view because it is so complex. This is also what makes it so difficult to interpret and analyze. Michel Foucault's assertion that the body of the possessed individual is not so much the site of "the great duel between good and evil" (although sometimes that symbolism does emerge) as it is a "multiple body that is somehow volatized and pulverized into a multiplicity of powers that confront each other."[13] So in both categorical and specific dimensions, the subject of this essay is complex and potentially problematic. Faced with such difficulty, one is left to choose a working definition of ritual and then stick to it. Bell provides some guidance in her description of traits shared by "ritual-like activities." Formalism, traditionalism, invariance, rule-governance, sacral symbolism, and performance are characteristics that rituals, and ritual-like behaviors, tend to display to one degree or another.[14] Bell also offers a taxonomy of ritual, groupings that she calls "genres."

Exorcisms fit unquestionably into her "rites of affliction" genre, but this taxonomy is not particularly useful for the analysis of rituals *within* a given genre. More helpful is a method developed by Ronald Grimes based on the observation that "a ritual has density, or depth, requiring an interpreter to read or dig through it."[15] According to Grimes, a scholar may expect to find "layers" of varying richness in any given ritual. Grimes's method posits six potential layers, which he labels "ritualization, decorum, ceremony, magic, liturgy, and celebration."[16] Although not definitions, Bell's list of traits and Grimes's modal layers help first to identify ritual through an examination of behavioral traits, then to assist in interpreting the internal dynamics of the ritual via an evaluation of the relative thickness of its modes, and finally to provide

---

11. Bell, *Ritual*, x.

12. Levack, *The Devil Within: Possession and Exorcism in the Christian West* (New Haven, Connecticut: Yale University Press, 2013), 3.

13. Michel Foucault, *Abnormal: Lectures at the College de France, 1974–1976* (New York: Picador, 1999), 207.

14. Bell, *Ritual*, 139–68.

15. Ronald L. Grimes, *The Craft of Ritual Studies* (New York: Oxford University Press, 2014), 205.

16. Grimes, *Craft of Ritual Studies*, 204.

a basis for comparing one ritual with others by nesting each ritual within a space within the larger context of genre. By integrating Bell's work with Grimes's, one is able to create a useful frame for considering Mormon exorcism. This combination also allows us to recover the "multivocality" of the rituals—what Barbara Gerke describes as "the variety of ritual experience of the different participants taking part in one and the same ritual."[17]

For example, Mormon exorcistic rites fit with Bell's genre called rites of affliction, and within that category, they show high degrees of traditionalism, sacral symbolism, and performance, all of which are carried out in what Grimes would label a "magically-inflected" mode.[18] I add a fourth dimension to this analysis, in addition to genre, trait, and mode, that I call the schema of ritual work. For the purposes of this essay, ritual may further be thought of as an embodied act that accomplishes three types of "work": practical, symbolic, and cultural. The first two kinds of work are generally known to, and accepted by, ritual practitioners. Scholars, in addition to exploring those two levels of meaning, must also identify and interpret the cultural work a ritual performs. In other words, scholars must find out what purposes the ritual serves beyond those put forth by practitioners. Another way to think about cultural work is that it does not rely on a belief in the supernatural processes or efficacy of the ritual. If one were to look at the practice of confession of sin, for example, psychological catharsis would be one type of cultural work that is performed.

When analyzed together, these three types of "work" provide scholars with a wealth of insight into the world views of the practitioners as well as the broader cultural context in which the ritual is performed. In the case of exorcism, for example, the practical work is the expulsion of a demonic force, the symbolic work may be the demonstration of a god's total power over a cosmic enemy, and the cultural work may be the expression of dissatisfaction with powerful elites or consist of allowing women an opportunity to speak in a world where discourse is

---

17. Barbara Gerke, "The Multivocality of Ritual Experience: Long-Life Empowerments Among Tibetan Communities in the Darjeeling Hills, India," in Axel Michaels, ed., *Ritual Dynamics and the Science of Ritual: II: Body, Performance, Agency, and Experience* (Wiesbaden, Germany: Harrassowitz Verlag, 2010), 425.

18. "Magic" is a problematic and hotly contested term. Grimes uses it to describe ritual actions that are "causal, means-end oriented and causal." Grimes, *Craft of Ritual Studies*, 204.

dominated by men. The possibilities for each kind of work are manifold and depend on each individual ritual act. My basic approach is to recount the event based on the documentary record, set the event in its historical context, identify the practical and symbolic functions of the exorcism via an analysis of typological models and any innovation/deviation from those models, and identify the cultural work performed by the possession/exorcism drama. For the sake of readability, I do not explicitly lay out how each case fits within the model. Rather, I have analyzed the cases using the general methodological approach described above without overt references to it.

SATAN IN EARLY MORMON DOCTRINE

Joseph Smith's understanding of the nature and purpose of the Devil is summarized best in a revelation that he dictated in early 1832 indicating that "satan [is] that old serpent even the devel who who rebelled against God and saught to take the kingdom of our God and his christ wherefore he maketh war with the saints of God and encompasseth them round about, [and] he made war."[19]

Of particular importance for Mormons were the elements of this story dealing with the warfare between Satan and "the saints of God." From the earliest days of Smith's ministry, Mormons were taught to believe that this was a literal, physical war in which the Devil and his angels sought to possess the bodies of those on earth.[20] In order to understand why possession and exorcism became entrenched in Mormon practice at a time when Evangelical Protestant denominations to which Mormonism was closest culturally were leaving the practice behind, it is necessary to understand that the notion of possession was, for Mormons, thoroughly grounded in their theology of the body.

Smith famously taught that embodiment was a reward for those spirits who had successfully "kept their first estate," by which he meant those who had sided with Christ in the pre-mortal war in heaven and had elected to come to Earth. The time spent on Earth was to be the continuation of the cosmic test, but no matter how poorly an

---

19. Vision, Hiram, Ohio, Feb. 16, 1832, handwriting of Joseph Smith and Frederick G. Williams, *Joseph Smith Papers*.

20. In Smith's teachings, the Devil's angels were those spirits who chose to follow him when he was cast out of heaven. They are, then, of the same heavenly family as human beings, but without physical bodies. See chap. 4, herein.

individual performed, all would be the beneficiaries of a bodily resurrection. Satan, and those who followed him, were denied the sublime blessing of embodiment, and thus sought to get a body, even temporarily, through possession.

In 1841, Smith taught that "we came to this earth that we might have a body. ... The great principle of happiness consists in having a body. The Devil has no body and herein is his punishment. He is pleased when he can obtain the tabernacle [body] of a man and when cast out by the Savior he asked to go into the herd of swine showing that he would prefer a swine's body to having none."[21] Two years later he again addressed the subject, vividly linking possession with the disembodied of Satan.

> When Lucifer was hurled from Heaven the decree was that he Should not obtain a tabernacle nor those that were with him, but go abroad upon the earth exposed to the anger of the elements naked & bare, but ofttimes he lays hold upon men binds up their Spirits enters their habitations laughs at the decree of God and rejoices in that he hath a house to dwell in, by & by he is expelled by Authority and goes abroad mourning naked upon the earth like a man without a house exposed to the tempest & the storm.[22]

These sermons, considered together, tell us several important things that aid in understanding the theological underpinnings of Mormon belief in possession and exorcism. First, the Devil is being punished through his own disembodiment. He, along with those who followed him, is exposed in some way to suffering and pain as a result of lacking the shelter provided by a mortal body. Second, part of the war that Satan wages against humankind in general, and the "saints" in particular, is to attempt to deprive them of their own body by literally taking it over. Smith's reference to swine in his 1841 sermon is a gloss on the story of the "Gerasene demononiac" (see Mark 5). Jesus, asking the name of the demon, was told that their collective name was "legion for we are many." Upon realizing that they were about to be cast out, the demonic legion requested that Jesus cast them into a herd of swine grazing on a nearby hillside. The biblical accounts offer no explanation of why the demonic spirits made the request, but Smith fills in the gap

---

21. Joseph Smith, Sermon, Jan. 5, 1841, reported by William Clayton, *Joseph Smith Papers*.
22. Joseph Smith, Sermon, May 21, 1843, reported by Howard Coray, *Joseph Smith Papers*.

by linking this event with his own notions of the joy of embodiment, even if that embodiment is brief and unclean.

It is not clear just when Smith came to these conclusions about the Devil, his angels, and the human body. All one may say with certainty is that, by the early 1840s, Smith had settled on them, and that they remained with the church for many decades. In an 1856 discourse, Brigham Young, Smith's successor as LDS Church president, said that "the Devels were cast out of heaven to this earth & they are still around us. Their condemnation is that they can never have a tabernacle but they seek to get into the tabernacle of all men they can."[23] A 1909 editorial in the church-owned *Deseret News* echoed these sentiments, proclaiming that "there are numerous instances of possession by evil spirits." Such events, the author claimed, represented attempts by "the evil one" to "imitate the greatest of all miracles—the miracle of incarnation."[24] Gordon B. Hinckley, who served as LDS Church president from 1995 to 2008, said that the story of the possessed boy and the herd of swine was designed to demonstrate "the worth of a human body.[25]

The connection between embodiment and possession lives today also in Mormon ritual life. The LDS temple endowment ritual contains a drama which enacts the expulsion of Adam and Eve from the Garden of Eden. In the LDS version of this story, it is Satan himself who convinces Eve to eat the forbidden fruit and it is Satan who is cast out and cursed by God, but not before Satan threatens to "take the spirits that follow me, and they shall possess the bodies thou createst

---

23. Wilford Woodruff, Journal, June 22, 1856, MS 1352, CHL. In this, as in several other things, Young disagreed with LDS Apostle Parley Pratt. Pratt, in his influential 1855 book *Key to the Science of Theology*, argued that it was not the spirits who had followed Lucifer to Earth who possessed humans but rather the "spirits of the departed, who are unhappy, [and who] linger in lonely wretchedness about the earth. The more wicked of these are the kind spoken of in Scripture, as '*foul spirits*,' '*unclean spirits*,' spirits who ... sometimes enter human bodies, and will distract them, throw them into fits, cast them into the water, into the fire, &c. They will trouble them with dreams, nightmare, hysterics, fever, &c. They will also deform them in body and in features, by convulsions, cramps, contortions, &c., and will sometimes compel them to utter blasphemies, horrible curses, and even words of other languages." Parley P. Pratt, *Key to the Science of Theology* (Liverpool, England: Franklin D. Richards, 1855), 115.
24. "Spirit Possession," *Deseret Evening News*, July 3, 1909, 4.
25. Truman G. Madsen, *The Sacrament: Feasting at the Lord's Table* (Provo, Utah: Amalphi Publishing, 2008), 135.

for Adam and Eve."[26] The drama thus clearly indicates that possession is Satan's goal and that he and his never-embodied followers should be expected to make good on the threat.

For Smith, ideas about the Devil and possession were not simply abstract speculations. He had claimed to have performed exorcisms for at least a decade before giving the January 1841 sermon. The New Testament prompted Smith and his followers to place the practice of casting out evil spirits among the gifts and signs that follow the "true church" of God. A revelation dictated by Smith in late 1830 stated, "I am God and mine arm is not shortened and I will show miracles, signs, and wonders, unto all who believe in my name and whoso shall ask it in my name, in faith, they shall cast our Devils."[27] For Mormons, this revelation was a reiteration in modern times of the promises given to the followers of Christ in antiquity.

This is an example of "traditionalism"—the act of linking a group's current practice with older practices in an effort to claim a special connection with the earlier group.[28] For Mormons, exorcism was part of a constellation of traditionalistic acts intended to link Mormon authority and practice with ancient Christianity. Eventually, the power to cast out devils would come to be viewed as a male priesthood duty, although cases of women given permission to cast out devils did occur. Throughout the nineteenth century, Mormons unabashedly believed and taught that casting out devils was part and parcel of the signs that follow believers and, therefore, a sign of the true church. Eventually, the performance of exorcism came to be viewed as a duty that fell under the umbrella of the Mormon higher priesthood. The issue of priesthood authority is one in which Mormons differed from Catholics as well as Protestants. There are a wide variety of Protestant views on priesthood and authority that vary from group to group. Luther, for example, believed that while "the power of the keys belonged to all believers, he confined its use to church

---

26. Joseph Smith introduced the "endowment" ritual in 1842, but it is unclear when the lines regarding possession were added. Summaries of the ritual date to the 1840s, but none purport to be actual, reliable transcripts. It may not be possible to document how early the line entered the ritual.

27. Revelation dated Dec. 7, 1830, Manuscript Revelation Book 1, in Robin Scott Jensen, Robert J. Woodford, and Steven C. Harper, eds., *Revelations and Translations: Manuscript Revelation Books*, vol. 1 of the Revelations and Translations series in the *Joseph Smith Papers* (Salt Lake City: Church Historian's Press, 2012), 384.

28. Bell, *Ritual*, 145.

officers." Calvin argued that there was a qualitative difference between the "extraordinary" powers manifest by Christians in the apostolic era the modern "ministry of the church [which was] ordinary in nature … one not of special powers but of preaching of the word." Unlike most Protestants who insisted on the idea of an informal "priesthood of all believers" and tended to reject the need for special authority to mediate between God and human beings, Smith believed that such God-given authority was an absolute necessity, that this priesthood had to be conferred by the laying on of hands, and that Smith himself had been ordained to the priesthood during visits from John the Baptist, and Peter, James and John.[29] Smith argued that Roman Catholicism wielded a perverted and powerless priesthood authority and he further distanced himself from Catholics as well as most Protestant groups on the issue of priesthood by creating a lay priesthood and rejecting a professional clergy.

FROM JESUS TO JOSEPH SMITH: TRACKING THE
MORMON UNDERSTANDING OF POSSESSION AND EXORCISM

In Erik Midelfort's seminal essay on possession cases in sixteenth-century Germany, he proposed that scholars had for too long been satisfied with generalizations regarding belief systems. When studying possession, he argued, "we need to ask exactly whose beliefs we are studying."[30] In the case of Mormon possession, we have to begin with the faith's founding prophet. Joseph Smith's ideas and beliefs about the Devil and demonic possession derive from three sources. First, the synoptic gospels in the New Testament, second Roman Catholic tradition, and finally Anglo-American Puritan folk belief. Possession and exorcism were key events in the narratives of Jesus's ministry, and are clearly linked in the stories with Jesus's godly authority. Only with the rise of Jesus and the Jesus movements did exorcism become a centrally important component of any Near Eastern religious system.[31]

---

29. David D. Hall, *The Faithful Shepherd: A History of the New England Ministry in the Seventeenth Century* (Chapel Hill: University of North Carolina Press, 1972), 8–11.

30. H. C. Erik Midelfort, "The Devil and the German People: Reflections on the Popularity of Demon Possession in Sixteenth-Century Germany," in Steven Ozment, ed., *Religion and Culture in the Renaissance and Reformation* (Kirksville, Missouri: Sixteenth Century Publishers, 1989), 103.

31. Graham H. Twelftree, *In the Name of Jesus: Exorcism Among the Early Christians* (Grand Rapids, Michigan: Baker Academic, 2007), 27.

The New Testament synoptic gospels all "agree that exorcism was an important aspect of Jesus' ministry and go so far as to suggest that Jesus' dealings with the demon-possessed is of central significance in understanding Jesus and his ministry."[32] The New Testament contains approximately fifty references to exorcisms performed by Christ or his followers. These cases, particularly the five most detailed examples, "provided scripts that demoniacs and exorcists followed" for centuries.[33] One of the chief reasons for the rise of exorcism as a centrally import-ant practice within Christianity is the concomitant rise of a being who represented the personification of evil. No such figure exists in the He-brew Bible, but by the time the New Testament gospels were written, such a figure had emerged and was given the name Satan, the Hebrew word meaning "obstacle."[34] And as the figure of Satan emerged, so did the notion that he had with him an army of disembodied spirits. The writers of the New Testament gospels each used the character of Satan to meet his own rhetorical needs, elaborating the character as required.[35]

Smith's second source for his tripartite demonology was Proto-Orthodoxy/Roman Catholicism, which influenced Smith in two ways: the diagnosis of possession and the belief that diabolical attack and possession were evidence of God's favor. The "symptoms" of possession manifested in nearly every Mormon account match with the Roman Catholic diagnostic lists that developed completely outside of the bib-lical context. Even a cursory reading of the New Testament, however, reveals that Satan's role, and the role of demons, possession, and exor-cism, remain rather vague and hint at a fuller cosmology that is never completely articulated in the earliest Christian texts.

By the Medieval period, Roman Catholicism placed great emphasis on the practice of casting out demons, which remained multiform until the sixteenth century. The Roman Catholic Church finally produced an offi-cial manual of exorcism, the *Ritual Romanum,* in 1614. This publication

32. Graham H. Twelftree, *Jesus the Exorcist: A Contribution to the Story of the Historical Jesus* (Eugene, Oregon: Wipf and Stock, 1993), 3.

33. Levack, *Devil Within*, 33. The five most detailed exorcisms in the New Testament are found in Mark 1:21–28, Matt. 8:28–32, Mark 7:25–30, Mark 9:14–29, and Mark 3:22–27.

34. Neil Forsyth, *The Old Enemy: Satan and the Combat Myth* (Princeton, New Jersey: Princeton University Press, 1987), 10.

35. For a detailed discussion of the role of the Satan character in the New Testament, see Elaine Pagels, *The Origin of Satan* (New York: Vintage, 1995).

was, in part, an effort to reclaim exorcism from the hundreds of freelance exorcists who had been casting out demons among Catholics for centuries. By the early modern period, a constellation of symptoms that Roman Catholics in particular found persuasive had emerged. Things such as levitation, contorted limbs, knowledge of previously unknown languages, changes in the voice, stiffness of limbs, and extraordinary strength formed the core of the diagnostic criteria used by Catholic exorcists.[36] Although Smith probably did not know the Catholic origin of possession symptoms, the ideas were so potently transmitted into Western culture that they became part of his cultural inheritance.[37]

Catholicism also provided another source for Smith's ideas about the Devil. The second-century Christian apologist Justin Martyr argued that Satan and his demonic legions were responsible for the persecution of Christians. The demonic forces accomplished this goal by tricking Jews, Pagans, and heretics into attacking Christianity. Justin thus emphasized the notion that the intensity of persecution against Christians served as an index of the tradition's "truthfulness." Also, Justin's diabology served as a boundary-maintenance device as he began to "articulate a distinctly Christian identity, the borders of which are defined against" the Devil and his "angels."[38] Given the importance of the demonic presence to early Christian identity, it is not at all surprising to find that a ritual of exorcistic combat emerged as well. One of the ways in which these early Church Fathers incorporated exorcism into the liturgical life of the early Christians was by attaching exorcism to baptism. By the early fourth century, for example, there is evidence that candidates for baptism were first given a "prebaptismal anointing" with explicitly "exorcistic" purposes.[39] Despite the inclusion of an exorcistic element in the baptismal rites, Christians from the time of Justin Martyr continued to place the ritual dispossession of adults near the heart of the Christian experience. Smith adopted an almost identical posture

---

36. Levack, *Devil Within*, 6–15.

37. Parley Pratt produced the same type of diagnostic list in 1855 in *Key to the Science of Theology*, 115–16.

38. Annette Yoshiko Reed, "The Trickery of the Fallen Angels and the Demonic Mimesis of the Divine: Aetiology, Demonology, and Polemics in the Writings of Justin Martyr," *Journal of Early Christian Studies* 12, 2 (June 2004): 154.

39. Maxwell E. Johnson, "The Apostolic Tradition," in Geoffrey Wainwright and Karen B. Westerfield Tucker, eds., *The Oxford History of Christian Worship* (Oxford, England: Oxford University Press, 2006), 39.

as Justin Martyr: demonic attack was a sign that God's true church was interfering with Satan's nefarious plans. Smith did not derive these ideas directly from Justin. By the nineteenth century, they were deeply embedded in Christian thought. For the purposes of contextualization, however, it is helpful to identify Justin as one of the originators of an idea that came to figure so prominently in Smith's thought.

Finally, Smith inherited the particular diabological views of his Puritan forbears and the Anglo-American folk culture, including the rich vein of "cunning folk" tradition that they brought with them to North America. The Protestant Reformation marked an important turning point in the history of Christian diabolism. Although Protestants carried a very strong belief in a literal Devil and in the reality of possession and exorcism, they eventually made the political decision to cede exorcism to the Catholics where it could take its place among other "superstitions, like consecrations, blessings, and holy water."[40] Centuries of lived tradition proved tenacious on this point, however. Despite the fact that the Anglican Church abolished the office of exorcist in 1550, recent studies have indicated that this "termination did little, if anything, to curb the belief in demonic possession" which persisted intact in Europe as a facet of "lived religion" into the eighteenth century.[41] English Puritans held to the belief that "signs and wonders" had not entirely ceased, but their disdain for ritual meant that miracles connected with healing or exorcism had to be dealt with via less obviously ritualistic methods.[42]

In the American context, Catholic-style possession and exorcism dropped away and were replaced by a new, Puritan style of imagining and combating evil. Seventeenth- and eighteenth-century New Englanders believed strongly in a literal Devil, one that, as in Europe, worked most often through the agency of human beings, but belief in possession was less widespread. Seventeenth-century New Englanders used the phrase "diabolical possession" to describe instances in which

40. Jeffrey Burton Russell, *Mephistopheles: The Devil in the Modern World* (Ithaca, New York: Cornell University Press, 1986), 91.

41. Ryan Stark, *Rhetoric, Science, and Magic in Early Eighteenth-Century England* (Washington, DC: Catholic University of America Press, 2009), 28.

42. On the issue of cessationism and its effects on Protestants of all stripes, see Ralph Del Colle, "Miracles in Christianity," in Graham H. Twelftree, ed., *The Cambridge Companion to Miracles* (New York: Cambridge University Press, 2011), 235–51.

the Devil manipulated human beings in a wide variety of ways. Puritans thus conceived of "possession" in a much broader sense than the Catholics did and Mormons would. To early New Englanders, possession suggested that the Devil could enter into a contract in which he took possession of a person, in much the same way that one would take possession of a piece of property and then use it to do his bidding.[43]

Frequently, the Devil was believed to enlist the help of humans who would sign a pact with him and, thenceforth, would be granted supernatural powers that allowed them to afflict other human beings.[44] As in Europe, these beliefs contributed to the prosecution and execution of accused witches. Almost always, "diabolical possession" cases were believed to be caused by witchcraft and were therefore met not with exorcism, but with a quest to identify and punish the witch. Unlike Catholic and, later, Mormon, approaches to the problem, Puritans tended to define the combat between the forces of good and the forces of evil locally, rather than cosmically. "Diabolical possession" served as a warning of witchcraft in the community, and it was the latter that was seen as the true threat and which generated community action.

The symbolic expulsion of evil is important to any religious community, and in sixteenth- and seventeenth-century New England, "diabolical possession" served the larger project of the witch-hunt. In fact, among the most common acts of a possessed person in seventeenth-century New England was to produce specific witchcraft accusations.[45] Puritans invested witch-hunting with all of the symbolic

---

43. See, for example, the case of the possession of Hartford, Connecticut, resident Ann Cole. Cole's "possession" led to no dispossession ritual, but it did launch the second-largest witch hunt in New England history. A wide range of primary source material dealing with the Cole case is published in David D. Hall, ed., *Witch-Hunting in Seventeenth-Century New England: A Documentary History, 1638–1693* (Boston: Northeastern University Press), 148–69.

44. W. Scott Poole, *Satan in America: The Devil We Know* (Lanham, Maryland: Rowman and Littlefield, 2009), 3–32, passim. There is some debate among scholars about the frequency of demonic possession in Colonial America. W. Scott Poole argues, as I do, that the occurrences were so infrequent and so insignificant in comparison to the reports of witches' contracts with Satan that they cannot be properly understood as a live element of the early Puritan world view. Others, like Richard Godbeer, attribute much greater significance to the possession accounts from the period. Although the issue remains disputed, it has highlighted the need for greater scholarly study of the subject. For Godbeer's perspective, see Richard Godbeer, *The Devil's Dominion: Religion and Magic in Early America* (New York: Cambridge University Press, 1992).

45. For a detailed discussion of "possessed accusers," see Alison Games, *Witchcraft in Early North America* (New York: Rowman and Littlefield, 2010), 65–71.

value that other communities placed in exorcism. They found the solution to the "Devil problem" not in ritual expulsion, but in an increase in godly living on the one hand, and the detection and destruction of witches on the other.

Most American Christians, both Catholic and Protestant, from the early colonial period through Smith's lifetime, shared "a belief in spirits and a belief that the boundaries between the human and spirit realm are permeable to these entities and can be penetrated by them."[46] They differed greatly, however, on the nature of these spirit beings, the types of things that these spirits did once they "penetrated" the human realm, and what humans could, and should, do to get rid of them. In general, Catholics experienced a more ritually dense religious life than did their Protestant contemporaries, and the ritual density of Catholicism provided more evidence to Protestants of the spiritual bankruptcy of Catholicism. Given this history, it is unsurprising that relatively few Protestant American religious figures in Smith's lifetime believed in possession and exorcism in the narrow sense of bodily possession and ritual expulsion. Even Catholics, who in Europe championed the practice of exorcism, found themselves shying away from the practice in the American context. American Catholics, from the mid-nineteenth century until the Papal condemnation of "Americanism" in 1899, found themselves dealing with a tsunami of practical, logistical, and educational challenges and internal schisms resulting from the collision of Irish, Italian, Polish, and German Catholicisms.[47] As if this were not complex enough, Catholics also had to face the horrors of Nativist persecution. All of this shifted exorcism to a much lower level of priority than it enjoyed among Catholics in Europe.

Belief in a literal Devil waxed and waned among the most dominant American religious groups of the late eighteenth and early nineteenth centuries, but the practice of exorcism was almost unheard of. The most fundamental reason for this was the phenomenon of "cessationism"— the belief propounded by leading Protestants that miracles had ceased after the death of Christ and the original apostles. Protestants argued that Catholics hid Christ in a thicket of "superstitious," miracle-inducing rituals; Protestants claimed to strip such things away and so leave

---

46. Amanda Witmer, *Jesus, The Galilean Exorcist* (London: Bloomsbury, 2012), 23.
47. Patrick W. Carey, *Catholics in America: A History* (London: Praeger, 2004), 55.

their rational and reasonable Christ unobscured. One Protestant cum Catholic wrote in 1870 that Protestants "rejected miracles ... not because they were miraculous, but because they were *Romish*. They had no choice. If the miracles were real, the doctrines were true."[48] Protestants would certainly disagree with those stated reasons, but there is no question that mainstream American Protestants generally shied away from a belief in miracles. Historian Jenny Franchot argues that Protestants saw "a dangerous exhibitionism [that] hovered over Catholic ritual," and that the "Roman church staged magnificent theatricals to bedazzle and manipulate its flock." This theatricality offended Protestant sensibilities because "the priest's sacramental enactments, in making visible the invisible workings of spirit, violated the privacy of God's gaze, profaning his theatrical space with that of the human gaze."[49]

In the mid-eighteenth century, however, a major shift developed in American views of the Devil. The rise of Evangelical Christianity that occurred in tandem with the First Great Awakening, and its new emphasis on emotion, created a different type of space in which the idea of the nature and purpose of the Devil could grow and change. The new Evangelical understanding of God as a presence who actively sought to be a part of the emotional inner life of the Christian necessitated a corresponding reimagining of Satan as a being who fought against individual Christians in order to keep them from feeling God's love.

As with any type of religious belief, Evangelical notions about Satan spanned a continuum, the center of which shifted over time. At the most liberal end of the spectrum were those few who "spoke of Satan purely in a figurative sense, as an emblem of the human heart's sinful inclinations." An equally small number of people who believed that "the Devil could take visible form and even inflict violence" occupied the opposite end of the continuum. The majority of Evangelicals in the eighteenth century, however, "regarded Satan as an actual, but invisible entity, who raised evil impressions on the minds of those awake or

---

48. James Kent Stone, *The Invitation Heeded: Reasons for a Return to Catholic Unity* (New York: Catholic Publication Society, 1870) 76. For a discussion of Stone, see Robert Bruce Mullin, *Miracles and the Miraculous in the Modern Religious Imagination* (New Haven, Connecticut: Yale University Press), 109.

49. Jenny Franchot, *Roads to Rome: The Antebellum Protestant Encounter with Catholicism* (Berkeley: University of California Press, 1994), 188–89.

asleep."[50] The Second Great Awakening, which began around 1800, changed that landscape dramatically. For a time, the new dominance of Arminian theology and a belief in a very raucous form of religious emoting pushed the belief in a violent Devil into the Evangelical mainstream. From 1800 until about 1830, the belief that the Devil or his evil spirits could physically attack human beings was extremely common among the new Evangelicals populating the pews in Baptist and Methodist churches.[51]

As time passed, however, and the clergy became increasingly educated, ministers sought to "tone down" diabolism as part of a broader shift among Evangelicals away from such "superstitious beliefs" as witchcraft, divination, dream reading, and so forth.[52] After 1830, Evangelicals reported that the Devil most typically manifested himself in the thoughts of those seeking to commune with God. It is important to note that although cases of possession were reported by Methodists and Baptists during this period they were uncommon, and Evangelicals unsurprisingly sought to perform no ritual acts of exorcism, which most Evangelicals still viewed as carrying the "taint" of tyrannical Catholicism. Methodists at the highest level had long since characterized exorcism as irredeemably "popish" and, as such, something to be avoided and even mocked. The first Methodist bishop, Thomas Coke, wrote a deeply anti-Catholic letter to John Wesley in 1784 that featured the topic of possession and exorcism.[53] Encoded in the letter are all of the most salient pillars of Protestant anti-Catholicism that were common to the Trans-Atlantic world. Catholicism is never more obviously corrupt, according to this line of thought, then when one looks at exorcism. Coke seemed to revel in the absurdity of exorcism; he relished the unmasking of false rituals and the ridiculous and fraudulent dramatics of the woman "pretending" to be possessed. In the letter we encounter a view of exorcism shared by many American Evangelicals. It

50. Christine Leigh Heyrman, *Southern Cross: The Beginnings of the Bible Belt* (Chapel Hill: University of North Carolina Press, 1997), 57. It is worth noting that even at the height of American Evangelical belief in a physically violent Devil, the notions of bodily possession and exorcism were largely ignored.

51. Poole, *Satan in America*, 58.

52. Heyrman, *Southern Cross*, 73.

53. Thomas Coke, Letter to John Wesley, Apr. 17, 1784, Typescript, Papers of Dr. Thomas Coke, John Rylands Library, University of Manchester, Manchester, United Kingdom, PLP 28.5.16a. I am indebted to Christopher Jones for bringing this document to my attention.

was a distillate of the essential elements of Catholicism: corrupt clergy, bizarre rituals involving the body parts of saints, deception, forms of religion devoid of pious content, and a fundamental cynicism.

As the nineteenth century progressed, tension grew between liberal Evangelical theologians, who found even the concept of a personal Devil increasingly less useful, and conservative Evangelical voices. In May 1829, one year before Joseph Smith's exorcism of Newel Knight (below), the *Christian Secretary*, a periodical published by the Connecticut Baptist Convention, included an article that sought to fight the increasingly common Evangelical belief that the cases of possession and exorcism in the Bible were not literal. The paper had picked up the story from an English publication, *The New Baptist Miscellany*, published by the conservative Particular Baptist movement.[54] The article was clearly aimed at liberal Evangelicals as well as "the wise men of the world," and argued quite pointedly that "infidelity alone can refuse credit to the numerous passages which a perusal of holy writ affords in support of" possession and exorcism.[55] The conservative and defensive tone of the piece suggests that mainstream Evangelicals were moving away from literal belief in possession.

Even the most conservative of Evangelicals faced a dilemma, however. On the one hand, they believed that the exorcisms performed by Jesus were real. On the other hand, they had to reject modern possession and exorcism because of the Catholic overtones that those terms had acquired since the Reformation. In 1857, *The Methodist Quarterly Review*, a major publication of the Methodist Episcopal Church, published a translation of an article that originally appeared in Germany entitled "The Demoniacs of the New Testament" that hints at this tension, and also suggests a way to resolve it. The article points out that "the most remarkable miracle wrought by our Lord and Savior Jesus Christ is the cure of demoniacs; both because their state as being possessed by evil spirits is in itself most enigmatical, and because similar phenomena both before and after the time of Christ, are either wanting

---

54. Information on this publication is found in Rosemary Taylor, "English Baptist Periodicals, 1790–1865," *Baptist Quarterly* 27, 2 (Apr. 1977): 62. Taylor notes specifically that this publication's "reputation for conservatism was justified."

55. "Diabolical Possession," *Christian Secretary*, May 29, 1829, 8:19, 76.

altogether or extremely rare."[56] According to this line of reasoning, the very fact that possession and exorcism were phenomena apparently reserved for the time of Christ serves to make Christ's acts that much more powerful and miraculous. This approach cleverly accounted for a literal belief in the stories of the Bible, while simultaneously providing a devotional explanation for dismissing contemporary possession claims and rejecting exorcism as relic of an important, but bygone, era.

It was into this world of mainstream Evangelical retreat from a strong belief in the physical power of the Devil to possess human bodies that Mormonism was born. Joseph Smith not only disagreed with the dominant Evangelical view of possession and exorcism, he used their stance as a foil for his argument that Protestant rejection of exorcism was part of the larger problem of relegating miracles to the past. In Mormon belief, any attempt by Protestants to deny the modern presence of the promised biblical signs that would follow the true followers of Christ, including exorcism, signaled a state of Christian apostasy. Smith therefore flatly rejected the belief that the Devil lacked the power to physically afflict, much less possess, human beings.

The Smith family was divided over the topic of religion, with some members of the large family choosing to become Presbyterians, while others favored the Methodists. Smith, as a young teenager, was in crisis over both the religious fissures in his family and the inability to settle on a faith for himself. Seeking to find some relief from this stress, Smith said that he retired to a grove of trees near his family's home to pray. Smith gave multiple versions of the experience that he said followed that prayer. At least two details are present in enough accounts to give us a general sense of what he was claiming to have experienced. The first is that he was physically attacked by Satan; the second is that he was saved from this attack by at least one divine being.

The first mention of a demonic or satanic attack connected with Smith's "First Vision" is found in the second of his accounts of the event, which he produced in 1835. Smith wrote that he had retired to the woods to pray and ask God "who was right and who was wrong." Just as he attempted to speak his prayer, Smith's "tongue seemed to be swollen in my mouth, so that I could not utter." At the same time,

---

56. "The Demoniacs of the New Testament, [After the German of Dr. Ebrard by Professor Reubelt]," *Methodist Quarterly Review*, July 1857, 9:405.

Smith "heard a noise behind me like the sound of some one [sic] walking toward me. I strove again to pray, but could not; the noise of walking seemed to draw nearer."[57] Smith sprang to his feet and looked around but could see no one. He then attempted to pray again, at which time he was able to speak the prayer that brought about his vision. Smith's early stories of his First Vision bear the marks of Methodist conversion narratives from the first third of the nineteenth century, including the struggle with an evil force.[58] In an account of the vision that Smith dictated in 1838, the version that is now accepted as the "official" account of the vision, Smith added something significant. After describing the encounter with evil, he noted that he had feared that he was going to be destroyed not by anything "imaginary," but by "the power of an actual being from the unseen world, who had such marvelous power as I had never before felt in any other being."[59]

The vast majority of Methodist conversion narratives, and, indeed, Evangelical conversion narratives in general, describe experiences with the Devil and with God in heavily qualified terms that suggest the experience, while real, was not necessarily physical. Smith, however, moves the other way and, in the case of his encounter with the Devil, seems to be setting his experiences in sharp contrast with antebellum Evangelical ideas. Smith wanted the world to know that the Devil was an "actual" being that was not part of an "imaginary" or mystical world but one that had aggressively intruded into the physical plane of existence. The belief in an incorporeal yet physically powerful Devil who came armed with an army of disembodied spirits who had sided with him in the war in heaven became a significant Mormon view that served to set them apart from most manifestations of contemporary Protestant Christianity.

Case 1: Newel Knight

The remainder of this essay examines four cases of possession and exorcism, culled from the hundreds that I have collected. The cases

---

57. Karen Lynn Davidson, David J. Whittaker, Mark Ashurst-McGee, and Richard L. Jensen, eds., *Histories, Volume 1, 1832–1844*, Volume 1 of the Histories Series of the *Joseph Smith Papers* (Salt Lake City: Church Historian's Press, 2012), 116.

58. Christopher C. Jones, "The Power and Form of Godliness: Methodist Conversion Narratives and Joseph Smith's First Vision," *Journal of Mormon History* 37, 2 (Spring 2011): 88–113.

59. Davidson et al., *Histories*, 1:214.

span a wide historical range, a decision based on a desire to sample instances over the course of time rather than look in detail at historical change. Such work must be left for future projects.

This essay opened with a brief look at "the first miracle which was done in this Church, or by any member of it." This was the exorcism of Newel Knight in which the Devil himself was claimed to have been cast out, an act described by Joseph Smith as being "done by God and by the power of Godliness."[60] This occurred in April 1830 in Colesville, New York. Smith was staying with the family of Joseph Knight, a man who had earlier assisted Smith during his dictation/translation of the Book of Mormon. The Knight family were "Universalists," but they enthusiastically opened their home to Smith, and he used it as a base for his own missionary efforts in the region. Knight's son, Newel, was particularly impressed with the young visionary and had become close to Smith, and the two often engaged in conversations about the importance of eternal salvation. According to Smith, the younger Knight had finally consented to join Smith's church and to pray vocally at the next meeting. When the appointed time came, however, Knight refused to pray in front of the others but promised Smith that he would pray in the woods. Knight's trip to the forest did not go as smoothly as he may have hoped because he "made several attempts to pray, but could scarcely do so, feeling that he had not done his duty, but that he should have prayed in the presence of others." Upset by his inability to pray, even in isolation, and plagued by guilt over his failure to publicly perform the prayer at the previous night's meeting, Knight began to feel mentally and physically unwell. By the time he reached his home, his

---

60. Joseph Smith History, Draft 2, ca. 1838–1841, in Davidson et al., *Histories*, 1:384. For reasons that are unclear, Knight did not offer his own account of the possession/exorcism in his autobiography. Instead, he simply reproduced Smith's account of the events. It must be noted that there are potential problems with the document containing the account of the Knight exorcism. The account is recorded eight years after the event itself, which involves two points of concern. The first is the simple, and common, tendency for events to be misremembered as time passes. There is no question that Smith performed an exorcism in 1830, because the *Palmyra Reflector*, a New York newspaper that mocked Smith and his followers relentlessly, published a piece in the June 30, 1830, edition that satirized the event. Second, and more complex, is the possibility that Smith, having developed and refined his theological notions on the subject of Satan, the body, and God, between 1830 and 1838, may have read the newer ideas back into the earlier event. Despite the potential for problems with this source, it is the only extant first-person record of the event, and thus, the one with which we must work.

"appearance was such to alarm his wife very much." Knight's wife sent for Smith, who found the young man behaving strangely. Also, noted Smith, Knight's "visage and limbs distorted and twisted in every shape and appearance possible to imagine."

Knight's possession experience began, much as Smith's did, with an attempt to pray in the hopes of eliciting a divine manifestation. Knight's encounter with the Devil soon expanded well beyond the story Smith told of being bound by an unseen, but very real, being. According to the account, Knight's body was both levitating and contorting. Both of these phenomena are widely reported as part of possession experiences worldwide. What is more interesting, in the case of Knight, is that the Devil's chief aim in possessing Knight's body is not the possession of a body *per se*, but rather the possession seems to act as a means by which to administer abuse to the body. The satirical *Palmyra Reflector* account supports the idea that the most salient element of the event was the pain that the Devil inflicted upon Knight. The *Reflector* quoted Knight as saying that his "flesh was 'about to cleave from my bones' — the muscles, tendons &c. could no longer perform their different functions — the habitation of Satan, was about to be laid open to the light of day, when the prophet interfered."[61]

If one reads these accounts in light of the 1841 and 1843 sermons given by Smith, the two notions—the Devil seeks a body as a pleasure and a refuge that has been denied him and the fact that Devil inflicts such severe physical pain upon that body—are clearly in conflict. As we will see, few Mormon accounts of possession that occur later, especially in the 1840s and after, contain any mention of physical harm done by the possessing spirit to the possessed body. In fact, LDS Apostle Wilford Woodruff recorded in 1840 an incident in which he claimed the Devil struck him on the head and tried to choke him. He later went back and re-edited the entry to downplay the pain inflicted by the Devil.[62] It would be irrational to expect Knight to have any idea what Smith would eventually conclude about the nature of possession. When considered in that light, it is not surprising that we find

---

61. Dogberry, *Palmyra Reflector*, June 30, 1830.
62. For a discussion of Woodruff's retrofitted journal entry, see Benjamin E. Park, "'A Uniformity So Complete': Early Mormon Angelology and Microhistorical Theology," *Intermountain West Journal of Religious Studies* 2 (2010): 30.

a disconnect between Knight's behavior as a possessed man and what Smith later taught about the nature of possession. In religious cultures, such as that found in Roman Catholicism, in which the expectation of behavior of both the possessed and the exorcist are clearly and repeatedly articulated, one finds relative consistency of both elements of the exorcistic performances over time. Although Mormonism shares with Catholicism a belief in bodily demonic possession, within Mormonism, only the basic pattern on exorcism remains constant; the nature of possession consists of a kind of "free-lance" performance in which the possessed individuals behave according to his or her own socialized beliefs in possession. Over time, the act of exorcism remains relatively stable, while the possessed persons' behaviors follow a widely variable script.

In addition to the issues surrounding the body, the Knight account also reveals the basic pattern that would form the basis of most Mormon rites of affliction, both exorcistic and the much more common healing rituals. In Newel Knight's case, the ritual actions consisted of the following: Smith touching Knight (in this case by grabbing his hand), Knight demonstrating sufficient faith to be delivered of the spirit of the Devil, and the invocation of the name of Jesus Christ to accomplish the deliverance. With a few notable exceptions, Mormon exorcism accounts generally do not describe any particular ritual action being performed, and there is no official rite of exorcism. Early accounts tend to emphasize the power of the invocation of the sacred name of Jesus. By the twentieth century, the ritual of exorcism was usually performed in the same way that healing rituals are, namely by holders of the higher or Melchizedek, Mormon priesthood laying their hands on the head of the afflicted and commanding the evil spirit to depart in the name of Jesus and by the power of the holy priesthood.

It is difficult to tell what this experience meant to Knight, because he left no account of it, and Smith's account is potentially unreliable given the obviously propagandistic purpose for which it was recorded. Presumably, based on his subsequent baptism into the Mormon faith, the exorcism provided evidence both of the reality of Satan and the power of Smith to fight the Devil and win. It is worth noting that in August 1830, Knight himself diagnosed his aunt as being possessed by the Devil, and he exorcised her, using the same method that Smith had used on him only a few months earlier.[63]

It is somewhat easier to surmise what this event, and its retelling, meant to Smith. Joseph Smith was interested in establishing the Kingdom of God on Earth, in imitation not only of Jesus and his early followers as described in the New Testament, but also as a "restoration" of all holy practices authorized by God from the beginning of time. Smith was adamant that Satan and his host of angry and disembodied followers were particularly interested in fighting the truth, and the more opposition Smith faced, the more obvious it was that he was God's true prophet. In fact, Smith explained his own possession experience just before the First Vision as evidence that Satan hated him personally. "It seems as though the adversary was aware, at a very early period of my life, that I was destined to prove a disturber and an annoyer of his kingdom; else why should the powers of darkness combine against me? Why the opposition and persecution that arose against me, almost in my infancy?"[64]

Smith apparently saw his fight with Satan not as a contemporary Evangelical may have, as a personal struggle for an individual soul, but rather as a battle set against a cosmic backdrop in which two individuals with special powers fight over the fate of humankind. Neil Forsyth demonstrated that these sorts of stories are as old as humanity itself, and they formed much of the basis of the ancient Christian combat myths that developed around the battle between God and/ or Christ, and Satan. Probably via the New Testament stories, Smith saw himself in the role of not only of kingdom builder, but kingdom destroyer. The exorcism of Newel Knight, or at least Smith's 1838 telling of the story, signals this not least of all through the presence of Satan himself. Knight is not simply afflicted by an evil spirit. Knight claimed that he saw Satan himself leaving his body. He had, in some sense, an experience that was an inversion of Smith's First Vision. This

---

63. Knight's aunt had taken to her bed and was in tremendous pain. Knight became convinced that the woman was possessed by the Devil when she claimed that she was about to die "for the redemption of this generation, as Jesus-Christ had died for the generation in his day." Knight concluded that "Satan had ... put a lying spirit in her mouth." Newel Knight, "Autobiography," 189–94, MS 19156, fd 1, CHL.

64. Joseph Smith, History, 1838–1856, vol. A-1, created June 11, 1839–Aug. 24, 1843; *Joseph Smith Papers*.

story was important enough to Smith warrant a prominent place in the church history that he began dictating in 1838 precisely because it represented, in miniature, the entire claimed purpose of the "restoration of the Gospel of Christ": to drive Satan from the world through the special authority invested by God exclusively in Smith and the church he founded. [65]

The prominence granted to exorcism in the New Testament, coupled with Smith's own self-understanding as the prime embodiment of God's power on Earth, led Smith and his followers to view possession and exorcism as a natural, and even necessary, component of their collective mission. In fact, aside from the Knight account, the other exorcisms performed by Smith in his lifetime were either not reported at all or reported in a completely offhand manner, without further commentary, as if their reality and symbolic value were both obvious. In a March 1831 letter to his brother Hyrum, Smith wrote that "this morning after being Colled out of my bed in the night to go a small distance I went and had and an awful strugle with satan but being armed with the power of God he was cast out and this woman is Clothed in hir right mind the Lord worketh wonders in this land."[66] In the letter, Smith intentionally echoed the language of Mark 5:15, in which the Gerasene demoniac was "clothed and in his right mind" after being exorcised by Christ. In this case, as with the Knight exorcism which had occurred less than a year before, Smith's mission of establishing the kingdom of God was enacted, bodily, in the form of an exorcism.

Case 2: The Pomfret Branch

Smith was not the only Mormon exorcist at work in the 1830s. In 1839, the same year that he recorded his exorcism of Knight for his official history, a newly-baptized sixteen-year-old Latter-day Saint

---

65. Non-Mormon observers bristled at the use of the Knight story to strengthen Smith's prophetic bona fides. In response to the 1909 *Deseret News* article mentioned above, a Catholic newspaper, *The Intermountain Catholic,* published a piece entitled, "The Obsession of Newel Knight." Although the author of the article accepted the reality of both possession in general and the possession and exorcism of Newel Knight in particular, he rejected the belief that the exorcism was evidence that "God approved of the teachings of Joseph Smith." Rather, he argued that "the expulsion of the evil spirit derived its effect from the name of Jesus, not from any grace inherent in the Mormon Prophet." "The Obsession of Newel Knight," *Intermountain Catholic,* July 17, 1909.

66. Joseph Smith, Letter to Hyrum Smith, Mar. 3–4, 1831, *Joseph Smith Papers.*

named Lorenzo Brown participated in a dramatic series of exorcisms. Brown joined the church in 1838, although his family's association with Smith began several years earlier, when Smith and fellow LDS leader Sidney Rigdon hid in the family's house for several days. Brown's father joined the church in 1835, but Lorenzo waited three more years. In early 1839, while the majority of the Mormons were in a temporary settlement in Quincy, Illinois, Brown and his family and a handful of other members of the LDS Church constituted a very small and isolated branch of the church at Pomfret, New York, a village in far-western New York situated along the shores of Lake Erie. The branch consisted primarily of Brown and his extended family, with nearly the entire branch being related either through blood or marriage. The branch met for church services in the Brown home and these meetings were the scene of an unusually large number of charismatic events, especially healings and glossolalia. "We were blessed spiritually with the gift of tongues, through which, and the interpretation, we learned many things." Brown recalled that several hymns were revealed via glossolalia "one of which was given through myself and interpreted by Sister Esther Crowely."[67]

While the practice of glossolalia was not uncommon in early Mormonism, this branch seems to have had more than a passing interest in various "gifts of the spirit." Brown himself made a point of recording that his father's was "a family that often had things in the future made known to them and were singular in this respect. My grandfather predicted the day, hour, and minute of his death, for some years previous. A certain individual, of veracity, has certified to the fact of standing by his bedside with a timepiece to compare time and found it exact. Also, his son John was said to have great spiritual exercises in mind."[68] Family lore preserved other similar stories, including one in which Lorenzo Brown's father "one night after he had got his clothing damp, was sitting with his back to the fireplace drying his clothes and thinking about religious matters when an angel appeared to him and told him to join none of the churches because the true church was not on the earth

---

67. Lorenzo Brown, Diary and Autobiography, Jan. 29, 1839, MSS 497, Perry Special Collections, BYU. Brown also notes that his first exposure to Mormonism involved seeing "an elderly man speaking in tongues."

68. Brown, Diary and Autobiography, Jan. 1, 1856, 1.

but would be in the near future. Some time later he heard Mormonism preached and recognized it as the true gospel. It was through him that the Browns, the Crosbys, and the Mumfords joined the church."[69] The charismatic gifts claimed by Benjamin Brown played a major role in converting to Mormonism all of the persons involved in the exorcism events reported by Lorenzo. The members of the Pomfret branch thus not only shared tight familial connections, but also an interest in charismatic spiritual gifts as described in the New Testament.

It is not surprising to find out that the members of the Pomfret branch also found an opportunity to cast out evil spirits. According to an affidavit that Brown wrote in 1839, and which was signed by various witnesses to the event,

> On this day passed a marvelous scene before the Elders of Israel viz., Benjamin Brown, Henry More and Melvin Brown who was called to cast out Devils which had entered Sister Crosby after praying and fasting 17 hours by the power of the Holy Ghost one was cast out which was seen and felt for he attacked all of us shook Br. Brown on the side and in the face seized Br. More on the arms which made them sore for some time also Brother Melvin on the shoulders and arms so that he could but just stand his arms was sore for some time the Devil was seen in the room for some time at length entered into Brother Melvin while [illegible] with such power that it seemed as he would be pressed to death. He could not speak but made signs when we [?] and laid hands on him and cast him out in the name of Jesus Christ when he came out he came snarling like a dog. On the 18th we cast out 37 [demons] in a variety of forms and noises some like dogs cats hogs pigs and snakes. These was seen by many of the saints and heard and the room became darkened like a mist and the smell was like brimstone and more filthy it affected our eyes so that we had to wash them also our mouths much affected some heard noise like thunder and saw it lightening some were punched in the face others in the arms others heard him gnash with his teeth, so this was many witnesses both men and women in the Lord Jesus Christ.[70]

---

69. George H. Crosby Jr., "What I Remember of the Benjamin Brown Family," n.p., 1933, copy in my possession. While stories of various supernatural experiences persisted in Brown family lore, the story of the exorcism apparently dropped out, since it was included neither in Crosby's 1933 account nor in Lorenzo Brown's own 1856 summary of his life.

70. Lorenzo Brown, "Account of the Healing of Sister Crosby," MS 5645, CHL. Although the document is undated, it must have occurred in early 1839, before the members of the branch relocated to Nauvoo, Illinois, to join the main body of Mormons.

This account is an example of the confluence of Mormon belief in the role of the priesthood authority, which allowed most adult Mormon males to act in a sacerdotal role, and charismatic folk beliefs that newly-baptized members of the church often brought with them into the church.[71] Most Evangelical Protestant sects with which the members of the branch would have been familiar did not believe in priesthood authority, and thus they relied primarily on prayer to drive away evil. Mormons, by contrast, believed that ancient apostles had restored the authority of the Holy Priesthood, which could be conferred on male members of the church, and which was an important component in most healing and other rituals that involved the laying on of hands. According to Brown's journal, most of the males in the branch had been ordained to the priesthood in January 1839, which would place those events close in time to the exorcism. The link between priesthood power and exorcism was not definitively linked at this point. However, the fact that only men who had been ordained to the priesthood acted as exorcists in this case suggests that, in the minds of the members of the Pomfret branch at least, the priesthood was a vital component of the ritual.

Whereas primitivists and revivalists of the early nineteenth-century in the vein of Barton Stone, would have certainly seen "struggles with Satan, sometimes of a very physical variety, as a precursor to their own conversion" and would thus have been prepared to accept the affliction of Crosby as a manifestation of the power of Satan, they would have responded to the possession with prayer and fasting.[72] The members of the Pomfret branch, however, as newly minted Mormons, felt that they had authority to lay on hands and cast the Devil out by the authority of God. The event Brown describes represents a hybrid event in which standard, familiar, and culturally acceptable interpretations of "demonic affliction" were met with a new and unusual view of lay priesthood authority that involved not only fasting and prayer but also

---

71. The issue of gender and blessings for health or exorcism is controversial. In 1842, Joseph Smith told members of the LDS Church's women's organization, the Relief Society, that the signs that follow believers, and he explicitly mentioned the power to cast out devils, "follow all that believe whether male or female." "Minutes of the Proceedings of the Sixth Meeting of the Society, 28 April 1842," Nauvoo Relief Society Minute Book, MS 7238, 33, CHL. Notwithstanding this admonition, exorcisms performed by women must at this point be assumed to be rare, and I found none in my research. There is, however, much more evidence of a long history of Mormon women laying on hands for the healing of the sick.

72. Poole, *Satan in America*, 42.

the laying on of hands and the declaration of the authority to act in the name of Jesus Christ. Like the Knight exorcism, of which these persons were almost certainly unaware, the participants in the Crosby event were pitting their new found faith and their belief in their power and authority as ordained representatives of Jesus Christ against the power of the Devil who was manifesting in ways that would have been familiar to them and to most of their neighbors. The events described by Brown represent a more chaotic scene and an event of larger scope than most do Mormon exorcism accounts. While the exorcism began as a relatively simple case of casting the Devil out of one person, it soon spun out of control, involving not only more than thirty-seven demons. It is possible that this chaos and scope have their roots in the lack of a strong institutional leader who could have dictated the pace of the events. Foucault argues that at the center of the scene of possession is the "confessor, director, or guide," an individual who orchestrates a scene of barely-controlled chaos through skillfully wielding "the powers of direction, authority, and discursive restraint."[73] Such a figure is absent from the 1839 account. With little experience of Mormonism, and Mormon priesthood organizational structures, outside what was essentially their own extended family group, the members of the branch seemed to lack an authoritative center. There had, in effect, many "priests" but no "Priest."

In addition to the prominent physical violence of the events, it is important to note that there appears to be a strong mimetic element to the events described in this account. On the first day, Satan was cast out of Melvin Brown and when he left he "snarled like a dog." The next day the events resumed, and in like manner, the thirty-seven demons exorcized from the various participants only left after they had caused the possessed person to move and make the noises of a variety of animals, including "dogs cats hogs pigs and snakes." The association of Satan with the animals described by Brown was an old one that had persisted in European and American folklore since the Middle Ages. According to Jeffrey Burton Russell, "[the Devil] was frequently identified with or associated with animals, sometimes following earlier Judeo-Christian tradition and sometimes because animals were sacred

73. Foucault, *Abnormal*, 206.

to the pagan gods, whom the Christians identified with demons."[74] The members of the Pomfret branch who were possessed by these demons were thus probably following a typological model that had informed the cultural world view of their families for generations.

In 1881, Benjamin Brown published another account of his experience in the Pomfret branch, which is important both for what it omits from and what it adds to the 1839 account.[75] The 1881 account completely drops any mention of anyone having seen Satan and any mention of smoke, nor does it include any discussion of animalistic behavior among the possessed. In recalling the incident nearly four decades later, Brown remembered it as a much less chaotic event that turned on an open battle between a host of demons that identified itself as "Legion" and the power of the priesthood. In the later account, Brown rebuked the evil spirits in the woman, which resulted in the woman rising "up from the bed on her feet without apparently bending a joint in her body, as stiff as a rod of iron." The possession event continued for nearly a week, but it reached a flashpoint when, according to Brown, one of the demons "reviled our priesthood ... saying to us, 'O! you have the priesthood have you? Well, then, cast me out, command me to come out,' trying to shake our faith, and thus incapacitate us to rebuke him successfully." Finally, after another round of laying on of hands, the demons fled. In this version, the action seems much more orderly as if Brown had introduced a level of order into his re-narration that was absent from the 1839 account.

In his published account, Brown offers two reasons for the possession. One of them was simply that the "Lord permitted [the demon] to exercise his physical power ... to give me experience of such facts, without which I could never have known," of the physical reality of the Devil and his minions. The second reason Brown offers is that the possessed woman had "given the Devil ground by encouraging a spirit contrary to the order of the Church, taking upon herself to rebuke the Elders, and he claimed his right by virtue of her transgression." In neither account does Brown provide details of the ways in which

---

74. Jeffrey Burton Russell, *Lucifer: The Devil in the Middle Ages* (Ithaca, New York: Cornell University Press, 1984), 67.

75. Benjamin Brown, "Testimonies for the Truth," in *Gems for the Young Folks* (Salt Lake City: Juvenile Instructor Office, 1881), 72–73.

Sister Crosby "rebuked the elders," but his mention of it in the 1881 account demonstrates that Mormons accepted the idea that any challenge of a female to the members of the all-male priesthood was an invitation to satanic control.

The typological model of a world in which Satan existed, possessed human bodies out of jealousy and rage, and could only be countered successfully by the restored priesthood of the only true church was confirmed in the 1839 account. A slight shift in world view is evident in the 1881 account, however, where the behavior of the possessed, and the manifestation of folkoric elements such as animalistic behavior, were apparently less important than the fact that she represented a threat to the order of the church as represented by the priesthood. The 1881 telling of the event seems less like a cosmic struggle than an effort to maintain order in an organization. The 1870s and 1880s were a particularly tumultuous time for Mormons in Utah. The United States government was cracking down on plural marriage, and the growing number of non-Mormons in Utah troubled church leaders. A general zeitgeist that centered on a fear of disorder prevailed, and it may explain the emphases in Brown's 1881 document. Apostle Joseph F. Smith, for example, wrote, "They [the American government] do not want us to be, religiously or otherwise, a separate and distinct people from the rest of the world. They want us to become identified and mixed up with the rest of the world, to become like them, thereby thwarting the purposes of God."[76]

The resistance to being "mixed up" with the world, of chaotic and confusing identity melding, could be remedied most thoroughly through a firmer reliance on priesthood order. It is suggestive that, as Christopher Blythe notes, 1882 saw the republication of a pamphlet that was most famous for its account of demonic obsession and possession of Church leaders in England in 1837.[77] In late 1879, Salt Lake Stake President Angus M. Cannon addressed a meeting of local church leaders in which "he dwelt upon the iniquitous practice of Church members going to law against their brethren, instead of submitting disputes to the tribunals of justice instituted by the almighty among his

---

76. "Discourse, Given by Elder Joseph F. Smith, in Paris, Idaho, 19 August 1883," *Deseret News*, semi-weekly, Oct. 2, 1883, 1.
77. Blythe, "Mormon Apocalyptic," 71.

people."[78] Cannon was referring to ecclesiastical courts, which in the nineteenth century handled disputes of all kinds among church members. The notes of this meeting were published in the *Deseret News,* giving them a wide readership. It is plausible that the tense atmosphere of late 1870s and early 1880s contributed to Brown's recollection. What is beyond dispute, however, is that by the 1880s, the power to exorcize was closely tied to the Melchizedek Priesthood, but not yet to any particular hierarchical position. This would change in the late twentieth century.

Case 3: The Devil, the Female Voice,
and Polygamy in the Southern States Mission

The mission fields have always provided cases of possession and exorcism. An event that occurred in the Southern States Mission in the late 1880s illustrates some of the unexpected perils that participating in the theatrics of exorcism entailed. In 1888, a Mormon woman reported that she was possessed by "a devil" and requested that the local missionaries perform an exorcism. The missionaries complied, laying hands on her head and casting the evil spirit from her. The missionaries reported that the exorcism was successful. It appears that she followed the script when the priesthood power cast the Devil out, thus reaffirming the truth claims of the LDS Church and the power of the missionaries over Satan and his forces. However, she then improvised on the script when she began to claim to be receiving divine revelation for the missionaries. These revelations appeared benign at first. She "revealed many truths to them pertaining to their labors, informing them how to avoid danger that threatened them, which they did."

She also predicted that a sick child in the area would be cured, and when that turned out to be true, the missionaries began to take the prophetic claims of this woman seriously. Unfortunately for the missionaries, the woman's revelations became much more grave. She claimed that God wanted one of the missionaries to take her as a plural wife and to bring her back to Utah with them when they returned in the fall. The missionaries took this so seriously that they wrote to LDS Church President Wilford Woodruff to ask his advice. Their chief

---

78. "Priesthood Meeting," *Deseret News* 29:633, Nov. 1, 1879.

concern was how to avoid being arrested for polygamy once the woman was taken as a plural wife. Woodruff did not respond to the missionaries directly, but rather sent their letter, along with a letter of his own, to the mission president. The mission president then investigated the matter, released the conference president, and gave the missionaries a "severe rebuke." The mission president concluded that the woman had been possessed *the entire time*, explaining that a second demon must have entered her immediately after the first one had been cast out. The mission president explained that

> The object of this evil spirit was to get these Elders to commit adultery with this woman. They had no right to receive revelations through this or any other woman. If the Lord had any thing to reveal to them, pertaining to their duties, it was their privilege to receive the revelation. The Elders are not sent out here to get wives, they are sent to preach the Gospel; and strictly commanded to let women alone. These Elders debased their priesthood in making it subject to the Devil, through this woman. This was a married woman, and had three children, which alone should have been sufficient for the Elders to know that they were being deceived.[79]

In this case, we have an example of possession being used for multiple purposes by different actors. First, the woman used her possession to get the attention of the missionaries, who duly and, to their understanding, successfully performed the ritual expulsion of the evil spirit from her. This allowed her then to begin giving the missionaries "revelations." It is clear that the woman was attempting to convince one of the missionaries to take her as a plural wife and take her back to Utah, either in spite of or because of the fact that she was married with three children. One might reasonably conclude that she presented her revelations in the hopes that the missionaries would believe they were divine, which they apparently did. The idea of possession was not re-introduced into the scenario until the mission president arrived, angry and still stinging from the letter he had received from Woodruff. The mission president then deployed the concept of possession to marginalize the "revelations" that the woman had received, causing the author of this account to retrofit the narrative to include a second possession.

---

79. James G. Duffin, Journal, Southern States Mission, 211–13, MSS 1696, Perry Special Collections.

It is important to recognize that the mission president could have chosen other ways to explain the situation. He could, for example, have simply asserted that the woman was lying in a transparent attempt to begin a relationship with one of the missionaries. The fact that he chose instead to explain the entire event as the result of demonic possession demonstrates not only the strength of belief in the phenomenon among Mormons in the late nineteenth century, but also the usefulness of possession as an explanation for failed or otherwise objectionable and unauthorized "revelation," something that had posed problems for Mormonism since its earliest days.[80]

Compounding the problem of unauthorized revelation, at least from the standpoint of the mission president, was that the false revelations were coming from a woman. Among the revelations that the woman dictated were several dealing with polygamy. She "revealed many truths pertaining to plural marriage. Told them it was of God; that it was pleasing in His sight when his servants entered into that order, that they would be blessed for so doing. & many other things pertaining to this holy order of marriage told them that this woman was a favored woman of the Lord." Although the mission president later asserted unequivocally that it was "the Devil ... giving these revelations through this woman," the pattern of the revelation and its subject matter would have been familiar to the missionaries. In fact, this very type of revelatory process had been used by men to convince women to enter into plural marriages with them from the time of Joseph Smith.

The inversion of the gender roles that pervaded this series of events was obviously of grave concern to the mission president. In this instance, an oracular performance was deemed demonic because, in part, at least, it was coming from a woman. Her revelations appeared to the mission president as subversions of the proper order, and, in fact, the missionaries' priesthood had been "debased" simply because they were convinced that the revelations of a woman were from God. The possessed woman, in the view of LDS authorities, was a partner with the Devil in this effort.

The case is unusual among Mormon cases of possession and exorcism

---

80. See, for example, the 1830 case of Hiram Page and his seer stone. Michael Hubbard MacKay and Nicholas J. Frederick, *Joseph Smith's Seer Stones* (Provo and Salt Lake City: Religious Studies Center and Deseret Book, 2016), 153–57.

STEPHEN C. TAYSOM

in that possession is *ascribed to* the possessed rather than claimed *by the possessed*. This unusual feature is significant, because, in this case, at least, it demonstrates how belief in demonic possession provided a mechanism for protecting the belief in divine personal revelation through literally demonizing subversive oracular speech.

Case 4: The Routinization of the Devil

The final case examined in this essay comes from the 1970s, a decade during which popular interest in possession and exorcism was intense. The 1973 release of William Friedkin's film *The Exorcist,* based on the best-selling book of the same name by William Peter Blatty, had wide-ranging cultural influence. Sociologist Michael Cuneo notes that in the 1960s "exorcism was all but dead and forgotten," but that by the mid-1970s it had "sprung back to life [and] exorcism was in hot demand."[81] American Catholics, who had been the major keepers of exorcistic practice among Christians for centuries, had shied away from the practice. Especially after the reforms of the Second Vatican Council (1962–65), American Catholics wanted to do away with the practice altogether. Few exorcists even existed within the dioceses of the United States. Cuneo links the publication of Blatty's book and the film upon which it was based to the possession boom. Cuneo even coined a phrase to describe this: "the Blatty Factor." What is interesting about this is that, in addition to a renewed demand for exorcism among American Catholics, American Protestant groups, too, began to show tremendous interest in the practice for the first time in centuries. Protestants called their dispossession rituals "acts of deliverance," and "deliverance ministries" began to spring up with the sole purpose of detecting possessed persons and, via prayer, verbal and physical interaction with the demon, and the use of apotropaic objects, expelling the demon from its host.

Mormonism was not immune to the Blatty Factor. In 1977, then-LDS Church Historian Leonard J. Arrington attended a dinner for a handful of people in Salt Lake City. Present at the dinner, and slated to address the group, was a man named M. Russell Ballard. Ballard had recently returned from serving as a mission president in Toronto, Canada, and had since been called as an LDS general authority. Ballard's

---

81. Michael W. Cuneo, *American Exorcism: Expelling Demons in the Land of Plenty* (New York: Doubleday, 2001), xiv.

remarks that evening focused on an experience he had while a mission president in which he performed an exorcism.[82]

According to Ballard, a woman who lived within the mission boundaries began to exhibit "signs of possession" during a group trip to the LDS temple in Washington, DC. She was behaving strangely on the trip down but was perfectly fine within the temple only to resume her behavior once she got out. Ballard eventually heard about this case from the missionaries who had been visiting the woman and trying to cast out whatever evil presence had possessed her, and he decided to visit her himself. When he arrived, even before he entered the house, the woman shouted, "Don't let that man in, don't let that man in!" This is an example of what Cuneo calls the "hero-priest" phenomenon. In *The Exorcist*, the demon that is possessing the young girl both fears and longs to fight with a *specific priest*. When that priest arrives at the house where the possessed girl lives, the demon cries out the priest's name in a tone of both agony and expectation, and, as Cuneo describes it, the presence of the heroic priest yields "an almost palpable sense of relief and gratitude."[83]

In the Ballard case, the possessed woman behaves in a similar fashion. The possessed woman recognizes that this particular individual is to be feared far more than any of the other priestly functionaries who had been involved up to this point. Additionally, she announces that fact in a loud voice just as Ballard arrives. This is close to the scene portrayed in *The Exorcist*. I do not know if Ballard ever read or saw *The Exorcist*. It is entirely possible, however, that the possessed woman had seen the film and was using it, as so many others did during this time frame, as the accepted typology for possession.

Despite the demonic objection, Ballard entered the home and "saw a face that was contorted in such a way that she was unrecognizable. She spoke with a completely different voice than her regular voice, a deep voice. She spoke in a different manner than she had ever been known to do previous to these attacks." Ballard accepted these signs as genuine. He instructed the woman's stake president[84] to lay his hands

---

82. All quotes from this section are from Leonard J. Arrington's Journal, Aug. 1977, MSS 10, Box 33, fd 1, Arrington Papers, Special Collections, Merrill-Cazier Library, Utah State University, Logan.

83. Cuneo, *American Exorcism*, 9.

84. A stake president is a lay ecclesiastical leader who presides over several congregations. A stake is roughly equivalent to a Catholic diocese.

on her once again. This blessing, unlike the ones performed by the missionaries, did have some impact. Ballard, who had by this point identified the possessing spirit as Satan himself, claimed to feel Satan leave the woman but remain in the room. Soon, however, the Devil returned and repossessed the woman. At this point, Ballard took over the exorcism himself. He laid his hands on the woman's head and carried on a "dialogue" with the Devil for twenty to thirty minutes before eventually casting him out for good, "not only from the body of the woman but from the room completely."

After telling this dramatic story, Ballard offered his interpretation of the events. The Devil possessing the woman had not wanted Ballard to enter the home because Ballard "was the ultimate Church authority in the region." This was also the reason that "the Stake President was not able to use his authority to banish the demon" completely. Ballard thus saw the entire encounter as one not of priesthood authority (because all of the men holding the Melchizedek Priesthood have the same authority) but of Satan's respect for hierarchical bureaucracy. At various levels of ecclesiastical administrative authority, the Devil seemed to respond differently. He apparently could ignore the missionaries completely but had to respond in a limited way to the adjurations of the stake president. But only Ballard, "the ultimate authority in the region," could command Satan to leave permanently.[85]

In addition to providing yet another example of Cuneo's "Blatty Factor" at work, this story has important implications for how late-twentieth-century Mormonism was coming to draw an increasingly sharp distinction between hierarchical position and priesthood power. It is unclear why the Devil, who seemed to wield considerable volition in this episode, did not continue to possess the woman until being cast out by the president of the LDS Church himself. The logic of the situation would seem to dictate that course of action. Naturally, there are practical problems with something like that. The Devil thus acquiesced to the highest ranking church functionary *who could conveniently present himself.* This is an important component of the story

85. A similar dynamic occurred during the possession of Nicole Aubrey in Laon, France, in 1566. In that case, it was the "demon" within the possessed person who demanded that only a Catholic Bishop could successfully complete the ritual. See Jonathan L. Pearl, *Crime of Crimes: Demonology and Politics in France, 1560–1620* (Waterloo, Ontario: Wilfrid Laurier University Press, 2012), 44.

because it suggests that Ballard, at least, believed that the Devil had to respect not only the authority of the Mormon priesthood, but also the logistics of the hierarchy.

This story was told at a time when the LDS Church hierarchy was expanding more rapidly than it had for more than a century. In October 1976, LDS President Spencer W. Kimball significantly expanded the third-highest body of LDS general authorities, known as the Quorum of the Seventy. In 1975, the First Council of the Seventy consisted of seven members. In 1976, the First Council was dissolved and replaced by the First Quorum of the Seventy, a group that had thirty-nine members, one of whom was Ballard. The reasons for this expansion, according to Kimball, were "the accelerated, worldwide growth of the Church," and the pressing need "to handle efficiently the present heavy workload and to prepare for the increasing expansion and acceleration of the work."[86] At the same time, the church was working hard to create uniformity in everything from building design to Sunday school lessons. Called "Correlation," this effort shifted control over local affairs to church headquarters and thereby increased the importance and power of general authorities vis-à-vis local leadership. Ballard's story of possession and exorcism fits well into the 1970s context that combined an increased popular interest in particular modes of possession and exorcism, an increasingly important and large church bureaucracy, and a tilt away from local autonomy to more a fully articulated model of uniformity and centralized control. Eight years later, Ballard was called to join the Quorum of Twelve Apostles.

CONCLUSION

By combining approaches from ritual studies with documentary materials dealing with possession and exorcism accounts from Mormon history, it is possible to locate Mormonism in the American religious landscape over an extended period of time. It is clear that Mormons in the American context drew on a wide arrange of intellectual, theological, and ritual precedents to construct a diabology and exorcistic ritual practices that differed from both Catholic and Protestant approaches

---

86. Spencer W. Kimball, "The Reconstitution of the First Quorum of the Seventy," Oct. 1, 1976; published online at www.lds.org/general-conference/1976/10/the-reconstitution-of-the-first-quorum-of-the-seventy?lang=eng; accessed Jan. 22, 2015.

to the Devil. Despite official silence on the subject of possession and exorcism, Mormons have maintained for nearly two centuries a vibrant mythos and ritual system that both acknowledges the possibility of possession and provides a ritual for remedying that possibility. Acknowledging the richness of Mormon exorcistic ritual action allows us to view possession accounts in a more nuanced, sophisticated manner. For Mormons, possession and exorcism function on multiple levels, from the cosmic to the practical. This study also shows that each case, while sharing general traits, also requires local contextualization to understand the unique and complex dynamics at work. Thus, Mormon possession and exorcism accounts reveal broad beliefs, like the ongoing cosmic warfare between God and the Devil, but they also illumine more pedestrian trends, such as the shift toward standardization and the sacralization of bureaucracy. Similarly, cases reveal sub rosa social tensions, such as the fear of women stepping "out of their places." When considered within a properly broad context, the cases also illustrate the interaction, often unspoken, between Mormonism and American popular and religious culture.

CONTRIBUTORS

David H. Bailey is a mathematician/computer scientist, now retired from the Lawrence Berkeley National Laboratory. He received a PhD in mathematics from Stanford University. His published research includes studies in computational mathematics, high-performance scientific computing, and financial mathematics. He has received the Sidney Fernbach Award from IEEE Computer Society, the Chauvenet Prize and the Merten Hesse Prize from the Mathematical Association of America, the Gordon Bell Prize from the Association for Computing Machinery, and the Levi L. Conant Prize from the American Mathematical Society. He and his wife, Linda, reside in the San Francisco Bay Area. "LDS Theology and the Omnis: The Dangers of Theological Speculation" first appeared in *Dialogue: A Journal of Mormon Thought* 37, 3 (Fall 2004): 29–48 as "Mormons and the Omnis: The Dangers of Theological Speculation."

Loyd Isao Ericson received his BS in philosophy at Utah Valley University and pursued an MA in philosophy of religion and theology at Claremont Graduate University. Since 2009 he has been the managing editor of Greg Kofford Books and has been published in *Sunstone, Element: The Journal of the Society for Mormon Philosophy and Theology,* and the *Claremont Journal of Mormon Studies,* which he helped to found. "The Challenge of Defining LDS Doctrine" first appeared in *Element: A Journal of Mormon Philosophy and Theology* 3 (Spring/Fall 2007): 69–85 as "The Challenges of Defining Mormon Doctrine."

Shannon P. Flynn is an independent researcher living in Gilbert, Arizona. He has a BA in history from the University of Utah (1993) and has been a student of Mormon history for over forty-five years. His areas of interest include all restoration branches of the LDS tradition, and especially the history of the LDS Church in Brazil, where he served a mission. "Three Sub-degrees in the Celestial Kingdom?" appears here for the first time.

Susanna Morrill is Associate Professor in the Department of Religious Studies at Lewis & Clark College (Portland, Oregon). She wrote *White Roses on the Floor of Heaven: Mormon Women's Popular Theology, 1880–1920*, along with other shorter works on Mormon women's history and culture. "Women at the Gates of Mortality: Relief Society Birth and Death Rituals" first appeared in the *Journal of Mormon History* 36, 2 (Spring 2010): 128–59 as "Relief Society Birth and Death Rituals: Women at the Gates of Mortality."

Blaire Ostler is a philosopher who is specialized in queer studies, and is a leading voice at the intersection of queer, Mormon, and transhumanist thought. She is an author publishing her first book, *Queer Mormon Theology,* and a podcaster at Sunstone. She is a board member of the Mormon Transhumanist Association, the Christian Transhumanist Association, and the Sunstone Education Foundation. "Heavenly Mother: The Mother of All Women" first appeared in *Dialogue: A Journal of Mormon Thought* 51, 4 (Winter 2018): 171–81.

Steven L. Peck grew up in Moab, Utah, and is Associate Professor of Biology at Brigham Young University. From 2019 to 2021, he was a visiting fellow at the Neal A. Maxwell Institute, also at BYU. He co-directed the Maxwell Institute's 2018 Summer Seminar and is author of *Evolving Faith: Wanderings of a Mormon Biologist.* His novels include *The Scholar of Moab, A Short Stay in Hell,* and *Gilda Trillim: Shepherdess of Rats.* "Crawling Out of the Primordial Soup: A Step toward the Emergence of an LDS Theology Compatible with Organic Evolution" first appeared in *Dialogue: A Journal of Mormon Thought* 43, 1 (Spring 2010): 1–36.

Boyd J. Petersen holds a PhD in comparative literature from the University of Utah. Since 2004, he has taught at Utah Valley University in Orem. He is the author of *Hugh Nibley: A Consecrated Life* (2002), *Myths of Male Mothers: Allegorical Renderings of the Birth Topos in Nineteenth-century Poetic Production* (2008), and *Dead Wood and Rushing Water: Essays on Mormon Faith, Culture, and Family* (2013). From 2016 to 2020, he was the editor of *Dialogue: A Journal of Mormon Thought.* "'To Destroy the Agency of Man': The War in Heaven in LDS Thought" first appeared in the *Journal of Mormon History* 38, 1 (Winter 2012): 1–50 as "'One Soul Shall Not Be Lost': The War in Heaven in Mormon Thought."

Kelli D. Potter is Associate Professor of Philosophy and a member of the Religious Studies Board at Utah Valley University, Orem, Utah. Her current work focuses primarily on the implications of heterodoxy for the nature of religious belief. "Mormonism and the Problem of Heterodoxy" first appeared in *Dialogue: A Journal of Mormon Thought* 49, 1 (Spring 2016): 41–63.

Stephen C. Taysom is Associate Professor of Philosophy and Comparative Religion at Cleveland State University. He has published numerous articles on American religious history and a book about Shaker and Mormon boundary maintenance strategies. He is completing a biography of LDS Church President Joseph F. Smith (forthcoming from the University of Utah Press). "'Satan Mourns Naked Upon the Earth': Locating Mormon Possession and Exorcism Rituals in the American Religious Landscape, 1830–1977" first appeared in a slightly different format in *Religion and American Culture: A Journal of Interpretation* 27, 1 (Winter 2017): 57–94.

Samuel R. Weber is a psychiatrist practicing in Utah. He has published elsewhere on topics related to Mormon history and mental health. He thanks the following individuals for their feedback on various drafts of his essay: Jonathan Stapley, Amberly Dattilo, and Christopher Blythe. "'Shake Off the Dust of Thy Feet': The Rise and Fall of Mormon Ritual Cursing" first appeared in *Dialogue: A Journal of Mormon Thought* 46, 1 (Spring 2013): 108–39.

ABOUT THE EDITOR

Bryan Buchanan works at Benchmark Books in Salt Lake City. After graduating from the University of Utah with a degree in Middle East Studies (emphasis in Hebrew), he has since been consumed by Mormon history. Among many other projects, he is currently editing the diaries of LDS Church President George Albert Smith and compiling a documentary history of the first fifty years of fundamentalist Mormonism.